# The New Job Security

# The New Job Security

## Five Strategies to
## Take Control of Your Career

## Pam Lassiter

TEN SPEED PRESS
*Berkeley • Toronto*

Ten Speed Press
Box 7123
Berkeley, California 94707
www.tenspeed.com

Distributed in Australia by Simon & Schuster Australia, in Canada by Ten Speed Press Canada, in New Zealand by Southern Publishers Group, in South Africa by Real Books, in Southeast Asia by Berkeley Books, and in the United Kingdom and Europe by Airlift Book Company.

Cover illustration by Regan Dunnick
Text design by Linda Davis/Star Type, Berkeley

Lyrics from "Facets of the Jewel" © 1996 by Neworld Music Publishers (page 121), from a performance at Northfield Mount Hermon School in September 2001. Used with permission from Noel Paul Stookey of Peter, Paul, and Mary.

Library of Congress Cataloging-in-Publication Data on file with the publisher.

Printed in the United States
First printing, 2002
1  2  3  4  5  6  7  8  9  10 — 06  05  04  03  02

## Dedication

*To Allison and Teel—my shooting stars.*

*To Barrie—my anchor.*

*To Jack, Susan, and Nancy—my home ports.*

# Contents

# Acknowledgments

I owe my first thanks to everyone who allowed me to participate in their career planning. Whether you were looking for your next job or continuing to develop within the same company, you let me share in your life and I thank you for your trust. You will see your stories in this book.

The journey to the publication of this book was a circuitous one. The early ideas were bounced off Bob Gardella, Dave Opton, Alan Webber, Melinda Merino, and Audrey Bryant. Audrey was a cornerstone in my planning. She led me to Jeff Brailler, who refined my initial thinking and in turn led me to Sharon Broll, an editor who was essential in clarifying my overall thinking and presentation. The competence of these people demonstrates the theory that answers always appear when you're ready for them.

Claudia Bruce knew the drill. Her knowledge of product management and publishing were instrumental. Pierre Mornell confirmed Claudia's recommendation of Ten Speed Press as the best fit with my message. I owe Pierre a big thanks for the introduction to Aaron Wehner, associate editorial director at Ten Speed. Aaron, you're a good listener as well as editor. Kirsty Melville, your strategic vision, support of your staff, and sense of the market as publisher can't be beaten. Most of all, Julie Bennett, my editor, you're the best. You walk the line between motivating and calming authors with great grace. Thank you for being my shepherd.

My two alliance partners have been rich sources of wisdom. Dave Opton, the executive director and founder of ExecuNet, is in the Hall of Fame as a rich source. Thousands of professionals have improved their work lives thanks to Dave's career information services. Caela Farren, president of MasteryWorks, and Tom Carl, the vice president, create systems that progressive companies use to integrate career growth with professional growth. These two companies demonstrate my belief that career management is a continuum, not a discrete task that you turn on like a faucet only when you're in job transition, and that you have the resources to take control.

My thanks to the professionals who contributed their specific expertise to the book, including George Davis, Joe Rich, Laura Morse, Randy Stevens, Ken Hablow, Bruce Walton, Diane Wilson, Al Silk, Monica Higgins, and Herminia Ibarra. You're all so smart. Susan Weiler brought her research expertise to bear with great skill and accuracy, even though I never gave her enough time. These are all generous, talented pros.

Myra Hart, you're in a class by yourself. Having the honor of working with you on the program you've developed for Harvard Business School alumnae continues to be an inspiration to me, as are you. You're making a difference in people's lives.

My final thanks go to the two people who pulled me through this year: Warren Radtke and Kathy Goodrich. Warren, I could relax when I knew that executives in transition were in your hands. You take good care of them. Kathy, where would I be without you? Your caring, follow-through, and ethics make me look good. Thank you both.

Thanks is too small of a word for my family. Allison, Teel, Jack and Susan, Nancy, and Barrie—you gave me the foundation I needed so I could pull this off. Your halos are glowing.

# The New Way to Achieve Work Success

If your work hasn't been much fun lately, we ought to talk. Are you stuck in your current job, unsure about how to move forward? Are you in transition between jobs, wondering how to land the right opportunity? If you are having trouble finding the satisfaction and meaning from your job that you once did, don't worry, *The New Job Security* can help. By mastering the five simple strategies that make up the New Job Security, you might just find yourself having fun at work again (or for the first time). The key is to realize that it's never too late. You spend most of your waking hours at work, so you owe it to yourself to do something you enjoy.

It's okay if you don't know right now what you'd really enjoy doing. It's enough to recognize that you're ready for something *different*, whether that means increasing alternatives for growth within your current company, getting more results from your job search, or moving into a new phase of work life where values and balance mean more than getting the corner office.

The experience of working with professionals like you—incredibly accomplished people who nevertheless need to learn simple career management strategies to accomplish their professional goals—is what drove me to write this book. Unfortunately, nobody teaches us how to develop career management strategies before we join the workforce and realize we need them to grow our careers. Even if you were lucky enough to pick up some basic strategies in college, they have a tendency to change. The good news is that you can change as well, and *The New Job Security* will give you the tools you need to effectively manage your career, not just for a single job hunt, but over your lifetime.

Is the idea that you'll want different things from your work as you move through your career anything new? No. What's new are the ways that people find jobs, whether they are looking for new positions within a company or trying to break into a company from the outside. What's new is the economy, where you're a hot commodity one year and yesterday's newspaper the next. What's new are the demographics: boomers are finding themselves in job searches at middle age, and Gen-Xers are discovering that the start-ups have stopped. What's new is the idea that not only are you responsible for your own career, you actually have a large degree of control over it.

Despite this New Job Economy, with its sharp transitions, intense competition, and high churn rate, too many of us are using old career management skills. People operating under the old rules have old habits and old mind-sets. They look primarily for approved job openings, typically through help wanted ads. They don't read marketplace trends and predict what skills they'll want to develop to be in demand. They don't know how to stay strategically in touch with their networks, and don't think to help their contacts when they don't need anything in return. They don't know how to negotiate win-wins to get the money and conditions they want. Instead, they believe that if they work hard, they will continue to be employed, the work will continue to be interesting, and, at the end of the line, their pension and the value of their stocks will have grown. This way of thinking is obsolete. In the New Job Economy, if you don't know the new rules you're out of work or at risk.

This book is your guide to the new rules for career management. Using information gathered from almost thirty years of experience as a national career management consultant, I have developed and integrated results-driven approaches for people who want to develop the New Job Security. Contrary to emerging popular opinion, there *is* job security out there. Its location has just moved. The New Job Security is centered in *you*, not in a company. It's portable. Once you've created New Job Security, you can:

- Move successfully within a company
- Move externally, with little trauma, to interesting alternatives
- Create multiple income streams, if you choose
- Shape jobs so they reflect your values and goals as well as your expertise

- Set up your career transitions (including eventual "retirement") so they're under your control rather than someone else's

To achieve the New Job Security, you'll need to develop the five new strategies that I teach in my practice, which thousands of people are now using successfully. Without these skills, you are at a significant disadvantage, both while you're employed and while you're in transition.

## The Five New Strategies

The order in which I've presented the five new strategies is not a coincidence. I begin by explaining how to lay a strong internal foundation, move increasingly into more external concerns, and end with steps to negotiating the conditions of your new (or revised) job. Once you master these five strategies, you'll continue to use them throughout your career to achieve the type of work life you want.

### Take Control

Taking control means having a plan for achieving your goals. Your goals and your plan may coincide with your company's needs, but it is not dependent upon them. Your expertise supports your plan, you can communicate it clearly, you are involved with the world outside of your company, and you actually attract new relationships along the way because you're having fun.

Professionals often say they're in control of their careers. It's poor form not to be, right? But listen to your language. If you hear yourself say, "There are no job openings," "I don't have the right qualifications," or "I can't move up in my company," there is substantial room for improving your control over your future.

### Market for Mutual Benefit

To market for mutual benefit means that you obtain your own objectives by helping other people obtain theirs. By helping those people whom you want to employ you, or in the language of product marketing, "consume" you, you get their attention and you differentiate yourself from the crowd. There are direct parallels between product marketing and your own career planning that not only will give you a structure for managing your planning but will also set you up for substantially improved career results.

## Stop Looking for Jobs

Stop looking for jobs that everyone else can see and respond to as well. Instead, find problems to be solved and trends to be captured, then shape work around them.

"What a relief," you say. "Looking for jobs wasn't working anyway." Well, we're not going to stop looking for jobs entirely, but we're certainly going to shift the percentage of time you spend on it. The number of approved job openings is finite. The number of problems to be solved is infinite. Which category would you rather go after?

## Network as the Norm

Networking as the norm means building a diversified set of relationships with people whom you are helping and who are helping you as part of your ongoing life.

Making the creation and maintenance of a network the norm in your life is no minor feat, is it? Anyone who has been through a job search knows that it's hard to start a network quickly, when you're under duress. How to build and sustain a network that is motivated to help you over the long term is both an art and a science and is essential to your career success. Don't worry. We'll talk about ways to connect quickly, too.

## Negotiate in Round Rooms

Negotiating in round rooms requires knowing your value, communicating it so you motivate your employer, and being flexible in how you reach your goal. Why in a round room? A round room can't trap you in corners. Staying away from strictly defined corners is important in negotiating. Your results in negotiating will improve as you make it easier for the other person to say "yes."

Negotiating strategies are simple and can become daily practices. You can put them to work quickly, and you can use them for more powerful results for the long term.

## Mastering the Five New Strategies

Mastering these five new job security strategies gives you three advantages: control, control, and control. At the most basic level, you'll have control of job alternatives in a highly volatile workplace. You'll also have control of your short-term career growth by knowing how to gain experience and build a reputation that has employers seeking you (instead of the other way around). And you'll have control over planning your long-term career, including deciding which skills could carry into an active retirement. The career goalposts keep moving, but your five new strategies will put you in control of where they're planted.

Throughout this book, I'll demonstrate the five new strategies with real-life examples. Names of people and companies have been changed to protect the innocent. Chances are you'll recognize yourself in some of the "needs improvement" examples. My goal is to have you see yourself in the "right" examples by the end of the book.

Some of the examples are based on professionals who were in job transition and others are based on those working inside companies to improve their work and careers with their current employer. *The same career management principles work, regardless of whether they are applied within a company or when transitioning between companies.* It's not as simple as being employed or unemployed, a binary mode, any longer. You always want to stay connected and competitive, more of an analog mode. Your strategies are for ongoing use. Your objective is to develop rapport with decision makers, define target markets (which can be other groups within the same company), network (with the top people in these groups), stop looking for jobs (spotting problems instead of job openings), and negotiate, regardless of whether you're employed or not. Translating the five new strategies into ideas and behaviors that can help you now, at this very moment, with your career is our immediate goal.

To ground the five new job security strategies in your own experiences, you'll find homework assignments scattered throughout the book. One of the great things about being a grown-up is that we actually appreciate and value learning. Stretching our minds with homework can now be seen as an enjoyable and essential exercise to develop new ideas and behaviors. Keep a writing pad next to you as you're reading so you can work on the homework assignments while the ideas are fresh in your mind. By the time you've finished reading this book, you'll have your own career global positioning system. It's about time that you thought systematically about your career, something that affects you over 60 percent of your waking hours. You now have your own workbook.

My hope is that you will integrate the five new strategies throughout your career so your job security has few surprises. First we'll evaluate old habits and mind-sets, then we'll explore how the five new strategies will establish New Job Security for the rest of your work life.

Let's get started.

# Old Dogs, New Tricks

*The only way to enjoy life is to work.*
*Work is much more fun than fun.*

NOEL COWARD

## Three Tales from the Front Lines

It's easy to slip into an Old-Dog mind-set, regardless of your age. What's an Old Dog? See if you recognize yourself in these scenarios first, then we'll evaluate whether you have any Old-Dog tendencies.

"What do you mean, a pink slip? Termination? Me? There's been a mistake." Gordon had been working for his current employer for more than twenty years, had been regularly promoted, had received good performance evaluations, and was doing the organic chemistry work that he loved. This pink slip, that wasn't even pink, had to be an error.

Sure, he'd seen his shares of stock in his publicly held company erode in value as earnings had slipped, but his chemical research was at the heart of the company's products. They couldn't keep the money coming in without the core products that Gordon's research helped produce. The idea of his job being vulnerable to some of the changes he'd seen in other parts of the company was so foreign to him that he had ignored the tremors going through his own division.

"Why me? This doesn't make sense!" But to his company, cutting Gordon made perfect sense.

Professionally, Gordon was in a holding pattern. He'd done most of his intellectual development in college, over twenty-five years ago. He'd gone to work for his current employer shortly after finishing his bachelor's degree in biology. He'd taken some workshops that his employer had offered, but not many, and not unless he believed that the topics would directly benefit his current work.

Staying in touch with professional trends outside of the company had been difficult for Gordon. He occasionally read articles in professional journals, and he took some graduate courses in chemistry twenty years ago. He found professional association meetings painful, so he avoided them. "Too many people are standing around, and there is too much chitchat."

Socially, Gordon was a private person. He did his job and kept in touch with a small group of friends. At work, he wasn't terribly interested in life in the other divisions, corporate politics, or company finances. He was interested in his research. "I thought if I just kept my head down and did my work I'd be safe." That approach proved to be fatal.

If Gordon had taken the time to look up from his work, he would have seen two warning flags waving wildly in front of him:

- Most of the people who worked with Gordon had advanced degrees, a master's or doctorate, while he had a bachelor's.
- His colleagues had degrees in chemistry, the department's main focus; Gordon's degree was in the less directly related field of biology.

Gordon had assumed that his increasing level of experience would offset his professional weaknesses, but his colleagues were becoming increasingly experienced also. When his company hit an economic speed bump, he was vulnerable.

Gordon is an Old Dog.

Penny could see it coming, but assumed she was safe. As the head of Human Resources for a well-respected, large, family-owned textile firm, she had been involved with laying off employees when a division was closed. She knew that textiles was not a growth industry in the United States, but her company's fabrics had been "hot," and she was loyal to the company's founder and president.

David, the president, had brought Penny into his company when she was making a career change, which had earned her long-term gratitude and allegiance. If there were layoffs, so be it. Penny would learn how to do them and be there to help David. She didn't want to abandon him when things got a little rocky. Besides, David would always save a space for her, even if the going got rough.

She had started her career as a teacher, and moving into human resources had seemed a logical fit for her nurturing, caring personality. Going to work and taking care of her young family had consumed all of her time. Now that her children were getting older, she could put more of her time back into her work. Even though the physical demands at home had lessened, the financial demands had increased, and would continue to do so.

Developing herself as a professional was a luxury for Penny. With all of the changes going on, taking care of a family and managing the day-to-day demands at work was enough of a challenge. Besides, she really didn't need to meet people outside of work to learn about different ways of handling the changes in her company. Budgets were tight, and she was sure that her mature industry and company wouldn't accept new practices anyway. "I'm swamped at work every day. I don't have time to get my job done, let alone figure out which new ideas are of any use or get to know new colleagues from outside of my company. If I ever need to, I'll figure it out then."

Penny is an Old Dog.

---

Michael is twenty-six years old and, by all measures, he should be a hot commodity in the job market. After finishing his undergraduate degree in finance at a major university, he headed for an investment-banking firm to get some firsthand experience. He followed through on his original master plan of getting three years of work experience, then applying to business school for a master's in business administration (MBA) degree that would make him eligible for some of the most prestigious and well-paying career paths available.

As the source of our economic wealth continues to shift from manufacturing to information and services, the "knowledge worker" continues to rule. Graduates of well-regarded MBA programs comprise an available pool of knowledge workers that the world's best companies target for bright, motivated hires. Michael put himself on the path that leads to these high-level jobs by accepting admission into a world-class MBA program. When he started classes, however, he discovered that he had become a little fish in a big pond. He's in classes with people who are as smart as or smarter than he is. His first job successes have paled as the bar has moved higher. As he moves toward completion of the first year of his program, he's competing for coveted summer internships with companies that could catapult him to long-term career success.

I met Michael in a networking seminar I presented to MBA students. He was clear about his own goals. "I want to be a consultant with a professional services consulting firm. I want to design strategy for Fortune 500 companies, become a partner, and reap the rewards." What *he* wanted, he could articulate. When I asked him, "Why should a company hire *you*?" there were five seconds of dead air. That's a long time for an aspiring consultant. He hadn't thought about *the company's* needs. Most of his fellow students are targeting the same consulting firms, investment banks, well-funded start-ups, and a select group of other companies. How is Michael going to get their attention and differentiate himself from the rest of the pack?

Michael is on the verge of becoming an Old Dog.

As you can see, being an Old Dog isn't about age, experience, when and where you got your degree, or what your plans are for the future. It's about attitude. It's about an orientation to the outside world. It's about how you think about your career.

## Are You an Old Dog?

Complete the following evaluation and find out whether or not you're an Old Dog. You'll see where you're at risk in managing your career so you can take corrective action before any career fires break out.

You might find the questionnaire frustrating because it doesn't have a

"Maybe" or a "Sometimes" column. That is done on purpose. It's designed to force out your latent opinions, even if you're undecided about your answer. Check "Yes" if you agree with a statement or "No" if you don't, even if it's a borderline reaction. Don't think too long about each question. Your first reaction is usually the most accurate one.

## WORK RISK / OLD DOG ANALYSIS

|  | Yes | No |
|---|---|---|
| 1. I anticipate being with my current company for the next 3 years. | O | O |
| 2. I work in a growth industry. | O | O |
| 3. I am aware of general business trends and how they're affecting my competitiveness. | O | O |
| 4. I can clearly articulate the needs of targeted employers (current and potential). | O | O |
| 5. I am in touch with a cross-section of relevant professionals outside of my current/former company. | O | O |
| 6. I know my top 5 marketable skills. | O | O |
| 7. I am comfortable with the concept of networking. | O | O |
| 8. I am computer literate. | O | O |
| 9. I am considered the right age for the work I want to do. | O | O |
| 10. I know what skills are considered hot in my profession. | O | O |
| 11. I have changed how I am doing my work in the past 3 years. | O | O |
| 12. I have been in the job market within the last 5 years. | O | O |
| 13. I think about how I can be of help to others before I contact them. | O | O |

### If you're in transition . . .

| | Yes | No |
|---|---|---|
| 14. I know what my passions are, and where they are reflected in the marketplace. | O | O |
| 15. I'm comfortable with asking other people for help. | O | O |
| 16. I'm past feeling angry at my former employer or fearful and desperate about my future prospects. | O | O |

**If you're currently employed . . .**

17. I have anticipated how changes in my organization could
    affect my career.                                                    ○ ○

18. I accept that my company does not have the responsibility
    to develop my career.                                                ○ ○

19. I know that feeling essential, having high seniority, or being at the
    highest levels of the company are not guarantees of job security.    ○ ○

20. I am interested in and informed about the people in and
    needs of other divisions.                                            ○ ○

21. I understand my company's vision and goals and know how
    I can contribute to achieving them.                                  ○ ○

22. I can describe how I've contributed to corporate profitability.      ○ ○

**Old Dog Analysis**

*10 or more "No" answers:* You're thinking like an Old Dog. Time to start taking control of your own career planning. You've already begun by reading this book.

*5 to 9 "No" answers:* Be careful; your fur is beginning to gray.

*4 or fewer "No" answers:* Hot Dog! Your challenge will be to sustain your momentum.

How did you do? Did you check off "No" on the first five questions, decide that this was too much to deal with, then skip down here? If so, you're in good company with most other professionals. There is an easily learnable skill behind each one of these questions, however. We'll explore how you can learn and practice these skills in subsequent chapters. Knowing your markets, knowing your competition, and knowing how you should be developing yourself to reach your career goals will substantially lower your work risk for the long term. Let's consider your answers to the questionnaire. They will provide you with a benchmark to measure your future growth against, like weighing in at the beginning of a Weight Watchers program.

## The Ingredients of a Career

As you evaluate the results of your Work Risk: Old Dog Analysis, you will see three main themes emerge: change, skills, and attitude. These ingredients are constants. They will continue to be important even after you're settled in with work that you enjoy, not to mention enhancing your life in general. Being conscious of shifts in change, skills, and attitude can help you turn them to your advantage. Let's look at the themes of change, skills, and attitude so you can see how they affect your work life.

### The Only Constant Is Change

Your company is changing. Your industry is changing. Your work is changing. Are you changing? If you answered "No" to the following questions, you're running headlong into issues with change.

- *Business trends (#3)*
- *Needs of targeted employers (#4)*
- *Organizational changes (#17, 19)*
- *Your work style (#11, 12)*

You know your own job well, but you are not too concerned with what goes on outside your area. You may not be an early adopter when it comes to new technology or someone who rushes out to get the latest book on business management trends. As you get around to using a software application, some of your colleagues are already moving on to the next upgrade. Or maybe you're a new technology whiz, but have no idea what is going on outside of your department. Change is not something you welcome.

Whether or not you like change is irrelevant, unfortunately. It's here. It's fast. You can't ignore it because "I just have one more year until . . . (restructuring, the kids are out of college, promotion, retirement, et cetera)." Putting off learning something new now may hurt you later. Learning doesn't have to swallow up your time. You'll get some ideas later in the book about how to do your own on-the-job training.

Gordon and Penny, in the earlier stories, did not explore outside their organizations, or even their jobs, to keep in touch with the changes in their professions. They did not change their skills although company needs were changing rapidly around them. Consumed by day-to-day work, they were unprepared for major changes in the outside world that they had ignored (such as textile manufacturing moving to Asia or external competition). Not only are they Old Dogs, they are sitting ducks (to mix a metaphor).

Granted, understanding that the world is changing doesn't necessarily mean that you want to jump in. Most people don't like change. Change can be uncomfortable. Change can make you look awkward, either intellectually or physically. Remember learning to ride a bike? You were learning a new skill, and probably had the bruises to show for it. But your desire to ride overcame the frustration of not knowing how to do it, so eventually you mastered the technique.

Change will hit you at both the macro level (economic shifts) and the micro level (skills). Being willing to adapt to, and even anticipate, these changes will make you a desirable employee. Changing work-related skills feels just as unwieldy and maybe even more dangerous than balancing on two wheels. You have an acquired body of expertise and a professional reputation. It can be scary to admit that there are things you don't know. For example, as you are mastering a new spreadsheet at work, you may discover that you need the help of someone three levels lower than yourself in the organization who knows more about the spreadsheet than you do. Can you accept her help and use this as an opportunity to model to others the importance of learning new skills? You've got to.

**Anticipating change and welcoming it will promote your success in dealing with it.**

Whether you are looking for a new job or trying to hold onto the one you've got, integrating change is continual. You're used to being an expert, but now your area of expertise is changing, or has disappeared altogether. That hard driveway where you mastered the art of bike riding has now turned to sand. It may be of some comfort to realize that you're actually used to this. You deal with change all the time. You would never have gone off to school, gotten married, had children, or changed jobs if you couldn't accommodate change. Changes that *we* choose, plan, and control, we embrace. Changes that happen *to* us, we resist. Anticipating change and welcoming it will promote your success in dealing with it.

The ongoing change that you'll encounter in the marketplace can be mastered with ongoing skill development and the attitude that change is to be welcomed. Remember trying an ATM (automated teller machine) or buying something on the Internet for the first time? Did you feel awkward? Odds are that you now take these skills for granted because they're part of your normal operating behavior. Being a Top Dog means continual learning and, hence, continual risk. But better to risk feeling out of your depth than stagnating completely. Using change to your advantage will be intellectually challenging, will allow you to grow, and may even be fun. Not only will you stave off boredom, but you'll have more job options, more chances for promotion, and more potential retirement activities to enjoy. On the other hand, if you're cursing change instead of using it to your advantage, you'll be an Old Dog soon.

## Do You Have What It Takes?

Related to the theme of change is the theme of skill development: what your skills currently are and what they need to become. The following questions are all related to skill development. (Note that some of the questions relate to more than one theme; they overlap.)

---

- *Job security (#1, 2)*
- *Networking (#5, 7, 13)*
- *What's marketable (#3, 6, 8, 10, 11)*
- *Your contributions to profitability (#21, 22)*
- *Looking for a job (#9, 12, 14)*

---

The above aspects of skill development are all learnable. Given the right information, the right approaches, and the right vocabulary, you can network effectively, develop hot skills that you enjoy using, and know how you're profitable and what your options are at any given moment.

Learning what skills are essential for your success and then acquiring them shouldn't be put off until you're unemployed. It is much easier to learn new skills when you work for a company that supports your ongoing development because the company realizes it is in their best interest to have competitive employees. Companies can supply you with new equipment, colleagues who can answer questions, tuition remission, opportunities to attend conferences on new approaches, and the ability to demonstrate results with your new skill. Gordon and Penny could have made themselves attractive job candidates and improved their performance results if they had taken initiative to develop their skills at their current companies.

Regardless of whether you are in transition or currently employed, your concern will be the same: "Where will I get the time to develop new skills? I'm barely keeping my head above water." In Stephen Covey's book, *The 7 Habits of Highly Effective People* (Simon & Schuster, 1990), he tells a story about an exhausted woodsman who had been sawing down a tree for five hours. When asked why he didn't stop to sharpen the saw so the process would go much faster, the woodsman replied that he didn't have time. De-

## Identify which emerging skills will be important in your field, then get them.

veloping your skills on a continual basis is like sharpening your saw. If you're not expanding your professional repertoire, you're at risk of becoming an Old Dog. For career success, you don't have the luxury *not* to continually improve. According to Covey, "This is the single most powerful investment we can ever make in life—investment in ourselves, in the only instrument we have with which to deal with life and contribute." You won't be developing skills randomly, however.

Identify which emerging skills will be important in your field that are of interest to you, then get them. If an employer doesn't provide the time or funding for your education, invest in yourself. You're worth it.

### A New Attitude: Avoiding the Inverse Security Monster

Underlying the themes of change and skill development is the theme of attitude. After all, a new *attitude* is what will propel you to *change* your work-related *skills*. The following questions relate to your attitude. Look at them again; you have more power than you realize.

---

- *Job market (#12)*
- *Your network (#5, 7, 13, 15)*
- *Your interests in other areas of your company (#20, 21)*
- *Feelings of anger, depression, desperation, or obsolescence (#9, 16, 22)*
- *How your company takes care of you (#18, 19)*

---

As you choose what you want to do, start looking externally, whether it's outside of your current department or outside of your current type of work, rather than keeping your head down as Gordon and Penny did, or focusing on what you want rather than what the companies want as Michael did. Your attitude and your results will change for the better.

Gordon's downward focus, "If I keep my head down, I'll be safe," was a dangerous attitude. If you're currently employed, especially if you've been working for a company for a long time, you may be at risk and not even know it. You may have fallen prey to the Inverse Security Monster. The Inverse Security Monster creeps up on you slowly as you get comfortable in your work, become immersed in the day-to-day details, and start forgetting about that competitive edge that got you into the company in the first place. The blinders start to slide into place as you look down rather than out. You're taking employment for granted. Inverse Security means that *the longer you work for one company, the more insular and at risk you can become* unless you are actively managing your career. The Inverse Security Monster can consume your competitiveness, making transitions to another job slower and tougher. It's easy to defeat the Monster, but you have to be awake at the controls to do so. If you've been with a company for a long time and want to stay hot, learn the new career management skills and consciously pursue your growth and success as a professional outside your company as well as inside it by building your reputation and your network. Being known and respected both inside and outside of your company helps you and your company, and brings your job security where it belongs: within you. (P.S. Your friends whom the Inverse Security Monster has already eaten won't be thinking of career management, so do them a favor and show them this paragraph. You can rescue them.)

> **The longer you work for one company, the more insular and at risk you can become.**

Other ways that attitude can affect your work success are easier to spot and correct. You may have given up on certain job marketing approaches that you've tried before, probably when you were looking for work, that did not work well for you. Networking with some people whom you didn't know firsthand is an example. Conversely, you might have an approach or two that once worked wonders for you, so you're assuming they will work again, such as a direct mailing that landed you a job. Suspend attitudes based on your past history while you read this book and reevaluate them when you've finished. Staying receptive, curious, and confident will save you a lot of time. You won't be repeating practices that no longer work in today's job market, and you'll be opening doors on your first attempt.

You'd still have training wheels on your bicycle if you didn't have the right attitude. You were willing to accept the awkward feelings that come with trying something new to reap the rewards that come with mastering a new skill. Openness to change and a sense of humor will make the journey from being an Old Dog to a Top Dog a pleasant trip. Having fun along the way will attract people to you. Attitude drives everything.

## What Is the New Job Security?

The New Job Security is a work agreement that you make with yourself. The first step is to consciously agree to take the initiative in your work life, to set your own course and direction for your current employment and future alternatives. No, this doesn't mean that you're telling your boss what to do and everybody else to get out of the way. It does mean that you have your own professional goals and fallback plans. You decide how you're going to play to win, and you tweak your strategy according to the cards you are dealt. In the meantime, you have your criteria for decision making. As you transfer the control of job security to yourself, you'll develop an overall strategy to help you succeed. You'll learn how to develop a demand for your services, in your current company or a new one, so you will always have choices. You'll identify goals and the skills that you'll need to reach them. You'll develop backup plans to help you trump the challenges that will inevitably appear. Anticipating change will position you where you want to be before shifts in the economy or company occur. You are a step ahead of everyone else. Watch out world . . . a ringer has arrived.

What's the bottom line? The New Job Security comes from *you*. It is within your control, not your company's. Does all this sound like a tall order? Actually, it isn't. All five of the new strategies you'll see in Jim's story are learnable. Once you practice them until they come naturally, you'll be prepared for change. You may even create it.

Jim moved from Old Dog to Top Dog status with impressive speed and skill. In his early fifties, he left his senior administrative position at one of the world's most prestigious hospital systems because his division had been restructured and it became clear that Jim wasn't going to fit in with his new boss's operating style. He had always done a little consulting on the side to improve operational efficiencies for health-care product manufacturers, so now was his chance to develop that business. He knew how to do it, so he did. Promoting a consulting business over several years came easily, but it didn't bring the job satisfaction that Jim needed. He wanted to be part of a team, and he wanted a more predictable income, even though his current one had increased substantially.

Getting into a larger, for-profit company when you're an independent practitioner with not-for-profit experience is a major challenge.

He started out by doing a direct mail campaign, sending unsolicited letters to potential employers, and he got no results. Old Dog tactics. Jim began to feel discouraged and trapped in the job he had created, but didn't want any longer. As he started learning and practicing new career management skills that oriented him toward marketplace needs, his results changed. He targeted where he wanted to be and what he needed to do to get there. He repackaged himself in both his verbal and written communications. He networked deliberately, not randomly. Within months, he had accomplished his goal: a job in the for-profit world, developing business in the new healthcare practice of one of the world's fastest growing information storage companies.

The story doesn't end there, however. Within fourteen months, Jim was laid off. When a company's cycles clash with an economy's cycles, something is bound to give, and the most recent hires are usually the first to go. But Jim's attitude was entirely different this time around. Jim had the presence of mind when he was given his termination notice to be complimentary about his experience with the company that laid him off. He told the senior-level executive who eliminated his job, "On a 1-to-10 scale, this job was a 12. Thank you for the opportunity to have been part of this team. I really enjoyed it." The executive immediately started scrambling to find a way to save Jim from the cut list. Jim didn't want to be saved if the rest of his department was gone, but he left with great references.

The layoff didn't catch him off guard. Jim was tracking business, industry, and company trends long before the announcement was made. He had interviews lined up. He was much more competitive than before he took the job because he developed a strong network, developed new, highly marketable skills, and could clearly articulate how he would be an important part of his next employer's success. Jim wasn't going around to companies asking them what jobs they had open. He had a specific plan about how he wanted to combine his skills with targeted companies' market opportunities and how he wanted to set them up to capitalize on emerging business. Companies were drooling over his ideas. By the way, the company that laid him off offered him a different job one month later. He was now in a position to negotiate his conditions. What would you do?

Let's take a look at the five strategies that emerged in Jim's story. His positive, externally oriented mind-set (Take Control) kept him in touch with his markets both inside and outside his company even when he didn't need them. The ideas that he presented to companies as he was developing new relationships were based entirely on identifying and meeting *their* needs, not his (Market for Mutual Benefit). Not waiting until there were official job openings but finding solutions for companies meant that people were eager to hear his ideas and create work for him (Stop Looking for Jobs). He already knew the people and the companies that he wanted to approach before the cutbacks came at his company (Network as the Norm). He did not discuss compensation until a job offer was imminent, when he could negotiate to achieve his personal and financial goals (Negotiate in Round Rooms). Practicing the five new strategies makes Jim highly desirable. You can be too.

When he learned new career management strategies, Jim's results changed. Using his five new strategies, he stopped acting desperately, he started planning and networking strategically, he identified work he loved doing and who was having problems getting that type of work done, and he discontinued his old pattern of sending out direct mail. As his information base and confidence grew, people sought him out. And he made sure that the skills he needed within his profession remained sharp. Whether it was new product knowledge or relationships with potential clients, Jim stayed in front of where he saw the growth coming. It worked.

## Planned Careers, Not Pinball Careers

In order to develop your own portable job security, you'll create a master plan during the course of this book, a strategy that you can use to direct your career. First, let's get on the same page in defining how a job is different from "work" or "a career" so you can distinguish between them as you make your plans. As Richard N. Bolles said in his seminal work, *What Color Is Your Parachute?* (Ten Speed Press, current edition): "A career is technically your total life in the world of work. . . . A job is a particular kind of work in a particular field or occupation, where you set your hand to particular tasks using particular skills."

In other words, a job has well-defined parameters, typically with a job description. When you started reading this book, you were probably focusing on your next job. That's important and needs to be done. The best jobs come, however, when you're not thinking about them one at a time, not grabbing at a job just to have one, but thinking about future jobs in a sequence. "How does this job set me up for where I want to go?" is a question that you'll want to be able to answer. Although the next chapter, dedicated to Strategy #1: Take Control, will ask you to think with a longer term perspective about where you want to go, let's keep it more immediate right now to show how you can start to increase your reputation and alternatives.

---

**H O M E W O R K**

### ☞ What Does the Future Hold?

Think about a couple of jobs that you would consider having *two* jobs from now. They could be logical extensions of your current work or fantasy jobs that you've been contemplating. Sources of inspiration for potential jobs can come from your current organizational chart, from jobs friends have that sound interesting, from titles in higher-level help wanted ads, or from titles you run across in business publications that you're reading.

This is where you can start using that writing pad mentioned in the introduction. Your answers to the following questions won't be obvious all at once, but the act of writing down your ideas and documenting your research will give you a base for your future plans.

- Jobs that sound interesting two jobs from now: (list at least three)
- What characteristics does this work have that make it sound interesting?
- What kind of skills does this work require? (If it isn't listed in a help wanted ad, ask people who might know.)
- What could I be doing in my current (or next) job to set me up for the job after that?

You'll want your next job to help build the management and technical skills, the connections, and the industry knowledge that will set you up for your subsequent job. Use the requirements of your second job from now (even if it's what you want to do in retirement!) as a test for whether you need to begin shifting some of the content of your current one or, if you're in transition, whether the job you're considering fits with your future plans.

Thinking about your future, about where you want to be heading, even if it's just two jobs away in the same company, starts putting you in control. If you're employed, your boss may tell you what the company has in mind for you. He or she may want you to replace someone, to move to a different location, or to expand or consolidate your division. In some ways, isn't it a relief that someone else is doing the hard work of deciding the best place to apply your skills? But stop and think before you answer your boss. Is that new position heading you in the direction you have in mind for your future?

If you're in job transition, a job might fall into your lap early on in your campaign. Uncle Frank is happy to put your inventory management skills to work in his warehouse, even though his wire and cable aren't your first-choice products. The good news is that the job is available now, it pays you a decent wage, and it ends the job campaign. But stop and think before you answer your uncle. Is the job heading you in the right direction?

**If you jump from industry to industry and function to function, you're spending more energy on learning curves than on mastery.**

The problem with both of these examples is the lack of a plan. They're reactive decisions. Whole working lives can be filled up with a series of reactive decisions, something I've labeled pinball careers because the outcome is determined by what they bounce off of. A career bounces off the boss wanting you to do something for the company, a convenient job offer, the relative that wants to help, or the recruiter who calls. They're not bad options, they're just accidental. Saying "yes" without comparing the opportunities to your goals can lead to a random series of jobs without a compelling expertise. A random series of jobs with a random series of skills doesn't build up the reputation that you'll need to take control of your career.

Taking control of choices about where you work and what you do will come more easily as word gets out that you're a star. A pinball career doesn't give you the time to build industry knowledge and professional relationships. If you jump around from industry to industry and from function to function, you're spending more energy on learning curves than on mastery. This doesn't mean not to jump if you aren't happy, but it does mean do research up front so you can limit your major changes. If you can, stick to one main direction for at least a good stretch of time. A straight path allows you to get some traction in your area of expertise and industry; you'll light up your professional scoreboard. You're a pinball wizard.

## Wrap-Up

The good news is that you *can* learn new tricks. You've already learned if you're at risk in your work life with your Work Risk: Old Dog Analysis. You've learned that change, skill development, and your attitude are constant career planning forces that you can turn to your advantage. You'll be taking the initiative by preparing yourself now for the job *after* the next one . . . no pinball careers. Gee, I guess you're not going to be an Old Dog after all.

The key to your success, however, lies in putting your plans into action. You might be able to name every skill you need to be eligible for a vice presidency, but until you successfully lead a major initiative, until you manage your profit-and-loss responsibility well, or until you develop relationships with new customers that bring in business, your plans will stay on the shelf. Thinking happy thoughts, like Peter Pan, will not make you fly. Break down your goals into minor behavioral changes that you can make today and you're on your way. Set up a meeting to go over your new market development ideas, join a subcommittee in your professional association, or give a lead to someone in your network. Your career management success rate won't change until you attach physical behaviors to your plans and goals.

**Your career management success rate won't change until you attach physical behaviors to your plans and goals.**

What does the future hold for your career management? People are looking for their next jobs and planning their careers in a whole new way. The five new strategies in this book are subtler and more persuasive than any interviewing tips or how-to-write-your-résumé ideas that you learned years ago, if you were fortunate enough to get any career training at all. The five new strategies go far beyond the concepts taught in outplacement seminars, college alumni groups, and self-study programs. They will teach you how to develop yourself not only when you need a job, but also while you're on the job and into an active retirement. Career management is no longer just a between-jobs task. It's something you need to think about for the long term, and it is within your control. Welcome to the New Job Security.

## STRATEGY #1

# Take Control

*Ninety percent of the game is half mental.*

YOGI BERRA

"I've never had to look for a job before. They've always come to me. My company has always offered me something or recruiters have called. This is not what I had in mind at midcareer." This is the lament of the professional. I hear it frequently, and you may have experienced similar emotions yourself. The lament expresses a loss of dignity and a loss of control, but that's about to change.

## Overcoming the Past

Underneath the shock, surprise, anger, and resentment (if you've been terminated by a company), and the apprehension, frustration, and feeling that you're trapped (if you're currently employed but unsatisfied with your work), comes a small element of fear. "What if the right company doesn't come along? How will I handle rejection? How will I maintain my lifestyle and the plans for my family? Will I be able to land something that is at least as good as my old job?" Or, "What if I want to apply for a job outside my division, and my boss decides that I'm being disloyal? Will people become suspicious if I start trying to build relationships in another department? What if I apply for a position and don't get it?"

The pain is real, the fear is real, and the stress of transition is real. I often recommend Elisabeth Kübler-Ross's book entitled *On Death and Dying* (Simon and Schuster, 1997) as reading for executives going through difficult career transitions. Dr. Kübler-Ross outlines seven stages that we go through when facing death or loss. People ending a job, especially if they've been with the company for a long time, experience a similar series of emotions. You can't force yourself through the stages, nor can you will yourself into the final stage of resolution until your mind is ready. However, I'm going to ask you to put most of your painful feelings in a box that you access only when you're at a safe time and place with a small group of trusted people. Although addressing these feelings is critical to healing, sharing the pain with a broad group of people can actually stretch out a process that you'd like to end quickly. You want to generate positive action and referrals in your network, not an "ain't life miserable?" type of sympathy.

The first strategy is about taking control. If you've been laid off and you can demonstrate to your professional community that you haven't been leveled by your former company's decision, that you can even understand why they needed to make some tough calls, and that you now have a chance to focus on new, interesting work, how do you think you'll come across? *Strength attracts strength.* You're demonstrating strength by seeing both sides of the story and moving on to the future. You'll be easier to talk to if you keep your emotions on the positive side, and you want to be easy to talk to right now.

The more you appear forward-thinking and the less you air your dirty linen, the more you can engage your colleagues and friends in discussions about where the growth is in your industry and the economy and the faster you will move into your future job. When you are in that new job and engaged in interesting and challenging work, your pain will truly disappear. "My old company actually did me a favor by terminating me" is a reaction that I frequently hear a year after the event. Amazing what time and an action plan can do.

If you see yourself in the executive's lament at the beginning of this chapter and you feel inexperienced when it comes to job hunting, try looking at things from a different perspective. This is your opportunity to plan what you want to do for work, rather than react to what the marketplace throws in your lap. Congratulate yourself if this is the first time you've had the chance to approach your career in this way; you're going to learn a process that will serve you well for the rest of your life. You're going to be in control. What may have been a pinball career up until now—beginning with an offer from a recruiter in your senior year at college, then bouncing off various unplanned events—is about to become a planned career that meets your own as well as a company's needs.

Start taking control by giving yourself a way to answer a hard question that other people will inevitably ask when you're least prepared for it. The question is "What happened?" and it usually arises right after you've left a company. This is your most vulnerable time because you're often in pain if you've been terminated or feeling somewhat at loose ends if you have chosen to leave. People will hit you with "Why are you leaving?" or "What do you want to do?" right away because they want to be helpful as soon as they hear your news. You run the risk of losing their attention and referrals if you're not prepared to answer them, but who's thinking rationally at a time like that? After completing the assignment below, you will be.

Work through this exercise now if you're anticipating leaving your job for whatever reason. Even if you're currently employed and talking to people outside of work to gather information, they'll inevitably ask you, "Why do you want to leave?" This will give you more control during times of change so you're prepared. Try drafting several versions of your answers until you arrive at something you like that is both honest and positive. Another blank copy of this exercise can be found in Appendix A.

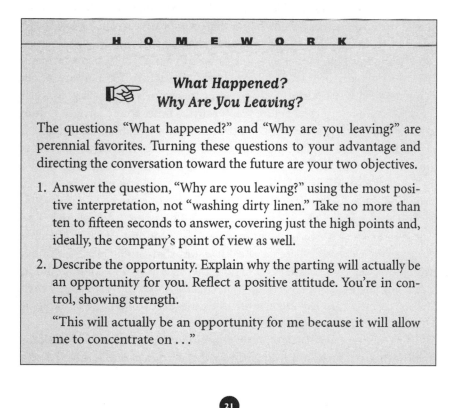

## H O M E W O R K

### What Happened?
### Why Are You Leaving?

The questions "What happened?" and "Why are you leaving?" are perennial favorites. Turning these questions to your advantage and directing the conversation toward the future are your two objectives.

1. Answer the question, "Why are you leaving?" using the most positive interpretation, not "washing dirty linen." Take no more than ten to fifteen seconds to answer, covering just the high points and, ideally, the company's point of view as well.

2. Describe the opportunity. Explain why the parting will actually be an opportunity for you. Reflect a positive attitude. You're in control, showing strength.

    "This will actually be an opportunity for me because it will allow me to concentrate on ..."

3. Envision the future. How will the companies that you're considering benefit from your transition and from your unique set of skills?

"As a result, I am looking for a company that . . ."

4. Ask a question. It gets the other person talking and moves the conversation toward future possibilities. Relate your question to the positive characteristics you mentioned above in number three. Make your question broader than just asking about a job opening.

If you're talking to a company representative, your question can be: "Am I correct in assuming that you . . . (have plans to introduce X products, want to convert to X type of system, and so on)?"

If you're talking to a friend or colleague, ask: "Are you aware of any companies that want to . . . (grow their international sales, turn around their operations, and so on)?"

See what you just did? You changed the topic. You're now talking about the future and business needs rather than your past—a much more useful place to be. People don't need to hear all the details about why you're leaving a company. Don't waste valuable time with good lead sources by focusing too long on history. You now have a structure for coming across strongly, positively, and quickly to someone who is expressing concern. Practice saying your spiel before you hit prime time. You're already gaining control over your presentation and the impression you make on others.

Taking control of planning your career is an ongoing, iterative process, not a "let's do it and get it over with" step. Just like organizations have rolling business plans that get updated every year as conditions change, you should too. Control, or the power to direct your career, is not absolute as you well know. You clearly don't have 100 percent control over what happens to your work, your company, or the economy. It's as difficult to manage the downside (such as health issues that might take you out of work) of your career as it is to handle the upside (wild economic boom cycles). If you ever think you're in total control, think of a card game where an unexpected card can change the outcome. You control the variables as much as you can, then you play your hand.

The exciting part of consciously choosing your own career direction is that I can guarantee, and I don't throw that term around lightly, that you have more control over turning your goals into satisfying work than you realize. I've watched thousands of professionals move from asking vague questions, such as, "What job openings do you know about?" (dead silence from the listener) to clear, direct queries: "What do you know about these thirty companies on my target list or this group of people who work in them?" That's a giant shift in control. You're not asking someone else to do your thinking for you. Guess which question gets a better response? Knowing where you're headed and how you're going to make a difference in a company demonstrates your control of your own career management.

Three attitude statements, once mastered, will give you control of your career planning.

---

- *"I know my value, and I'm reinvesting in myself."*
- *"I'm the boss; I set, maintain, and adapt my own career master plan."*
- *"This might actually be fun."*

---

If you actually feel and believe the three attitude statements, you'll increase your sense of control and your success with developing exciting career choices.

## "I Know My Value and I'm Reinvesting in Myself"

Let's define "value." I'm using the word on two levels. The first level is an intrinsic one: You value yourself as a competent, intelligent human being, independent of any associations with your work or your employer. It may seem obvious to be telling you, a professional, that you're of value. You wouldn't be where you are today if you weren't. I'm continually saddened, however, to see the number of highly competent people who start doubting themselves personally when their affiliation with a company is removed. "I've not only lost my job, I've lost my identity," one senior-level professional confided in tears, describing why he was having trouble projecting a positive image when meeting people. He had lost touch with why he was, and is, of value. Tapping into your true sense of self-worth will make a dramatic difference in your success in the marketplace, a self-fulfilling prophecy. If you're not projecting confidence now, fake it for a while. It's amazing how faking success, knowing that you're going through a temporary blip, can actually reestablish your personal sense of value.

The second level of your value is your uniqueness and worth in the job market. This will show on your résumé, and you need to continue to develop your value if you want to stay competitive. It doesn't matter whether you are currently employed or in transition. Having hot skills is what it's all about. The great people at a major high-tech manufacturing company that I outplaced, who I trained to set up and run their job campaigns, didn't have a clue that their skills were obsolete until they were laid off. With an average tenure of twenty years, they were still drafting mechanical prototypes on drafting tables with pencil and paper. They were not computer proficient, and they weren't aware that AutoCad had taken over their industry. They had stopped learning. They were becoming obsolete and increasingly unemployable, but didn't recognize it.

Here are the warning signs of obsolescence. Do you see any of these things happening in your career?

- **Complacency**
  Losing touch with your sense of value starts with feeling complacent in your current job. You've mastered it and people trust you, so you keep doing what you've learned to do over the years. You never think, "Will I still have this job next year?" or, "What can I do to improve?" because you are comfortable. Habit and repetition set in rather than growth and pushing the envelope. You stop learning new skills to do your job better like you did when you were first hired, and you just do the same things you did last year. You're starting to experience a lethargy that comes with continued employment. You're in a long-term relationship, and you start taking it for granted.

- **Isolation from Outside Networks**
  As you become engrossed in a new job and build professional and personal relationships with your colleagues, relationships with people outside work may diminish. You may not feel the isolation because you're still active, but you're becoming increasingly at risk. This is the onset of the Inverse Security Monster. The more you feel secure because you have been at a company a long time and the more you drop your connections with the outside world, the less secure you actually are. You feel secure because you're not looking for a job, but the Monster preys on those who become complacent. You're losing your paths to other com-

panies, to external information, and to your competitive edge as you get comfortable.

- **Losing Touch with Your Strengths**

  Why does (did) the company value you? Why would the marketplace value you? How have you grown recently? Can you communicate your value clearly? This does not mean bragging, by the way. It means getting results. (You'll be thinking through your value to others in the following homework.) When I ask highly talented professionals to identify their strengths, often they can list only four or five points. They've lost touch with their unique personal value. If you can't identify your strengths, you can't communicate them to others. Expanding your awareness of your skills not only makes you feel good, it's a basic part of product knowledge. Having the right vocabulary to express your talents to your audience will increase their "consumption" of you as a desirable commodity.

  > **The more you feel secure because you have been at a company for a long time and the more you drop your connections with the outside world, the less secure you actually are.**

- **Losing Confidence**

  This doesn't mean that you aren't good at what you do; it means that you don't realize how good you are, so others don't either. When professionals enter the marketplace, by choice or not, articulating why they're the best choice for a company is typically a challenge. Lack of confidence when in transition, especially at the professional level, can create failure. The confidence that comes from knowing what value you bring to a company—whether you're in transition or employed—and being able to articulate and deliver on that confidence, is what vanquishes the Inverse Security Monster.

## Knowing Your Value

If you're dubious about either your personal or professional value at this point, or what you have to offer, you're not going to represent yourself well to potential employers or to your boss during performance appraisals. Do "product research" on yourself before you approach major decision makers so you can communicate quickly and clearly why you're of interest. Being unsure about what you have to offer, as in the following example, can cost you good leads and relationships.

The president of a technical company received a telephone call from someone who had spent a long time networking into him. "This guy found four handshakes that eventually led him to me. He worked hard setting up relationships with people who would tell me to take his call.

"When it was time for the telephone appointment, he started the conversation by giving me a five-minute overview of his career, then saying, 'John [a mutual friend] promised that you'd be a good guy to talk to, that you were bound to have some ideas for a guy like me.' Then there was dead silence while he waited for me to come up with ideas for him. I had been prepared to help him with some referrals, but when I heard his total lack of focus and confidence, I lost interest. He wanted me to figure out his life for him. I don't know what a 'guy like me' is, and I'm not sure he did either. I wouldn't bother my friends by referring him unless I thought he was bringing them something of value."

Lack of clarity about his own value and expectations of the decision maker caused this professional to lose an interesting connection. You'll know better. One big moral of this story: never say "like me"! This all-too-common error combines the sin of not knowing or expressing your personal and professional value with the sin of asking the listener to do all the work for you. You end up irritating the listener and blowing a good lead. How much better it would have been if the job seeker had asked the president about trends in the industry, how he would respond to certain challenges in his field, what the most important skills would be for someone in financial management, to identify the two greatest challenges in his company (more about this in Strategy #2: Market for Mutual Benefit), *anything* other than ". . . ideas for a guy like me."

## Knowing and Communicating Your Value

The homework below will help you identify your strengths and value, then will clarify your focus and direction. You will be able to present yourself well, and "like me" will be history.

H O M E W O R K

## ☞ *Know Your Value*

Here are three ways to start capturing your value, strengths, and skills. Start with your professional attributes, then add the personal ones too. Go for volume first and refine later. After brainstorming, your goal for this exercise is to develop a clear definition of your top five to seven strengths, a concise way to communicate them, and a back-up vocabulary for those listeners who may need to hear things from a slightly different angle to understand your message.

1. **Skill Inventory.** Jot down your skills, strengths, and assets. You won't think of all of them at once, so keep adding to the list. Synonyms count. Give yourself a reward if you list more than twenty skills.

   *Examples of skills:* have in-depth expertise (in your discipline), build strong teams, meet deadlines consistently, develop products that sell well.

2. **Ask Friends.** Isn't it ironic that our friends and colleagues typically know more about our strengths (and weaknesses) than we do? Ask people who will be honest with you about their perceptions of your main talents. Tell them ahead of time that you're doing some "product research" and will be happy to return the favor; they may come up with more thoughtful responses. They may introduce ideas that you would never have thought of on your own.

3. **PAR Story.** The Problem–Action–Result (PAR) format has been around for years, and it still works. A PAR story succinctly describes an accomplishment that you're proud of. It's a way to discuss your successes without bragging because you're just telling a story. PAR stories are also very flexible; one story can describe multiple skills. Start by writing one story about a success at work using the following format.

•••••••••••••••••••••••••••••••••••••••••••••••••••••••••••••

Strength that I'm demonstrating in this story:

Describe a **P**roblem.
("Sales were going downhill and we couldn't get our new products out of R&D . . .")

Describe specific **A**ctions you took to resolve the problem.
Speak in bullet points, very simply and clearly. Use "I" rather than "we."
("The first thing I did was to call the team together . . .")

Describe the **R**esults of your actions.
Quantify them whenever possible.
("As a result of the new systems and revised products that I introduced, within two quarters we were able to increase . . .")

### *What additional strengths, skills, and assets does this story demonstrate?*

•••••••••••••••••••••••••••••••••••••••••••••••••••••••••••••

Once you've written one PAR story, write four more stories about four of your skills using the blank form found in Appendix B. If you select strengths that the marketplace values, you'll be well prepared for the main content of any interview or performance appraisal.

You're a valuable commodity and you have multiple strengths. Which ones will your decision makers value the most? Write out your stories so you can see your accomplishments, then refine and practice them. Build up the bottom section on the PAR stories about the additional strengths that your skills demonstrate, and you'll be sure to sound good to an interviewer, too. You'll be prepared to adapt the same accomplishment to different listeners with different needs.

The stories and your skills are like multifaceted diamonds. Turn the diamond around and show the listener the appropriate facets. One employer might want to hear about your leadership skills. Great. Tell him or her a story. Another employer may be interested in your technical expertise. Fine. Tell the same story with a different statement of the problem and relevant action steps. The results, how your company came out ahead, might actually be the same. You don't need a hundred stories to prepare for job interviews. You need five that you have taped in your brain, along with the additional strengths these stories demonstrate. You're being honest, you're being brief (two minutes, max), and you're being interesting and entertaining because you're just swapping stories.

You now have insight into the first attitude statement: "I know my value, and I'm reinvesting in myself." You have identified your strengths and your value, and you can communicate them to others. The last part of the statement, "I'm reinvesting in myself," is critical. How are you going to reinvest in yourself so your value continues to soar? Continuing to educate yourself, staying in touch with economic and business trends, and developing a broad set of connections are just a few of the ideas that will be presented throughout this book. And you're worth it.

## "I'm the Boss; I Set, Maintain, and Adapt My Own Career Master Plan"

Feeling like you're the boss of your own career may be a concept that you've already accepted, perhaps even welcomed. Being responsible for setting, maintaining, and adapting your overall career direction, though, can sound pretty serious. You can achieve this, however, if you can do two things: describe what type of work you want to do (function) and where you want to do it (industry). Knowing these two objectives is a true indicator that you have a sense of career direction. "Not fair," you say, "I'm in general management, and my skills can be applied to many companies. Show me an interesting job, and I will tell you how I can do it." Sorry. It doesn't work that way for people making the hiring decisions. You've just tried to be all things to all people.

Allen entered the office greatly discouraged and left even more so. He had been referred to an international executive search firm and expected help in positioning himself. He'd been given a courtesy meeting because he had hired this firm to conduct senior-level searches on multiple occasions. Having sold off several of the companies that he had been running for a worldwide security products manufacturing holding company, he was ready to make his own transition. He'd been traveling constantly for his international job and being the Guinness Book of World Records–holder for frequent flyer miles was not his objective.

Much to Allen's surprise, the search firm didn't offer the type of help he was expecting. Allen thought that he would walk away with his choice of the searches that matched his skills. He didn't. Not only do search firms not work that way, this one didn't believe that he was focused enough to present to its clients.

Allen had received a rude shock from the search firm. Puzzled that his excellent track record hadn't been an immediate hit and embarrassed by being in the position of needing help rather than giving it, he couldn't understand why the search firm wasn't being helpful. "I really can do anything. I've run several companies and would be happy to do that again if I didn't have to travel so much. I'm excellent at motivating people and turning around operations. The company or industry I go to doesn't matter. These strengths will work anywhere."

Is Allen right? Yes. Does it matter to the employer? No.

Companies, boards, and especially search firms want specific, relevant experience. They want people who have done the same type of work in the same industry as theirs, ideally with their competition. This matching of function and industry between the candidate and the position is what I call the "round hole-round peg" phenomenon. Is it fair? Maybe not. But it's the norm, so you might as well take advantage of its predictability and strategize to meet it.

This doesn't mean that you can't change fields or industries. People do it all the time. It does mean that your chances of getting what you want at the level and salary that you want will improve if your presentation clearly identifies why you are transferable and what value you bring. Your audience is not interested in figuring out new ways you might fit with their company. Do the figuring for them. Allen developed one résumé with one set of examples and vocabulary for industrial manufacturing firms, then a separate résumé that used many of the same examples but used vocabulary designed to meet the expectations of electronics firms. Remember how your accomplishments and strengths are like diamonds that you can rotate to show different facets to different people? That's just what Allen did. He ended up looking equally attractive to both groups of companies because he did the thinking for them. If you keep your message simple and clear, using the industry's vocabulary and referring to their needs and profitability, you'll do well. More about this in Strategy #2: Market for Mutual Benefit (see chapter three).

## Being Mushy Backfires

Do you agree with the old adage, "You can't be all things to all people"? If so, look at your résumé and listen to how you describe what type of work you'd like to be doing. Are you keeping yourself open for any possibility? In an effort not to lose any potential jobs, I see many executives who are too broad in their approach to the market. The fear is that if you commit to a specific type of work or to working within a specific industry, you'll be pigeon holed. You'll miss out on other jobs that a company has open that might be a fit. Right? Wrong. The paradox is that the more you try to increase your choices within the job market by generalizing about what you can do for people, the less other people can be of help. Contrary to what Allen believed, a potential employer wants someone with specific industry experience, someone who has the right moves, the right connections, and the right attitude so the company's investment in you can pay off right away. Can you imagine an athlete trying to keep the sport in which he or she specialized a secret? The more clearly you can describe your skills, cutting down on any mushiness, the more employers will respond to you.

The most common place for mushiness to creep in is in résumé design. How many people are leery of putting an objective as the first section of their résumé? To avoid stating an objective out of fear of losing opportunities is like being a shy boy at a school dance and never approaching the group of girls. You might have gotten a lot of attention, but you won't because you're not being direct.

Many head hunters and human resource professionals have told me, "If job seekers can't figure out what they want to do and tell me in their résumé, I'm not going to do it for them. I'm going fast. I'm skimming. I don't have time to analyze their wishes if they don't look focused."

Meet the employers' needs. Supply an objective. This will also help you focus the rest of your résumé, and will continue to hone your skills in communicating your strengths. "I want to increase sales for an instrumentation manufacturer, preferably one that would like to grow its international markets" is what you would tell someone verbally. Your résumé objective would be "senior sales management for instrumentation company," with supporting bullets about sales successes in the body of the résumé and an international or management bullet thrown in for flavoring. So much for being all things to all people.

## A Sense of Direction

There are two main points you'll want to communicate to others. These are the two directions we identified previously in "I'm the Boss; I Set, Maintain, and Adapt My Own Career Master Plan."

---

- **Function:** *What do you want to do?*
- **Industry:** *Where do you want to do it?"*

---

Let's see how this plays out. After some brainstorming, Allen came up with the following list.

---

| Function:<br>What Do You Want to Do? | Industry:<br>Where Do You Want to Do It? |
|---|---|
| *Jobs that might be a fit*<br><br>CEO, president<br><br>General manager, division president of several companies<br><br>Consultant<br><br>Running U.S. operations for an international company | *Categories of companies with which I have (or want) experience*<br><br>Electronics manufacturing<br><br>Holding company<br><br>Companies going through transitions: acquisitions, mergers, divestitures<br><br>Security product manufacturing<br><br>International technical companies with plans to expand into the U.S. market |

---

Read the list vertically rather than horizontally. Allen first thought through the function category. Titles he had already held or might consider holding showed up. His industry list worked the same way. Including some items in each category that he had actual experience in was important. They'll eventually be his "round peg" category in a job search, or the part of his job search that will move the fastest since search firms and companies prefer candidates who are currently in the same function and industry as the open position is. Including some new items of interest was helpful, too. Allen could follow up and research a new function or industry to see whether or not they were truly greener pastures. Beware of changing industry *and* function at the same time. There will be serious salary and job content implications if you're a rookie in both categories.

Take a look at Allen's two columns. Do the left and right columns interact? Might Allen be CEO/president of a company in the right column? Might he become a consultant to several of them? Yours could give you multiple options as well.

Clarifying your own industry and function is the next step. At this stage, it's just brainstorming, something between you and your notes. If you have a dream that you'd like to think through, write it down. In addition to round-hole–round-peg (same function, same industry) target markets, you might want to consider the "circus clown" opportunities. Not that you would want to be a circus clown (would you?), but there may be a fantasy job you have been thinking about for years. Why not check it out now? I hate to see someone kicking himself or herself five years after a major job change saying, "Why didn't I just check out that other idea when I had a chance?" There will always be bad days at even the most perfect job, and you want to feel reassured on those days that you made the right call, sort of like dating other people before you get married. Have you always wanted to start your own company, turn your hobby into a vocation, do something socially relevant? Test-drive some creative ideas now, along with the more traditional ones. You will learn if it fits with your goals, values, and strengths in comparison to your other alternatives.

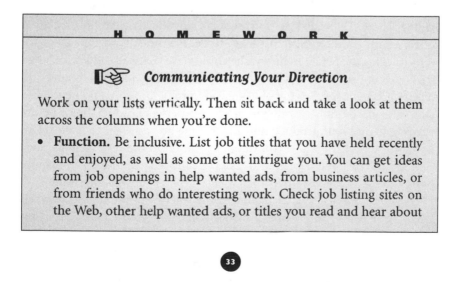

## H O M E W O R K

### 🖎 Communicating Your Direction

Work on your lists vertically. Then sit back and take a look at them across the columns when you're done.

- **Function.** Be inclusive. List job titles that you have held recently and enjoyed, as well as some that intrigue you. You can get ideas from job openings in help wanted ads, from business articles, or from friends who do interesting work. Check job listing sites on the Web, other help wanted ads, or titles you read and hear about to find out what titles are being used for the work you love. Forget about geography and where they're located; just start doing some market research.

- **Industry.** List any industry in which you have experience at this point, even if you don't love it. (Okay, leave one off if the memory of it makes you ill.) You will be of greater value when you have knowledge of an industry, and you don't want to eliminate any just yet. By industry, I mean the category of work that your employers were in: General Motors is in the automotive manufacturing industry. AT&T could be broken down into different parts of the telecom industry, such as broadband, wireless, or residential services. Warning: High tech doesn't count as an industry. It's too broad. Break it down into the type of work you have done.

  Next include any new industries that sound attractive to you. Moving to a new industry takes a little more work, increasing your need to network and to educate yourself, but it can be done.

Being clear about which industries interest you, and checking off your favorites, will set you up for the target marketing described in Strategy #2: Market for Mutual Benefit.

The next step is to start assessing the viability of the industries you've checked off. You'll be spending a good deal of time, maybe a lifetime, with some of these industries, so it's time to start being painfully analytical. What is the future of your favorite industry? You have a lot at stake in deciding where it's headed, so you want to be collecting data on its health during your market research phase. If Penny, the second Old Dog, had done this for the textile industry, she could have changed industries before she was branded. "Why did you stay in [insert dying industry] so long?" interviewees are asked. It's the old slide rule problem. You could be the best slide rule maker in the world and produce a perfect product, but if no one is going to buy your product, how much time do you want to waste developing those skills? I'll give you ways to respond to the interviewer's question in this book, but it's easier to take your industry's pulse on an ongoing basis and then act accordingly than it is to explain yourself afterwards.

As you progress in succinctly describing what you want to do and where you want to do it, you're taking firmer control of your career's direction, decreasing your susceptibility to a pinball career and increasing your potential for job satisfaction. Being the boss feels good.

## Finding Stability in the Center of Your Web

The choices you listed above for your function and industry preferences are a Big Deal. Being clear about them not only gives your career direction and lets you communicate it to others, the choices are a critical part of your job security safety net. In her book, *Who's Running Your Career* (Bard Press, 1997), Dr. Caela Farren, CEO of MasteryWorks, Inc., suggests building your function (job) and industry into a systems approach to career management, analyzing how changes in one part of the work system (your industry, chip manufacturing, is facing an economic slump, for example) can affect another part of the system (your company needs to eliminate your division to cut costs). You become much better at predicting what's going to happen to your work and your job's stability if you stay tuned to the whole system.

**THE WEB OF WORK**

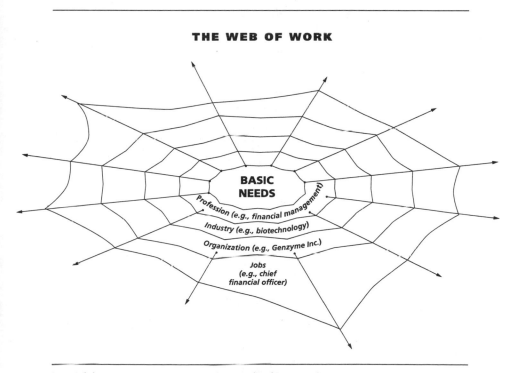

From *Who's Running Your Career* by Dr. Caela Farren (Bard Press, 1997).

Take a look at the four levels—profession, industry, organization, and job—of your system. Defining your own web will help you predict areas of instability and will suggest where you might spend some time building your expertise. Taking a systems view of work is something a lot of your competition hasn't thought to do yet.

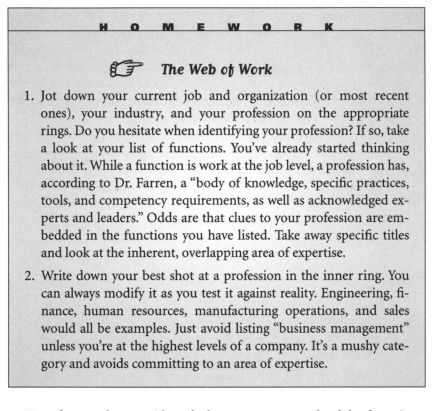

**H O M E W O R K**

☞ *The Web of Work*

1. Jot down your current job and organization (or most recent ones), your industry, and your profession on the appropriate rings. Do you hesitate when identifying your profession? If so, take a look at your list of functions. You've already started thinking about it. While a function is work at the job level, a profession has, according to Dr. Farren, a "body of knowledge, specific practices, tools, and competency requirements, as well as acknowledged experts and leaders." Odds are that clues to your profession are embedded in the functions you have listed. Take away specific titles and look at the inherent, overlapping area of expertise.

2. Write down your best shot at a profession in the inner ring. You can always modify it as you test it against reality. Engineering, finance, human resources, manufacturing operations, and sales would all be examples. Just avoid listing "business management" unless you're at the highest levels of a company. It's a mushy category and avoids committing to an area of expertise.

Now that you have an idea of where you are on each of the four rings, here is the $1 million question. Of these four circles, which one is the least stable? Which one changes the fastest and is the least dependable? You've got it: jobs. Jobs come and go. Even though that is the rung of the web that we obsess over the most, it's the one most likely to disappear. Jobs are eliminated or created to meet specific needs that may change over time. As Caela Farren points out, if you focus solely on your job, you miss the system's signals—the interactions of the four levels of the web that tell you your job is going to change. Heads up. It is important to be externally oriented, which means that your radar screen is scanning for blips at all four levels. Gordon, the Old Dog in the first chapter, thought he'd be safe while keeping his head down, staying internally oriented. Wrong direction.

As you move toward the middle of the circle, your stability increases. Companies certainly come and go. You've seen Digital Equipment Corporation, hundreds of dot coms, community banks, and many other firms disappear in recent memory. Industries stay around longer. Look at your own list of industries. Financial services, manufacturing, telecommunications, medicine, retail, and many others have been around for a long time. Although they have changed many of their products, services, and approaches, their modern purpose is still very similar to their original mission.

The profession circle is your core circle. Farren's work is based on the importance of defining and developing mastery of your profession, your stability in the midst of chaos. Try it. It works. Professions, she demonstrates, are based on meeting human needs and do not disappear. They are your stability in the new job market. Becoming and remaining an expert in your profession is what brings the world to you, a much preferable situation to reaching out to all of the world. Stabilize the center of your web, your profession, and you will be better able to weather job market storms.

In addition to riding out work-related storms, clarifying your core area of interest where you will build your expertise cuts down on pinballing. The competence that you're accumulating in your field is part of building your reputation, an essential part of the New Job Security. Your knowledge and your abilities to solve problems and generate ideas or new business opportunities will attract others to you. You don't want the doctor who is operating on you to be doing on-the-job training, nor do you want to be the continual rookie in your profession, jumping from sales to operations to management to finance and so on. Commitment to a profession (not a specific job) will pay off.

Can you change your profession if you change your mind about your career plan? Yes. You may have to make some salary, job level, and reputation-building trade-offs, but if you pursue a path and determine that it's not the right one, you're not stuck with it. Just don't change too often. For the meantime, let's assume that you have a chosen profession, function, and industry, and we can start moving you closer to the actual marketplace.

## Getting the Word Out So People Actually Respond

You're about to hit prime time, so you want to look like you have your act together, which, of course, you do. There are two types of collateral that you're going to use frequently during your career management to describe yourself: a brief story about your work (your Elevator Story) and your résumé. Your Elevator Story and your résumé are verbal and visual proof that you know where you're heading. The act of thinking through both of them, of structuring how you want to describe yourself to others, is an end in itself. Even if you're happily employed, having both of these at your disposal is part of being the boss of your career. You can use your Elevator Story any time you want to expand upon "What sort of work do you do?" You can use a résumé when you're employed as a bio if you're publishing some research or an article, speaking to a group, or doing some approved consulting on the side. Updating them is also much easier than starting them from scratch, so spend some time on them now, regardless of whether you're settled or in transition, and you can build on them over the years.

## AN ELEVATOR STORY WITH A PENTHOUSE

The Elevator Story refers to the answer you would give a potential employer if you were asked, "What do you want to do?" while on an elevator ride. You would need to be concise and brief, wouldn't you? You're going to be explaining to current acquaintances and to new people what type of work you're interested in, and you'll want to do two things: clearly describe your goals and motivate people to be of help. This story works when you're employed as well. You'll have a killer answer to "What type of work do you do?"

I've adapted the generic instructions that typically go with an Elevator Story, "Tell people about yourself in two minutes," to a more specific format that will yield greater results. Two additions, giving some results and asking a thought-provoking question, will set you apart from those who play their Elevator Story tape upon request, then let silence fall. You're going to engage people in a conversation that not only teases them with your skills and entertains them with some humor, but asks them to interact by offering their opinions about business—much less aggressive than hitting on people for names and job openings. You've just gone straight to the top with your Elevator Story, to the penthouse level where the successful, confident people hang around.

Let's walk through the format, then you can get started on your own story.

- Introduction

  The first sentence is an umbrella statement. "I have over _____ years' experience in _____." If you have a lot of experience, use your years in your profession as an opening qualifier. "Over twenty years" is as large as the number needs to get. You might start sounding a little too geriatric otherwise. If the number of years is small, say that you have "in depth" or "extensive" experience.

- **Three skills**

  Keep it simple and conversational. "What I particularly enjoy doing is _____." Pick out three strengths that you know will be of interest from the ones you came up with in your homework earlier in this chapter, and give them a phrase or a sentence each. "What I particularly enjoy doing is getting teams that have never worked together before to surprise themselves with their own successes. I also like to untangle a customer's technical problems so they're thanking me a year later. And I enjoy selling against stiff competition. I must thrive on abuse." Not only did you introduce humor, an important element to keep people listening to you, but you also implied as many as ten additional strengths, such as leadership, happy customers, and strong sales results, without bragging. Once you have one Elevator Story comfortably taped in your brain, you can switch your three skills to your listener's interests. Stay away from boring expressions such as "I like exceeding customer's expectations." Eyes will glaze over.

- **Two results**

  "As a result, I have been able to _____." This is the part that is really going to sell you. Listeners remember the results more clearly than the rest of the story and can resell you to their colleagues on this alone. Look back at the PAR stories that you wrote earlier. Pick from the bottom line, literally. If you can get some numbers or profitability into your results, so much the better.

- **Question**

  "Are you aware of any _____?" This is an important conversational tactic. Most people don't think to continue their Elevator Stories by lobbing the ball back into the listener's court for some useful information. You're smarter. "Are you aware of any professional service firms, like accounting or consulting firms, that might want to grow their business in some new areas?" Note that you *didn't* ask for job openings. That's a dead end. You did something much more difficult and much more effective: You did the thinking by defining the type of company that might have an interest in your background, then asked a question that he or she is likely to have an opinion about. (You'll get more details on this approach in the chapter on Strategy #3: Stop Looking for Jobs.) Good questions do not come easily. They take tweaking and refining until you receive answers that give you truly helpful information. Weren't you wise to capture the opinions of a person who was interested in you when you had the chance?

Now for your own Elevator Story.

---

### H O M E W O R K

### ☞ *Creating Your Own Elevator Story*

Create your own Elevator Story. Another blank copy of this form can be found in Appendix C.

- **Introduction**
  "I have over _____ years of experience in _____."
- **Three Skills**
  "What I particularly enjoy doing is _____."
- **Two Results**
  "As a result, I have been able to _____."
- **Question**
  "Are you aware of any _____?"

---

Once you have roughed out an Elevator Story that you like, try it out with a friend or at a social gathering. The more you become comfortable with it, the less you have to think about what you're saying and the more you can concentrate on your audience. You're getting the word out to your network, plus now you have an answer to the dreaded interview question, "Tell me about yourself." Just change the last question to "Is that the type of background you're looking for?" It will be.

## A BETTER RÉSUMÉ APPROACH:
## PRESENTING YOUR SHARP SKILLS

The other piece of material that you're going to need to describe your work is a résumé. This is not a résumé-writing book, however. There are plenty of those already. I'll pass along the key to success that results in résumés that are pulled out of the stacks and that receive consistent compliments.

You can take it from there. The key is *product marketing*. It seems so obvious, but no one else is doing it. You're in luck. Here's the three-step drill:

1. Define your target markets. (Use your industry listing, or categories within them, for this.)
2. Define the needs of these targets.
3. Present your product (you) in terms of their needs.

Sounds pretty simple, doesn't it? It's the opposite approach from how most people design résumés, however. Most people will list everything they have ever done and hope that the readers see something that sparks their interest. This is the throw-everything-on-the-wall-and-see-what-sticks approach. And it makes one, giant fallacious assumption: that the recipients of the résumé are actually going to read it. They aren't. They may skim it. But they're not going to spend time reading every word or figuring out what you really want to do and where the best places are for you in their company. They're not mean or insensitive; they're just busy. If you've been on the other side of the desk, you know firsthand that a decision maker may spend only five seconds per résumé. Design with this in mind, and you'll get more results.

Let's assume that you have already completed the first step. You've identified industries of interest in your earlier homework and you know your target markets or groups of companies with similar characteristics. The second step, defining the needs of these targets, involves some homework. You'll want to discover the hot buttons at the companies to which you'll be applying. There are two ways to learn about these needs:

1. Ask senior-level professionals in your targeted industries.
2. Analyze help wanted ads. (If you're at a senior management level, ExecuNet.com or CareerJournal.com are examples of websites that will have appropriate listings.)

When asking senior-level professionals about market needs, talk to those whom you will not be approaching for work. You're in a market research phase now, and you should not contact potential employers until you are fully armed. People such as friends, former employers, colleagues who have moved into other companies, or professional association members would be appropriate. In the process of exploring the job market, you're going to be talking with a lot of sources. Strategy #3: Stop Looking for Jobs and Strategy #4: Network as the Norm will delve into this further. One question you can ask is, "What are the four most important skills you'd be looking for if you were hiring a training director?" Ask them, "Where is this industry going to be in three years?" and similar questions. Listen to what they have to say. Take notes. After you've asked three or four people the same questions, some themes will emerge. *These* are market needs. Not only do the answers determine the viability of your function, combined with an analysis of help wanted ads, you'll have the body of your résumé.

---

**H O M E W O R K**

☞ **Who Has the Information You Need?**

- Whose opinions would you value about the type of work you want to do or the type of industry you're in or want to be in? (Ideally, these are people you won't be applying to.)

- Who knows about what's happening in your marketplace?

Set up some time to talk with your sources. Strategy #4: Network as the Norm will teach you how to make the most of an informational meeting.

---

You don't need to talk to people before you look at the help wanted ads, nor is the reverse necessary. You can work on the two approaches simultaneously or in whichever order makes sense to you.

The next way to pinpoint market needs, analyzing high-level help wanted ads, will be a secret weapon of yours. Here's what you do, but keep the secret so you can always outshine the competition. Find ten to fifteen high-level help wanted ads that you really like. It doesn't matter what part of the country they're from or even if they're a year old. Some of the places you can find them are in professional journals, on job boards, in newspapers, or on company websites. You may even include some that you've already responded to. Now start taking apart the fine print. I take notes when I'm doing this. Jot down the qualifications, the requirements, and the main functions of each job. Look for the patterns in ten to fifteen ads. By the time you finish, you'll be able to name the top five points that you need to prove in your résumé. These will become your Sharp Skills that convey your competitiveness. They're the overlap of your strengths and market expectations. You can tell PAR stories about accomplishments in these areas during interviews.

In the following example a senior-level engineer is targeting telecommunications companies. Our engineer might have this profile:

---

- *Profession:* Electrical engineering
- *Function:* Senior engineering management (VP, director)
- *Industry:* Telecom, wireless, networking

---

To track down market needs, our engineer might consider these three sources: the Sunday help wanted ads of a major city newspaper, a professional association that would carry listings for this function, or a website for senior-level job listings like www.ExecuNet.com or www.Career-Journal.com, the executive career website offered by *The Wall Street Journal*. I like ExecuNet well enough to host some meetings for them (more about the organization in Strategy #4: Network as the Norm). The newspaper had no ads at this level, once again confirming that newspapers are not the best source for higher-level openings.

Just skim the boldface text in these ads, and you'll see what the engineer has to consider (emphasis added).

## VP OF ENGINEERING IN TELECOM

Reports to CTO. **Lead development effort** for a second-stage software provider developing bandwidth management tools for broadband market. Responsible for **design, planning, and development** of one or more components of product applications. **Lead development teams** and senior developers in development and implementation of product components required by specifications developed and provided by product management and other sources. **Develop budget and project schedules** for all projects, monitor progress, and report status to senior management. **Hire, motivate, and appraise development team.** Ensure projects are completed **on time and to quality standards.** Facilitate **communications** upward and across project team, including project status, justifications for variances, and technical information. Serve **as focal point for other departments** on project status and other project information. Organize project through development of project plans. Ensure projects are completed according to product specifications and are properly documented. Ensure product **architecture and implementation are maintainable** and extendible. Ensure that documentation gets appropriate level of **technical review** support, **QA test** plans meet project requirements, and appropriate development procedures are followed. Must have degree or equivalent experience; graduate degree preferred. 15+ years in **software development**, with 7+ years in leadership roles. Experience in **C / C++ OOA&D** development environment. Ability to lead and motivate teams of developers. Experience with a variety of **development tools** (e.g., JDBC, Enterprise Java Beans). Proven experience in leading **software product development** projects. **Organization and planning skills. Outstanding communications skills, both oral and written.** Experience in a **startup** environment preferred. Experience in cable or communications industry preferred; reference ExecuNet in response.

## VP OF ENGINEERING
## WIRELESS COMMUNICATIONS
## COMPANY

**Lead design and analysis team** of 35 mechanical, structural, and electrical engineers and technicians in **new product development and modification** of existing product lines ranging from 1.2 meter through 34 meter in size. Must be able to provide **innovative design solutions. Management** experience a must. Assure all **project schedules and budgets are met; schedule and allocate design workload as well as develop and implement engineering standards** for all disciplines in an environment where designs are often modified and tailored to customer requirements. Must have **experience as VP**, director, or manager of engineering in $25M+ company. Ideal candidate has **supervised the engineering department that designs large structures.** Must have 10 years engineering experience. Must have BS engineering in structural/mechanical engineering. Must have strong management/technical leadership. Demonstrated success in standardizing designs as well as developing and implementing engineering standards for all disciplines within an engineering department. Must be **hands-on, high-energy shop floor person, who will ensure quality, on-time design project completion.** Ability to **prioritize and organize resources** is essential, as is the ability to **work under pressure and handle multiple tasks. Ability to communicate** and work effectively with all departments and at all levels within the company. Possess excellent business judgment, problem-solving abilities, and management skills; reference ExecuNet in response; paid relocation.

## DIRECTOR OF ENGINEERING
## NETWORKING COMPANY

The qualified candidate will be a critical **leader** in a fast-growing IP services and routing protocol organization. This company is seeking a senior individual with a strong background in the **networking** industry with a minimum of 8–10 years of experience with at least 6 years of management experience in software to direct a software routing protocol organization. Qualified candidates should have experience with **OSPF, BGP, IP, MPLS traffic engineering and/or RSVP signaling.** This individual requires in-depth understanding of **routing architectures and routing industry standards**. In addition, qualified candidates must have a proven track record of delivering a router to market. Additional responsibilities include developing **project schedules, recruiting, hiring, motivating, evaluating, and retaining software engineers.** This position interacts with a skilled **team** of hardware, software, and test engineers as well as **customers**, marketing, and industry leaders. Effective **communication skills**, flexibility, a strong **teamwork** approach, and the desire to work in a fast-paced startup environment are necessary for success. This role will report to the Vice President of Engineering and requires an MSCS/EE or equivalent. IEEE Job Site

Here's the exciting part. Even without knowing a thing about electrical engineering, I can tell you what Sharp Skills a senior-level engineering professional's résumé should include and can write an appropriate Elevator Story just by analyzing the trends in the ads. You can do it, too. Combine the recurring themes from the ads in your industry and function with the feedback you have from talking to senior-level professionals, and you'll have some killer communication materials and approaches.

Here are some themes that emerged in the senior engineer's ads:

- Demonstrates technical development leadership skills
- Manages projects so schedules and budgets consistently meet
- Creates and implements innovative design solutions
- Motivates teams to work well under pressure using strong communication skills
- Ensures that quality standards are met or exceeded in all projects

Your résumé should feature the trends you find in your industry. The following sample résumé format I developed (Sample #1) adapts easily to multiple functions and industries and is consistently well received. Take the themes that you found in your research and boldface them to catch the reader's eye when he or she is skimming. The more you can tie the themes to profitability, the better. The reader will quickly see that he or she cannot afford *not* to hire you. See how this market needs–based approach plays out in the format? This résumé is for people who are moving upward in their careers.

The second résumé format (Sample #2) should be used if you are making big changes in what you do or have limited experience. It downplays the "where" and the job titles and plays up the "why," your relevant skills. Remember, you are not thinking of your experience first when you design your résumé. It's the three-part drill you now know: identify (1) your target market, (2) what its needs are, and (3) what it wants to hear—in that order. You fit your experience to the needs of your market. When you draft your résumé, boldface the hot buttons of your target market so people can easily identify your selling points.

# THOMAS A. SMITH

123 Main Street
City, State, Zip

876.543.2100
tsmith@yahoo.com

## OBJECTIVE

Senior-executive position in biotechnology/healthcare industry

## SUMMARY

Experienced healthcare executive with proven expertise in creating new business, directing complex operations, managing finances, and developing results-oriented strategic plans. Strong record of increasing revenues and controlling costs in multiple-site operations. Recognized for leadership abilities, strong communication skills, and improving corporate profitability.

## PROFESSIONAL EXPERIENCE

**Biotech, Inc.,** Newton, MA, 2000–Present

### Senior Vice President of Operations

Responsible for field sales and operations of outpatient treatment centers and multisite GMP laboratories. Directed corporate departments of medical affairs, nursing, laboratory operations, and quality assurance and quality control for a start-up biotechnology company providing novel cellular immunotherapy for cancer. Performed corporate strategic planning, coordinated sales and marketing efforts, and assured optimal patient care. Implemented corporate-wide Quality Assurance Program.

- *Developed and implemented strategic plans* including financial and operational analyses, for refining operations of pilot site. Operational changes resulted in a 12% savings.

- *Opened multiple-site treatment centers* by establishing policies and procedures, hiring and training personnel, controlling costs, and managing sales staff in developing referrals and new patients, generating new revenue streams.

- *Focused marketing strategy* for introduction of new technology resulting in 74% increase in sales within a year.

- *Managed Materials and Process Review Board*, a multidepartmental, senior management committee that reviewed and approved all operational issues, including process development validations and policies and procedures, to ensure total quality management.

- *Developed new, multisite cGMP compliant laboratories* (current Good Manufacturing Practices) by combining expertise in FDA regulations with practical knowledge of protocol validations and sterility procedures.

- *Reduced cell-processing breakeven costs by 35%* by increasing protocol efficiency of internal operations and lowering staffing utilization while meeting cGMP regulations and maintaining quality of product and patient care.

**HPI Health Care Services**, Atlanta, GA, 1985–2000

**Senior Vice President of Operations,** 1998–2000

Directed all national operations, including fiscal responsibility for $60 million company providing management of hospital pharmacies, materials management, home infusion therapy, medical equipment, and nursing services. Developed new business ventures. Supervised 6 vice presidents and 1,100 employees in 106 sites nationwide.

- *Initiated capitated/cost guarantee contract resulting in sales of $27 million* by analyzing client's cost history, forecasting cost savings, and performing trend and financial analyses.
- *Negotiated management agreements to improve profitability* including 6 contracts that yielded $3 million net profit on an annualized basis.
- *Improved financial performance* by instituting strict budgetary controls and by implementing operational efficiencies, resulting in exceeding budgeted profits every year.

**Vice President of Operations,** 1995–1997

Responsibilities similar to Senior Vice President of Operations. Initiated computerization of billing areas, cutting billing time in half.

- *Created individualized marketing plans* for each account that resulted in a 20% increase in client retention.
- *Streamlined staffing patterns,* eliminating level of field management that resulted in savings of $500,000 annually while increasing revenue growth and client contact.

**Regional Vice President,** 1993–1995

Planned, implemented, and directed healthcare administrative services for Eastern Region. Translated corporate objectives into regional operational plans and goals. Assured quality care and optimal services. Controlled costs and maximized profits.

- *Achieved 27% increase in profitability* by tightening billing procedures and strengthening purchasing controls.

**Regional Director of Operations,** 1990–1993

Marketed and managed company's healthcare services across four-state area. Hired, trained, and supervised 77 healthcare professionals.

- *Surpassed sales targets,* increasing annual volume from $6 to $8 million and doubling profits within first year.
- *Introduced successful new services* with first national nursing home contract and new Home Health Care Services that generated $1 million in first year.

**Eastern Regional Director–Material Management,** 1988–1990

Promoted from Unit Manager (1985–1986) to Area Director (1986–1988) to Eastern Regional Director with responsibility for marketing and coordinating all equipment and material production, distribution, and logistics functions for new service line. Directed staff of 40 employees.

- *Developed and introduced new business* by identifying customer needs, then introducing new services that met expectations. Increased sales by $4.5 million annually.

### EDUCATION

**Master of Business Administration (M.B.A.)**
Xavier University, Cincinnati, OH, 1988

**Bachelor of Science**
St. Louis College of Pharmacy, St. Louis, MO, 1981

# MARY H. LAMB

74 Pasture Lane, Watertown, MA 02188     mlamb@aol.com     (508) 321-6789

## OBJECTIVE

Marketing/sales management position in food or hospitality industry

## SUMMARY OF QUALIFICATIONS

- *Results-oriented marketing experience* from designing strategic plans that clearly identified target markets, goals, and how to get there as well as from developing products and services that anticipated market trends. Introduced and promoted new product lines for companies that dramatically increased revenues.

- *Strong sales track record* that includes training and managing successful sales teams and negotiating contracts and prices to corporate advantage. Developed strategies that increased overall sales sixfold.

- *Ability to penetrate key accounts with industry relationships* developed over twenty years of experience. Credibility with professional associations, as a guest speaker and lecturer, as the subject of feature articles in newspapers, and from industry board memberships (AIWF) that create a strong referral base and access.

- *Product knowledge* from expertise in planning and implementing major events and from teaching college courses that emphasize product development and marketing.

- *Recognized presentation and communication skills* from unprecedented sales generated after product demonstrations and by consistent commendations from audience.

- *Create and direct promotional events.* Arranged cooking demonstrations by Julia Child and Jacques Pépin; the first food and wine festival at St. Andrews in Scotland for the hotel and travel industry; multiple trade shows and corporate functions; and all aspects of international tours. Increased visibility and sales.

## PROFESSIONAL EXPERIENCE

**Principal, Senior Marketing Director**

MBF Consulting–Atlas Fabrics Store, Inc., Worcester, MA, 1982–Present
Responsible for planning and operating a successful business primarily focused on management of special events, corporate and annual meetings, fund-raisers, promotionals, and trade shows. Designed and implemented marketing strategy, advertising and promotional campaigns, media coverage, and representation of the company to the public.

**Director of Public Relations, Consultant**

Kitchen, Etc., Dedham, MA, and North Hampton, NH, 2001
Developed and produced promotional activities for business and new products, including special events, product demonstrations, and favorable, free publicity in the media. Consistently increased sales over projections and improved company name recognition.

**International Tour Director**

Trafalgar Tours, London, England, 1987–1989
Primary responsibilities for media relations, tours, and major special event management for international celebrities. Produced a promotional video for new business development. Knowledgeable of values, culture, norms, and expectations of other countries.

## EDUCATION

**M.Ed.**, Suffolk University, Boston, MA 1987
**B.S. in Speech**, Emerson College, Boston, MA 1985
Graduate coursework in **Business Management** and **Special Event Management**, Bentley College, Waltham, MA

When you're changing fields or have recently graduated from school, you don't typically have a lot of relevant experience from an employer's perspective. The beauty of the second format is that it allows you to gather your hooks, or relevant selling points, from throughout your work and volunteer experience, then present them up front in one solid block. This looks much more impressive than the more traditional format if you don't have the right titles or companies to lead with. You're leading with the employer's needs and how you can address them instead. You just got his or her attention.

Read Strategy #2: Market for Mutual Benefit and Strategy #3: Stop Looking for Jobs before finishing your résumé. You'll get some additional ideas that will make your presentation even more powerful.

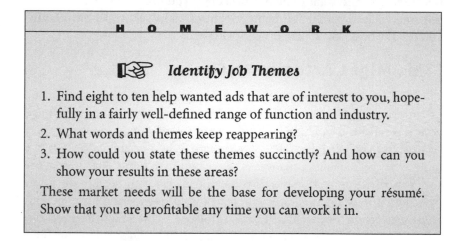

**H O M E W O R K**

☞ *Identify Job Themes*

1. Find eight to ten help wanted ads that are of interest to you, hopefully in a fairly well-defined range of function and industry.
2. What words and themes keep reappearing?
3. How could you state these themes succinctly? And how can you show your results in these areas?

These market needs will be the base for developing your résumé. Show that you are profitable any time you can work it in.

With these themes, you have just defined the Sharp Skills that the employers in your markets want you to have. Subtly show them you have these Sharp Skills every chance you get—in phone conversations, on résumés, in interviews. Keep testing them against marketplace needs every six months, even when you're settled. This is solid career management data that you'll want at your disposal so you don't become obsolete. Whether or not your employer wants to keep you at the cutting edge of these skills is up to you and her. Your company shouldn't train you in things that are not relevant to its best interests. *You* shouldn't stay with a company for the long term that doesn't want to keep you, and as a result itself, competitive. If certain Sharp Skills are important to you and your company isn't going to support their acquisition, find a way to get them anyway. Creativity counts as a Sharp Skill.

You are the boss. You now can set your career direction, communicate your function and industry clearly, and gather feedback that moves you forward. You can see your work from a systems perspective, and you know that your job stability will come from your professional expertise not from any one job. In addition, you can test your career decisions—such as "Which job should I take?" or "Do I really need an MBA?"—against expectations for your profession and avoid a pinball career. You know how to determine the needs of potential employers for your function and industry, and how to design your résumé and communications to meet their needs. By articulating a career direction, you're also demonstrating confidence. As discussed in the section on values, your confidence will pay off because strength attracts strength. People with ideas and connections will be attracted to you and want to help, especially if you overlay your clear direction and values with the third component of taking control—having fun. You *are* the boss, sort of like Bruce Springsteen.

## "This Might Actually Be Fun"

The third attitude statement is your final keystone to taking control of your career planning. Combine your sense of value and your ability to manage your career with having fun, and things start happening. Fun is not what you feel like you're having right now, though, is it? The ability to enjoy the journey as you're making changes is easier said than done. Fun is not a casual, superficial point, however. If you can truly get your head to the point of being curious about what you're learning, of wondering how you can help other people, of watching the marketplace and predicting its direction, you might actually start having fun. If you look like you're having fun, and are upbeat and positive with a sense of humor, people will be attracted to you. As you learn more about the overall marketplace, not just what surrounds your specific job, you'll be of greater help to people. Guess what starts happening to your number of leads, referrals, and points of recommendation as people start realizing that you can help them? They'll grow like wildfire. Your reputation is spreading. Having fun improves your results.

### *The Chemistry Factor*

We're getting into an area that I seldom see discussed, but which has a major impact on the results of any campaign that you might be contemplating: *what you are like to be with*. In fact, how people feel about being with you will typically be the primary driver in what opportunities become available to you as you progress in your career. Can you think of job openings, either internal promotions or external hires, that did not go to the most qualified applicant? Enough said. Chemistry, once again, rules. Use it to your advantage.

How you use the chemistry factor to your advantage gets back to having fun and what you'll learn in Strategy #2: Market for Mutual Benefit. If you can be enjoyable, comfortable, and fun for others to be around when you're in transition, you will increase your odds of reaching your goals. Here's the challenge: If you are truly unhappy with your work and want to move quickly, you will be feeling anxious. Feeling anxious lets out some sort of molecules into the atmosphere that scare off other people. Yes, your good friends will stick with you, but they're not typically the ones with job alternatives for you. You'd have a new job already if they were. You can build more connections if you relax.

Robert was two months away from being married. He had started up a company, so as CEO and founder he was managing what had become a good-sized operation. He sold it, made $40 million from the sale, then lost much of the money in different investments and alimony for an earlier marriage. He was now financially strapped. In addition to needing income, he needed something to do. Intelligent and highly accomplished, he didn't find being unemployed to be a good time. He was starting to get desperate about finding work. Pursuing help wanted ads, he waited, passively, for ads to come out, then mailed back responses with his résumé. A direct mailing had yielded nothing. His desperation increased.

Robert had decided to postpone his wedding until he could find work. All he could think or talk about was where he might get a job. According to Maslow's hierarchy of needs—a pyramid that shows that we have to meet our most basic needs at the bottom of the pyramid before we can rise to self-actualization—Robert was at the bottom level, in the survival mode. He was targeting lower-level jobs just to find something, anything. The harder he tried, the more elusive the opportunities became. It wasn't working.

Why wasn't Robert landing the interviews that he so painfully wanted and for which he was so very qualified? If you were on the other side of the desk, and someone approached you who appeared to be truly desperate for work, how would you react? Like a swimmer trying to grab a ball in the water, Robert was actually repelling his target by creating too many waves. Robert had another major challenge; he was using the two lowest-yield activities—responding to help wanted ads and sending out direct mail—to generate the activity for his campaign. We'll get to alternative campaign strategies in the later chapters. For the moment, let's focus on chemistry.

Socially, you'd much rather be around people who are relaxed, who have common interests, who can listen well, and who have a sense of humor, right? In other words, they're fun. Fun doesn't mean a slap-on-the-back camaraderie. It doesn't mean that you need to be a raging extrovert and the life of the party. It means that you're comfortable with yourself and enjoy conversations with others.

Professionally, it is no different. A relaxed, collegial relationship as an equal not only is more fun, but will also end up selling you better. "But," you're saying, "the name of the lead I just got is not my equal. She's two levels higher than I am and can kill my chances for any job opening I go after in the company in a heartbeat." All the better. If she wants to hire sycophants who tell her only what she wants to hear, you don't want to work there any way. You're an equal. *This is a level playing field.* The CEO is not going to talk to you simply because he or she has nothing better to do. If you are invited to a meeting, there is already something operating that makes you worth talking to; it could be networking connections, your expertise, your knowledge of a company that the CEO would like as a customer, or simply that he or she is desperate to fill an unadvertised job opening. Regardless, you have a lot more to offer than you realize, and figuring out what that is is your job. If you realize that your opinions and reactions to interviewers are just as valuable (or more so) than their reactions to you, you'll come across well. A confident mind-set builds the chemistry that leads to job offers.

In case your mind and body aren't in agreement yet, try the cocktail party mind-set. Think of meeting with someone at a company as an invitation to a cocktail party. (Note that I didn't use the word "interview." That just raises the bar for everyone.) At a cocktail party, you are open, curious, willing to meet new people, and have the freedom to walk away. The stakes are low; there is no such thing as failure. If you don't like someone, you talk with someone else. You approach the party thinking, "Maybe I'll meet some interesting people or some new friends." If you don't, it isn't the end of the world.

A meeting at a company is nothing more than a very small cocktail party. If you think of these people you're meeting as potentially interesting people or new friends, it puts you in control. You can evaluate them also. You'll talk about things that you have in common that might interest both of you, like you would at a cocktail party, and if you don't feel *your* interest building, it might not be a fit. During the meeting, let your sense of humor emerge. Relax and your body language will be at ease too. You won't sit waiting for the next question, like you're on a firing line. You'll be asking questions and interacting as you would with a potential new friend. Guess what happens to the other person's interest in you when you're relaxed, genuinely curious, and have some insights into what his or her company is doing?

## No More "Yes-Man"

By the way, I see many professionals show their support and enthusiasm for a company by becoming more of a yes-man (regardless of gender) during an interview than is normally their style. This isn't to your advantage, especially with higher-level positions. To challenge some of the decision maker's assertions, albeit in your professional and humorous way, will make him or her slow down and think about what you've just said. You may have just differentiated yourself from the pack, which is generally a good strategy. This should not be an in-your-face challenge, but rather a suggestion, such as:

- "I may have some ideas for you. Have you thought about doing . . . ?" (Insert a *brief* strategy that you think would work better than their current one and listen to their reaction.) This is the lead-with-an-idea-but-get-the-cannon-pointed-at-the-right-target-before-you-fire approach.
- "I've had a great deal of success doing something similar. Want to hear about it?" Wow him or her with a brief PAR story that ends with the same results that he or she wants.
- Reframe the problem. "Sounds like you have an open-system problem but you may not be getting the results you want because you're using closed-system approaches." You could even move to the whiteboard at this point and draw some explanations. This is a consulting approach, but you're using it now to show you bring fresh perspectives.

Remember, however, with any of these three methods for demonstrating your leadership and initiative that you don't want to give them all of the answers. You're selling too hard if you give your listener all your ideas early on, and you also risk the chance of losing them because they may not like your approach. If they *do* like your approach, you don't want to give all your ideas away immediately. Why buy the cow when the milk is so cheap? You want to draw out the other person in a meeting or interview so you can learn about his or her needs, then show your leadership qualities when they are relevant and in relation to those needs. You're enjoying the intellectual stimulation and the conversation along the way so you're still having fun, right?

It is your job to create this initial friendship if you want the relationship to continue. It starts at the beginning, with the first contact. You never want to create the image of being desperate, even if you feel that way.

### WAYS TO HAVE FUN IN A MEETING (FORMERLY KNOWN AS AN INTERVIEW)

- Prepare ahead of time so you can relax. (Research the company. Be prepared with five reasons why they should hire you and with several PARs to showcase your expertise. Have questions ready to ask them too.)

- Ask the administrative support person whether anyone else will be attending the meeting. "Will anyone else be joining us for the meeting? It would be really helpful to know the names ahead of time." Do research on the people you'll be meeting to learn about their backgrounds. (Enter their names into your favorite search engine, such as google.com. The higher up they are in the company, the more you will unearth.)

- If you landed the appointment because of a mutual acquaintance, ask, "Have you seen Sheila lately?" during that awkward first couple of minutes while you're walking back to the office. Avoid name-dropping, but see if you have friends in common. It will build trust and future references.

- If you have a choice, select a chair that puts you at the same eye level as the decision maker rather than something cushy and low.

- Notice something personal in the office and comment on it.

- Take a deep breath when you sit down and give him or her a chance to start the meeting. Have a couple of questions ready in case he or she doesn't lead. (Warning: In an informational interview, it is your responsibility to take the lead and have an agenda. In a job interview, the keeper-of-the-agenda shifts.)

- Socialize a little up front. "Is it true that you're the world's greatest golfer?" "How long have you been with (the company)?" The latter answer usually identifies his or her career path. Tune in; the answer might give you clues about possibilities for you as well.

- Some humor, your unique perspective on some of his or her issues (in other words, a light challenge), or some *short*, relevant success stories all play well during the course of the meeting.

- Relax physically. If you typically use your hands, do so. Move around in your seat. Lean forward to make a point. Write on the whiteboard. Keep them awake.

- Be confident. Even if you don't know something, present your response with assurance. "Gee, I can get back to you with that answer on de-bugging code. Do you typically have your CIO spend time on this? How do you balance the need for planning in this job versus the daily operations?"

- Ask thought-provoking, open-ended questions about the market, competitors, and plans. Sticking to questions about the potential job can get boring and doesn't challenge interviewers to think. Engage them in broader questions that they'll actually enjoy. Be prepared to initiate questions. Sitting like a bump on a log waiting for the interviewer to go down a list of questions doesn't position you very well as a leader. Remember, this isn't an interview. It's a cocktail party, and you're both asking questions.

- At the end of the meeting, ask interviewers, "Where do we go from here?" Keep mental notes during the meeting of what you can do to help them, whether it be an idea for a camp for their daughter or the name of an article in a business magazine. You want to nurture the relationship.

See how having fun and interviewing skills start blending? They should. Interviews will feel less like firing lines and more like meetings with friends as you progress. Your results will improve.

## Wrap-Up

When you combine the feeling of confidence that you do offer something of value with a sense of control over your direction in the marketplace and the idea that managing your career may actually be enjoyable, what happens? You're on your way to the New Job Security. The transfer of control to you has begun. One taciturn controller reported, "Although I never considered job hunting an enjoyable exercise, with this approach, it actually became fun. Is there a way I can make a living at this?"

STRATEGY #2

# Market for Mutual Benefit

*If you are not thinking customer, you are not thinking.*
PHILIP KOTLER

While giving the marketing section of my seminars, I've learned that the subject of marketing has a bad reputation in some quarters. Just like a couple of the people you once knew in high school, its reputation has been sullied because of who it is hanging around with and what people think is happening. Marketing has been hanging around with sales, and to many, sales is synonymous with high pressure, like telemarketing calls on Sundays. Being fast, manipulative, or slick are some of the connotations that professionals come up with when I ask them their impressions of marketing. If you agree with these negative associations, let me ask you to suspend your preconceptions for a while. Not only is marketing a fascinating discipline, it has direct implications for your career management.

In *Kotler on Marketing: How to Create, Win, and Dominate Markets* (The Free Press, 1999), Philip Kotler describes classical product marketing as "discovering unmet needs and preparing satisfying solutions." This idea has parallels that can make a dramatic difference in your overall work management. It's the conceptual base that I use for my career management practice (and doesn't hurt for life in general, either) that results in setting you, a professional managing your career, apart from the crowds. Can you think of yourself as a product in the marketplace? If you can objectify yourself this way, clear a lot of your emotions out of the way, and understand that you're looking for the right consumer, you'll have a much greater range of successful practices and approaches at your disposal. After an outplacement workshop I gave for a biotech firm, an accomplished Ph.D. came up to me and said, "One of the most striking things I remember from today is your saying that I'm a box of Tide on the shelf. I'd never thought of myself this way, but it actually makes what I'm going through easier." Let's see how it works for you.

## Marketing: The Four Ps Pay Off

Marketing is the planning strategy that transcends the selling process. Peter Drucker, an internationally renowned business strategist, once said, "The aim of marketing is to make selling superfluous." Although this may seem a trifle optimistic, it demonstrates the power that discovering unmet needs and creating relevant solutions can generate to pull people toward you versus the more painful "push" practices of cold calling and direct mailing. Why not use these ideas to build a demand for your services? Using the four Ps of product marketing will convince people to select you.

The four Ps—product, placement, promotion, and pricing—describe the optimum methods for driving product (you) consumption by various markets (your favorite industries that you listed in the last chapter). Take a look at how the four Ps help you analyze your situation.

### H O M E W O R K

### ☞ The Four Ps Pay Off

| The Four Ps of Product Marketing | Consumer Product Example | Professional Career Example | Your Strategy (Fill in the sections below.) |
| --- | --- | --- | --- |
| *Product:* Item or service to be consumed with specific features and benefits. Covers product research and development, including how new products are created or current products can be improved. | Coca-Cola. | Your strengths and assets that can be consumed (hired) and will benefit the consumer (employer). You can do your own product upgrades such as acquiring training and building new skills. | Features (your skills):<br><br><br>Benefits (how you differentiate yourself, your value): |

| The Four Ps of Product Marketing | Consumer Product Example | Professional Career Example | Your Strategy |
|---|---|---|---|
| *Placement:* Distribution methods. The channels through which the product reaches the marketplace. | Vending machines, grocery stores, fast-food chains. | Help wanted ads, networking, search firms, and direct mail. May include your geographic preferences. | Preferred ways to reach your market: |
| *Promotion:* Methods to develop awareness and consumption of a brand name (Coca-Cola) and specific products (Diet Coke and Classic Coke). | Media advertising, sponsorship of sporting events, and placement in movies. | Résumé, word of mouth, speaking engagements, writing for professional publications, and mailings. | Preferred ways to get your name to the top of the pile: |
| *Pricing:* Amount to charge for a product or service depending on production costs, margins, geography, competition, desired image, and what the market will bear. | Retails at approximately $1 per serving. | Compensation and benefits package. (Strategy #5: Negotiate in Round Rooms.) | Price (you're not cheap): |

Isn't this a great structure for your thinking? You can use this process to develop a marketing plan for yourself that cuts down on *reacting* and initiates *planning* and *strategy*. Warning: You're not going to have all the answers for the column about your strategy yet. You'll want to modify them as you continue reading this book and do some market research.

To get started, you need to define yourself as a product. Refer to the strengths and skills that you've already identified and build on them. Your strengths are no minor point. You use them to develop product differentiators. In other words, how are you, a software engineer, different from other software engineers that are in the marketplace?

During the implosions of the dot coms in 2000 and 2001, when high growth, Internet start-up companies were rapidly running out of resources and closing, presidents of those companies frequently called me. Each conversation would start, "I'm sure that I'm different from most of the people that you're talking to. I've been president of a small company that doesn't exist any longer, and now I want to run a more stable company." The problem is, they *weren't* different in their presentations. Everyone was sounding and looking the same even though each person, as an individual, was highly competent and unique. This is all part of product development. How does your experience at your company (and people in start-ups get a lot of valuable experience quickly) differentiate you? *You need to do the thinking for other people. They aren't going to exert the energy.* The more you've analyzed your "product" in relationship to market needs, including reinterpreting perceived liabilities as benefits, the more quickly and easily you can respond and articulate your fit.

Now how are you going to reach your markets; what distribution channels or placement are you going to use to let people know about you? I strongly suggest networking as your dominant method, but you'll want to consider search firms and relevant job listings as well. To continue, you must promote yourself in a very professional manner. A résumé is the most obvious vehicle, but helping others does wonders to motivate others to help you. More on that shortly. The final "P," pricing, is a topic that you don't want to blindside you. What are you worth in the marketplace? You can monitor this on an ongoing basis. The information will serve you during your annual performance appraisal as well as when negotiating during job searches. More on this in chapter six.

## You Can't Hit Bull's-Eyes If You Don't Aim for the Targets

Prior to delving into your own marketing plan, go back to your industry choices in Strategy #1: Take Control, and choose three or four target markets. Target markets are groups of companies with similar characteristics. Biotech, chemical manufacturers, insurance, commercial real estate, and telecommunications firms, for example, are markets that have their own separate problems, vocabularies, and needs. At least two of your choices should have some connection with your background. The greater leap you take from your roots, the harder the search and any salary transferability become. Allen, in chapter two, is a great example of someone who identified target markets. The list of industries in which he had experience became his list of target markets, as long as they were within his geographic constraints and preferred sales parameters. He enjoyed the industries he had worked in previously and was willing to continue searching within those industries locally.

Allen also listed some industry categories that were not exactly what he had been doing, but were close enough hits that the companies in these markets should be interested in his background (holding companies doing multiple transactions and international companies opening domestic operations that weren't in his specific area of expertise). That's a great idea for you too. Choosing some related-but-different target markets can open up your search. Ask yourself, "Who would be interested in my set of skills?"

## Who to Refer To: Your Referral Triangle

One way to brainstorm ideas for the related-but-different groups is to look at your Referral Triangle. Analyze the three categories of business that surround the companies in which you have worked: vendors, competitors, and customers. Where would your skills fit in these categories?

**YOUR REFERRAL TRIANGLE**

You probably don't want to work for all three of these groups, and your skills probably won't fit with all three. People in the retail industry, for example, aren't typically able to turn to customers for information, networking, or employment. People in business-to-business sales, however, may discover that they can change to another industry because they have the same customers in common. Look at the categories that are of interest and see whether any target markets make sense for you. A physician is surrounded by equipment, medications, software, and services that are targeted to improving his or her performance. One of these vendors may be interested in hiring a physician who knows the vendors' customers and has immediate credibility and who can suggest how the company might improve its products. Many is the doctor who has left private practice to work with medical instrumentation, pharmaceutical, or insurance firms. You may have people out there just waiting for your skills with a little repackaging.

Two other points about the Referral Triangle. First, even though you may not want to work for any of the vendors in your Referral Triangle, they may be great sources of information. Sales reps who come to your company probably aren't going to be the ones to hire you, but they know what's going on with their customers and their own company. The smart ones are usually willing to help you get into another company. You might consider them as a possible vendor.

Second, if you're in transition, have a noncompete agreement, and are concerned about even mentioning the names of the competition, don't worry about it too much yet. Time takes care of it as a rule. Your current firm is a source of references, experience, friends, and a lot of memories. Even if you consider working for the competition at some point, you would never breathe a word of competitive information to your new company, even without a noncompete, right? Your reputation is everything. You can talk with companies as long as it isn't flying in the face of some legal or ethical agreement. I've seen plenty of people take long enough with the interviewing and selection process that the noncompete was a moot point by the time the job offer was made, negotiated, and accepted.

When you start building your network in Strategy #4: Network as the Norm, you'll discover that you can revisit the Referral Triangle and apply it to each company for which you've worked to give you additional ideas for leads and connections.

## A Hit List of Your Target Markets

What's the point of researching multiple target markets simultaneously? Speed, options, control. If you explore one target market at a time, a sequential search, you might decide at the end of six months that you don't want to work in advertising firms, or maybe the economy has wiped out that sector. If you then begin to check out your second choice, you've just lost a lot of time. You're also losing options if you pursue one target market at a time. Within a geographic area, metro San Francisco, for example, no one target market can generate as many job offers as several markets combined. The number of companies that you'd truly want to work for within a given category, which happen to need you at the same time, is finite. The more people that you have pursuing you, the better. It ain't over until it's over, as Yogi Berra must have said about job searches, so you need the volume of choices that several target markets can generate. If you don't have enough companies going into the job "funnel" at the beginning of the search, you're not going to have any choices coming out. Choices lead to *control*. Working with multiple target markets lets you search faster, increases your options about where to go, hence giving you greater control over the immediate outcome as well as your ongoing work satisfaction.

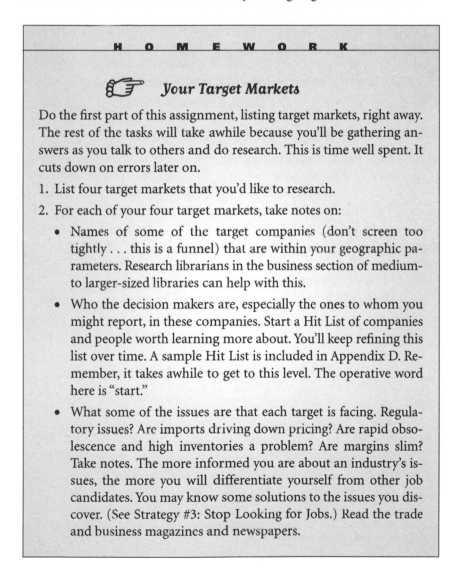

**H O M E W O R K**

### ☞ *Your Target Markets*

Do the first part of this assignment, listing target markets, right away. The rest of the tasks will take awhile because you'll be gathering answers as you talk to others and do research. This is time well spent. It cuts down on errors later on.

1. List four target markets that you'd like to research.

2. For each of your four target markets, take notes on:

   - Names of some of the target companies (don't screen too tightly . . . this is a funnel) that are within your geographic parameters. Research librarians in the business section of medium- to larger-sized libraries can help with this.

   - Who the decision makers are, especially the ones to whom you might report, in these companies. Start a Hit List of companies and people worth learning more about. You'll keep refining this list over time. A sample Hit List is included in Appendix D. Remember, it takes awhile to get to this level. The operative word here is "start."

   - What some of the issues are that each target is facing. Regulatory issues? Are imports driving down pricing? Are rapid obsolescence and high inventories a problem? Are margins slim? Take notes. The more informed you are about an industry's issues, the more you will differentiate yourself from other job candidates. You may know some solutions to the issues you discover. (See Strategy #3: Stop Looking for Jobs.) Read the trade and business magazines and newspapers.

- What their vocabulary is. What words do they use? Start morphing your experience into their language. Fund-raising, business development, sales, and marketing all have threads in common. Use words that your target market will quickly understand and value.

You will research many different sources, including publications, the Internet, and people in the know. Save any killer connections with decision makers for later on, once you have your market intelligence. Gathering information will help you eliminate the target markets that don't look that interesting as well as put you at the top of your game when you approach potential employers.

## The Marketing Circle

Here comes the fun part, breathing life and energy into your campaign by giving to others. As you give to others, they want to reciprocate, or give back. It's not a common practice when looking for jobs to think of your helping the employer *first*, often before you even have an interview. This concept, core to Strategy #2: Market for Mutual Benefit, will make perfect sense shortly. It is such a powerful driver of building relationships that your career will grow using this skill alone. Put it together with the other four career strategies in this book and you're going places.

It all starts with a simple circle, you on one side, a potential employer on the other.

**THE MARKETING CIRCLE**

## *Your Needs*

On the top half of the circle, start jotting down things that *you* want from an *employer*. You might start off with income, for example. How about challenging work? Try to define that one a little more. Flexibility, recognition—keep the ideas coming. Write these things down so you can see your expectations in front of you. A blank circle is included in Appendix E so you can play with it some more. Take a break, then come back to your list. Any new entries? Did you first think of things that you feel are missing from your current employer? That's natural. Now what about things your employer provides that you value but may take for granted, such as benefits, positive feedback, or work that you really enjoy doing?

Two areas that people often miss when they're developing their employment goals (yes, that's what you're doing) are the type of physical environment they like to work in and the type of people they want to work with. As to your physical environment, do you like a structured, formal downtown office, a converted warehouse with arcade games, or bunny slippers in a home office? Don't eliminate your second- or third-choice environments from your search yet, while you're still learning about the marketplace, but being comfortable with the environment you finally select is important. Surroundings can reflect culture and values, and you'll want yours to fit with your company's. What type of environment is important to you?

What type of people do you like to work with? Do you prefer to be on your own, do you want to lead a company of highly technical workers, do you want to be on an interdependent team with people having different skill sets with abilities equal to yours? If you clearly define your preference of colleagues and environment—having listed everything from the type of corporate culture you'd like to the type of boss you'd like—your odds have just gone up for finding the right future employer.

## THE MARKETING CIRCLE: YOUR NEEDS

Now, hopefully before you've gotten too far into your job market search, is the optimum time to define your preferences for your next employer. You have just developed a template. You can use this template as a measuring stick for potential offers, remembering that no company or offer is perfect. Deciding what you want from your boss and company now, early on, puts you at an advantage:

- When someone has an offer in hand, do you know what happens? The job seeker will subconsciously skew what he or she is looking for to fit the offer. Who likes to stay on the job market just for the thrill of the hunt? Accepting a job without honestly comparing it to your needs often results in your not lasting in the job for too long, or being unhappy with what you're doing.

- You have expectations that are important and need to be valued. They help level the playing field. The employer isn't the only one with some power.

- You have created the basis for questions that will be part of your meetings and interviews. If one of your goals is flexibility, for example, after they extend an offer you might ask, "I see some models of telecommuting in your company. Would you consider my doing the writing portion of this job from my home office, as long as your deadlines and budget were met or improved upon?" The way you ask the question and when you ask the question are important. We'll come back to this after we fill in the other side of the circle.

- You now know what topics to avoid for the early stages of any interviews. Your needs are a hidden agenda. "How can that be?" you ask. "If most of my needs aren't met, I'm not going to want the job." If you don't first meet most of *their* needs, you're not going to have a job offer to reject. Stay with me while we look at the other side of the circle, then we'll come back to this point.

## An Employer's Needs

First, the critical question: What does an *employer* want of *you?* Professionals in my seminars typically respond: skills, cultural fit, loyalty, and problem solving. These are all good answers and correct. There's something more, however. What's a one word definition of a successful company? Think about it.

**THE MARKETING CIRCLE: AN EMPLOYER'S NEEDS**

Inevitably, the right answer comes back: profitability. Profitability is the bottom line, in all senses of the word. If you can demonstrate that you're a profitable employee, do you think an employer will be interested in you? No doubt about it. Even if you want to work for a nonprofit, the managers will be sophisticated enough to know that they have to compete for market share (percentage of potential business) and bring in profits; it's how they spend their revenues and how they account for them that differs. Profitability, for better or worse, rules.

## *Proving Your Profitability*

The flashing neon light message from the marketing circle is that you have to show your profitability to attract the attention of a potential employer. "But," you say, "how I am I supposed to show profitability when my expertise is in researching molecular oncology? My job is to focus on scientific breakthroughs, not profits." Ah, the seeds of the answer are in the mission. Breakthroughs create profits. Profitability comes in many different forms,

**Showing your profitability will attract the attention of a potential employer.**

and it is your job to think this through and present it with confidence. You'll get more attention and better results if you take the initiative to translate your work into profitability for an employer, because they won't spend time on it.

How have you been profitable in your work experience? You have benefited your company(s) in more ways than you realize. Let's look at the two most obvious ways that you've been profitable.

### MAKING MONEY

How do you make money for a company? The following listing is certainly not inclusive, but it will start you thinking. Check off any items that may be relevant, and jot down any specific events that come into your mind. They may turn into stories (PARs) or hooks for résumés and conversations later on:

- You've increased your company's visibility in the marketplace (this includes speaking engagements, participation in professional meetings, writing for publications, and being interviewed).
- You've set up strategies, plans, and structures that enabled your company to reach its goals.
- You've closed a sale.
- You've built relationships with customers.
- You've initiated relationships with people or companies that might become customers.
- You've trained customers to use your product or service correctly, to their satisfaction.
- You've turned around a problem with a customer.
- You've developed products or services, sometimes with breakthrough thinking, that have responded to customer or market needs.

- You've researched data, technology, or information that has enabled you to improve the quality of a product or service.
- You've recruited, hired, and retained top talent.
- You've ensured that employees at all levels stay well trained and competitive.
- You've developed a structure that encourages employees to perform at their highest levels.
- You've set up a structure to access capital when it is needed.
- You've built relationships with financial markets.
- You've improved the reporting of information for better decision making.
- You've acquired, divested, merged, or spun off companies for your company.
- You've delivered a product or service to the market on time and under budget.
- You've done something for your company that others couldn't or haven't.

What else have you done?

### SAVING MONEY

The flip side of making money is not spending it! That's what creates profitability. You save money in multiple ways all the time for your company. Check off any of the following items that apply, and add more. Once again, jot down any specific incident that the examples trigger so you can refer to them when you're developing your résumé and thinking through responses:

- You've done more with less, including fewer people and limited time. (You're bound to have several examples in this large category.)
- You've integrated businesses, consolidated operations, or reduced overhead or operating expenses (another giant category).
- You've improved quality.
- You've streamlined manufacturing processes.
- You've reduced inventory, reduced scrap or waste, or reduced "bugs."
- You've improved field installation and/or service so fewer things go wrong.
- You've reduced purchasing costs by buying or budgeting wisely.

- You've reengineered processes so less time and effort are spent internally or on delivering your product or service.
- You've converted information systems so accurate information can be accessed quickly and easily.
- You've outsourced operations.
- You've managed reductions in force.
- You've structured compensation systems so they're competitive, but don't overcommit the company when revenues are low.
- You've thought of ways to do things faster, better, or cheaper (without lowering quality) that other people haven't.

You're pretty good, aren't you? Keeping track of how you are profitable isn't something you wait to do until you're between jobs. If you wait until you're between jobs to figure out why you're good, not only have you forgotten half of the things that other people would really value (and you've taken for granted), but you've buried any numbers or results that would make your work look really impressive. Track numbers whenever you can. Otherwise, track results and outcomes. A college administrator said that she "increased parent satisfaction, commitment to the institution, and word-of-mouth referral" by running outstanding parents' programs. You don't see any dollars listed, but you can visualize them flying out of the parents' wallets into the bursar's office.

## So What?

If you aren't sure that the above items you've checked off really get across your point about what a difference you've made, you haven't been specific enough yet. Saying that you've outsourced operations, for example, really doesn't describe the results. To get closer to an example of profitability, ask yourself "So what?" after each statement.

---

I outsourced the payroll operation.
> *So what?*

So we didn't have to do it in-house anymore.
> *So what?*

So I was able to eliminate two positions and transfer a third person to an open requisition that I would have had to fill anyway. She preferred the new assignment, too.

*So what?*

So we saved nearly $100 thousand in the first year alone, even deducting the cost of the payroll service. I freed up some space that another department could use, and we lowered our own headaches substantially. The employees don't really care about where their checks are coming from, as long as they come.

*Bingo.*

---

You just created a hook. A "hook" is a selling point that you can communicate quickly and clearly, which emphasizes results. The hook in the above example could be "I analyzed and implemented an outsourcing program for the company that resulted in providing superior services to our employees at 40 percent of what we had been spending. Are you looking at any cost savings programs?" Not only did you state your hook, you strategically followed up with an open-ended question on that topic to link its applicability to a target company. The conversation keeps going in the right direction.

## What Ifs

Before you start saying, "But, it wasn't just me . . ."

- **What if I wasn't responsible for the final outcome?**

  Many people are responsible for a final outcome; few feel that they are. Can a company turn out a successful product or service without numerous people behind it? Own your part. It will emerge as "I developed the prototype that went on to result in over $5 million in new sales for the company in its first year." You're not claiming credit for the entire process, but you can share in the glory of the outcomes.

- **What if the project got canceled, and all of my work was lost?**

  This happens. It can be crushingly disappointing, but even in the best companies, avenues of research, product development, analysis, and investment are sometimes dropped. Describe what you did accomplish, then stop the story. Though possibly incomplete, your hook is still valid. "I developed a new process for coating the boards that addressed some of the failures we were seeing in the field. It was the first time that anyone had been able to do that, and the VP of engineering was thrilled." You didn't mention that your division was sold before your idea was integrated into the product, but you could tell them, if they asked, what happened. In the meantime, you've proven your competency.

- **What if I hate to brag?**
  That's the nice thing about telling a PAR story (see Appendix B). You aren't bragging. You're telling a story. People typically talk in stories. Listen at your next social gathering, and you'll hear them. People enjoy listening to stories. You're not talking about you. You're talking about results.

- **What if I'm not in job transition, but am currently employed?**
  So much the better. You can start building your arsenal of amazing accomplishments now. Guess when it pays off? At your next performance appraisal. If you don't normally get appraisals, ask for one. You're going to know things about your results that your boss doesn't have a clue about.

---

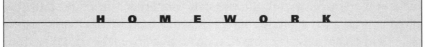

**H O M E W O R K**

### ☞ Track Your Results

Start a file somewhere in your computer or in a notebook, preferably one that is at your home. Record your results in it. Don't wait until they are major, earth-shattering events or you won't have many entries. Sometimes, surviving a day is quite an accomplishment. Stop taking things for granted; other people will value what you're ignoring.

Collect accomplishments first, then quantify them as you can. A PAR story is an easy way to get started. If you're part of a large project, track the results of the whole project. Ask yourself, "So what?" until your part is as close to the company's outcome as possible. The last sentence with the results is your hook.

List at least five ways that you have been profitable for companies in your career. End each example with a hook. If you prefer, you can fine-tune the results portions of your PAR stories until the hooks are sharp.

---

## The "Mutual Benefit" Part of Marketing

After a lot of preparation, you're now ready for the mutual benefit part of marketing. This is where it gets fun.

## THE MARKETING CIRCLE:
## SPEND YOUR TIME ON THE BoSoC

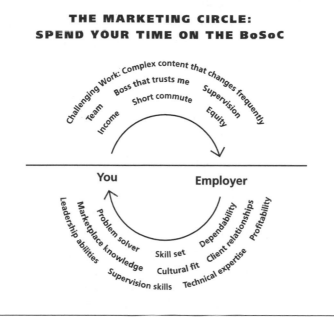

Okay, now that you have completed the whole circle, here comes one of the most important points in this book: When you're talking with people, especially potential employers, where are your conversations focused? On the top side of the circle or the bottom?

This is marketing at its best. *You're considering the needs of your target market (the bottom side of the circle) and presenting your product (you) in terms of those needs.* All your communications with potential employers (or a current one) should focus on their needs, the bottom side of the circle (BoSoC). This may sound cynical or harsh, but it works. They may care that you aren't being paid fairly or that you've just been laid off from your last job or that you have a bad boss, but that isn't going to motivate them to hire you (or promote you, or give you a raise, or help you get a job in a different department). Only staying attuned to their needs will motivate them.

In my seminars, when I discuss the critical nature of concentrating on the employers' needs, everybody agrees with me. Our own needs still sneak back into our communications, however. Disciplining yourself to communicate on the BoSoC is easier said than done. It takes practice.

## A Marketing Circle Quiz

Test yourself with the following four examples. Can you tell whether the examples represent needs on the top side (your needs) or on the bottom side (the employer's needs) of the marketing circle?

- In a résumé, the objective reads: Challenging position in a growth-oriented company.

  *Better objective:* Senior-executive position building global business through organic growth and acquisitions.

- During an interview, in response to "Tell me about yourself": "Well, I graduated from college in 1902, and I'll give you a capsule of my work experience since then . . ."

  *Better response:* An Elevator Story (see Appendix C). Select the strengths that best coincide with the needs you believe they have.

  *Best response:* "I have over fifteen years of experience doing (whatever it is they need that you do). So I don't bore you with my entire life history, would you like to tell me a little more about what you're looking for in this position, and I'll tell you where we overlap?" You're getting them to talk first. Good idea.

- During an interview with a biotech company, you're asked, "What sort of work have you been doing?": "I've been helping to develop the LR2000 for some time. As you may know, that, along with the Q2X work I've been doing, is going to be a big breakthrough in fiber optic technology." (The company you're talking with isn't in fiber optics.)

  *Better response:* "The work I've been doing sounds like it's very similar to some of the development work you're doing around the topical applications of XYZ. Am I correct in understanding that the compound's absorption is one of your main areas of interest? I can tell you about my work in that area." Forget the product names that are used in your old company and any vocabulary that your target market doesn't need (such as fiber optic, if that isn't their field). Use their vocabulary as much as possible. Emphasize sameness more than difference.

- Response by a job candidate to the question "What's your salary?": "I've been making $100 thousand, so I wouldn't want anything less than that."

  *Better response:* "I'm sure you pay competitively. What did you have in mind?" (See Strategy #5: Negotiate in Round Rooms for more info.)

See the difference? All four of the examples were on the top side of the circle, but the better and best responses moved them to the bottom side. All of the better responses focus on the bottom side of the circle (BoSoC) to motivate your listener. There are few of us who aren't motivated by our own and our family's best interests. Those of us who aren't are already in religious orders. The secret, however, is that by meeting someone else's BoSoC, you meet your own as well. This is Marketing for Mutual Benefit. Being helpful to other people, will, in turn, inspire them to be helpful to you. You're putting deposits in a bank for future withdrawals. You're accruing interest in the meantime, in all senses of the word. The help you offer now may have nothing to do with a job opening that you want. It may mean sending someone an article recommending a place to go fly fishing since you've discovered that you share this interest. But you're building a relationship and helping someone else. That's the great part I've been promising: helping others. You can meet peoples' needs (their BoSoCs) directly or indirectly. Either way works.

- *A direct BoSoC:* An employer is rolling out a new product in a month, but her director of media relations was just recruited away by another company. Given your background in advertising, you ask whether she'd like some help pulling together their promotional efforts in the interim. Note: You didn't ask for a commitment, you just offered to help. (See Strategy #3: Stop Looking for Jobs.) She's listening. She is in a corner and has to deliver.

  This same approach is golden at your current company. You can build relationships anywhere in a company, including with your own boss, if you identify needs and respond to them. Be careful! You don't have much spare time, so be very strategic about where and with whom you offer to help.

  In direct BoSoCs, as well as with your résumé and all telephone conversations with potential employers, it's safe to assume that profitability, or the path to it, is your underlying theme. Emphasizing ways to make an employer successful will have the ripple effect you want.

- *An indirect BoSoC:* You and a potential employer discover that you both have seventeen-year-old daughters who are going through the college-selection process. After hearing about his daughter's interests, you discover that you went to one of her first-choice schools. You say, "No guarantees, but I'll see if I can help." You'll want to meet the kid first so you aren't recommending her blindly, using up your good connections in the process. This is a quadruple win: the employer, his daughter, your alma mater (because you only recommend kids that you honestly think will benefit them), and you, the Nice Person. Deposits in the bank.

- *An out-of-office BoSoC:* I can't resist giving you an example of how Marketing for Mutual Benefit works in personal relationships, too. Your spouse doesn't want to do something that you want to do, such as go to the theater. You know that your spouse loves to get together with another couple, so you see whether they are interested in joining you if you can get tickets and if your spouse agrees. You learn that tickets are available, then you ask your spouse whether he or she would like to go to the theater with the other couple before you buy or commit to anything. This is how you Market for Mutual Benefit. You defined the needs of the target market (your spouse who likes to socialize with friends), and presented the product (night out) in terms of your spouse's needs. This works with teenagers, too.

## How Do I Know What Their Needs Are?

Good question. As President Bush said (both of them), "Espionage is a dirty business." You won't actually be doing anything clandestine, but it's in your best interest to gather information about your target markets from multiple sources. If you depend on a company's annual report or their website, you're reading only what the company wants you to see. One of my clients discovered that the defense contractor that was aggressively courting him was being indicted for fraud. The company had never brought it up in the interviews, obviously, so if he hadn't done his homework, he might not have known to avoid the company until it was too late.

How do you determine a company's needs? By reading and talking. On the reading side, the Internet takes much less time than traditional forms of research for accessing newspaper articles, investment analyses, and company reputations. The reference librarian in a good public library can be helpful. There's also a professional association of researchers, the Association of Independent Information Professionals, that you can contract to dig up information on your final targets. Their Web address is www.aiip.org. Susan Weiler, a professional researcher who has done great detective work for me (weilerinfoserv.com), recommends them as way to save time and to learn about resources that you might miss otherwise. They're not cheap, but you may find them worth the investment.

On the talking side, ask your friends and colleagues what they know about the companies that interest you. We'll get into this more with

Strategy #4: Network as the Norm, but finding contacts in and around potential target companies is the best way to check out the management team and the board, two groups that will determine your long-term well-being. You can research their backgrounds as well. This will help you establish what you have in common, such as going to the same undergraduate school or liking golf, for future conversations.

As you're doing your research, keep a list of the questions that occur to you about what's happening at the company. Their needs are not far behind. Why did the earnings slip for two quarters in a row? Will the product they're developing have a lot of competition? By doing your homework, you'll have a good idea about what their needs are, the bottom side of the marketing circle, before you ever talk to them.

A *warning:* When talking to an employer, don't state what you've learned in your research as a carved-in-stone fact. If you read that a mutual fund the financial services company you're targeting runs is doing poorly in the marketplace, address your concern in a question instead. "How are you thinking of responding to the anxiety in the marketplace about high-growth funds?" This typically works better than "Wow! You really got trashed in the market last week." You won't trigger any defensiveness, you'll show that you know that everything you read isn't necessarily accurate (except for some career books), and you'll gain information from them. Well done.

## This Is for Real, Folks

The satisfying thing about Marketing for Mutual Benefit is that you start off wondering, "Is this some sort of game?" and end up realizing that you're truly making the world a better place, one person at a time. You're actually helping other people. Sounds corny, but it's habit forming. This is not a game, nor should you start helping others within your professional network if it feels fake or insincere. You should be helping others because you want to, or you'll be frustrated when a favor is not noticed or is not repaid according to your timetable. The motivation must be internal. Helping others doesn't quit when you land a job, either. This book is about career *management,* not just finding your next job.

"Where do I find the time?" you might ask. Good question. The answer is to focus. You can concentrate on a finite group of people with whom you want to develop relationships, and refer others to different resources. You're just not physically going to have the time to help everyone, but you can at least give them some alternatives. In Strategy #4: Network as the Norm, you'll get ideas, including "The Sixty-Second Networker." It's doable. You

Market for Mutual Benefit as you continue in your day-to-day work. As you supervise others, you motivate them by meeting their needs, their BoSoC, such as letting them manage their schedules so they can do things like go to their kid's soccer games. They'll love you. If you leave a company, or have to turn down a company that's recruiting you, do so with good grace. When leaving a company, avoiding a meltdown will provide you with greater options in the future: references, networks, even rehiring or consulting. It happens all the time. Those are your benefits, or the top side of your circle. The company's BoSoC is a peaceful transition, among other things. If you're recruited and need to turn down a company or search firm, try to give the name of someone else who might work out and notify the other person that you did so. How many friends did you make with that transaction? You haven't taken much time doing any of this, but you've created a habit of helping others.

## Wrap-Up

A wonderful by-product of Marketing for Mutual Benefit is the way your reputation grows. When you make suggestions about how you can enhance someone else's profitability or help someone on a personal level, you'll gain much more than potential interest in you as a job applicant or promotable employee. You'll gain respect and recognition. You'll build trust because you took a risk on someone else's behalf. You've given something of yourself without expecting anything in return.

Of course, your kindnesses will be repaid in many ways. Not only will your bank account grow, people you have helped will tell other people about you as well. The moral of this Market for Mutual Benefit story is to *start now*. "Pay it forward" now. Start building the relationships and connections that will support you throughout your career now. Answer the needs of people within your target markets. You're no longer asking people to help you to fix your problem; you've regained your creativity and your dignity and taken control of your career. You're putting your safety net into place. That's essential to your New Job Security.

STRATEGY #3

# Stop Looking for Jobs

*To try to make the future is highly risky.*
*It is less risky, however, than not to try to make it.*

PETER DRUCKER

When professionals describe the pain they feel after having been rejected or, worse yet, ignored by multiple companies, their discouragement is palpable. "I was a perfect fit for their ad, and I didn't even hear back from them." Or, "After the initial screening by the search firm, they wouldn't even return my calls." Or, "I applied for a promotion in another part of my company, didn't get it, and now my boss has cut me out of the information loop."

There's an easy solution to feeling like roadkill. Stop looking for jobs.

People are always taken aback when I say this. "How can I? Job openings are real, and they're currently available. That's where the income, security, and opportunities are." Like Willy Sutton, who chose to rob banks because "that's where they keep the money," professionals know that a company is where the jobs are kept, and so help wanted ads or search firms must be the best way in. This is true sometimes, but not always. Posted, advertised job openings, regardless of whether they're listed on a company's website, in a help wanted ad, on a jobs listing board, internally, or with a search firm, are just a fraction of what's happening. The same happens with search firms. Not all companies can afford or choose to pay others to do their searches for them.

## Self-Abuse: Help Wanted Ads and Search Firms

When you're in transition, there's a natural tendency to go to help wanted ads and search firms first. They're obvious sources of approved, funded opportunities where you can shortcut this job search and get to work quickly, right? Not necessarily. Help wanted ads and search firms are only distribution channels for the job market. (Remember the "P" for placement in the four Ps of marketing?) They advertise but a fraction of the available jobs. And, bluntly said, neither channel to the job market is geared to help the job seeker. Their goal is to help the employer. They can be a source of abuse or disappointment for you. Once you understand the motivations of search firms and the employers behind the apparent job openings and realize that they aren't responding to *any* candidate (okay, a slight exaggeration) and that it's nothing personal, it gets easier.

> **Help wanted ads and search firms advertise but a fraction of the available jobs.**

Ross was definitely unhappy after his first attempts at looking for a job. He had chosen to leave his company in Germany where he was corporate vice president and general manager for an international manufacturer. He wanted to cut back on an overwhelming travel schedule and establish some longer-term roots in the United States than he had been able to develop while living in Europe, Singapore, Montreal, California, and Boston. It was time to settle down. He kicked off his campaign by responding to senior-level help wanted ads and contacting search firms. Then he responded to some more . . .

No one responded to him.

Ross was both surprised and incensed. He wasn't comfortable asking for help. He was reserved, formal, used to being in charge, and not fond of chitchat. To risk approaching people and then be ignored was the ultimate insult.

The problem was the channels he chose. Ross was putting all his energy into the two most visible channels to the job market, help wanted ads and search firms, which are the two that have the lowest yields (3 percent and 10 to 15 percent, respectively).

He rebalanced his time to develop a new network and expand his old one, no minor feat for someone who cringed at the thought of networking. He found a way to connect with others that fit with his highly professional, reserved image, and now has offers . . . for unadvertised jobs.

Before we talk about how to stop looking for jobs, let's talk about the best way to approach help wanted ads and search firms. You don't want to totally ignore these visible jobs, but you will want to spend your time where the work is likely to be: in creating jobs. The best campaigns use a combination of approaches or distribution channels, varying the amount of energy spent on each according to the odds of its paying off. Help wanted ads may get 3 percent of your time and search firms, 10 to 15 percent. You'll know the right percentages for you as your campaign progresses. First, however, the visible listings.

## Help Wanted Ads

Let's look at ads (regardless of their source—newspapers, online, or elsewhere) first. To the job seeker, the ads look like a straightforward request for skills. The odds of your receiving a request for an interview are extremely low, however. How could the returns be so low when you know that you're a great fit?

---

### WARNING

- *Just because you see a help wanted ad doesn't mean that there's a job opening.*
- *Even if there is an opening, everybody else is seeing the same posted ad.*

---

Companies use help wanted ads for a lot of different reasons besides filling a position. A company can demonstrate to the Immigration and Naturalization Service that they need a green card for a current, highly skilled employee if they can show that no one else in an applicant pool is as well qualified. A company might have a highly desirable internal applicant for an opening and place an ad as a confirmation that it has the right person. It may be trying to build its database and collection of résumés in case of a turnover. A blind ad (no company name listed) could even be a consulting company hired to find out what a client would need to pay if it recruited for the job described in the ad, in other words, a salary survey. You've seen "salary history must be included to be considered" in your Sunday morning reading or your cyber skimming. There isn't a salary survey behind every request, obviously, but you don't have to play a company's game by answering the salary question. (See Strategy #5: Negotiate in Round Rooms in chapter six for more information.)

The rule of thumb is to go ahead and respond, always to a specific name that you can track down if it isn't listed, but do not put your heart in the envelope or the email. Usually you can track down either the person who would be making the hiring decision or the senior human resources person (or both) from the company's website, a search engine, a directory in the library, or simply by asking the company's telephone operator. Spending a lot of time or emotional energy on a help wanted ad is not a good use of your resources. Have a generic response to help wanted ads in your computer that you can pull up when needed. Modify it slightly to fit if the ad is worth a little extra trouble, then ship it off. The most important part of responding to a help wanted ad is putting your network into action, if you really like something. This is a two-tiered response: responding to the ad so your résumé is in the official pile, and networking into the company at the same time. This shows that you follow the rules, but keeps you from getting lost in a stack on a desk in human resources. If you can contact someone inside the company, ask, "What is it like to work there? Who is handling the search? What's the management team like? What do you think of the products?" This will start building a relationship. You haven't asked the person to put in a good word for you yet, but see how the conversation goes. He or she might volunteer to do so, in which case you can graciously accept, assuming that his or her name and reputation is one that you'd like to have representing you within the company. If the person doesn't volunteer and you're comfortable asking, say, "Can I get you to put in a good word for me with [the hiring manager]?" He or she will typically be happy to do so. Regard-

> **The most important part of responding to a help wanted ad is putting your network into action if you really like something.**

less of how you respond to a help wanted ad, not investing yourself in it is psychological protection, not only because the ad may be a red herring, but because . . .

## Everyone Else Is Seeing the Same Ad

If you see an ad, so does your competition. If you're responding, so are they. It's not just your worthy competitor who's responding, but every Tom, Dick, and Harriet who may not be remotely qualified but feels like they are moving forward in their own job search if they respond to ads. With this group, you're not competing over who has the best qualifications, but rather for the attention and energy of the résumé reviewer (often one of the newer hires in the human resources department for the first screening). For every decent-sized ad in a major metropolitan newspaper, it isn't unusual for a company to receive hundreds of résumés in response. Job postings on the Internet can generate even more responses because there are no geographical limitations to the number of people who see the ad. How much attention are you going to get? Chances are that the most qualified people aren't selected to be interviewed because the human resources screener fell asleep before she finished reading all the résumés (ah, human frailty enters into the selection process more than we want to know).

The human resources department and the company will move at their own pace, which is rarely the speed you'd prefer. When they don't get back to you, it's not out of maliciousness, but because of the volume of responses. Even if you responded to an ad that wasn't real, or if someone had the inside track, the outcome is the same. Companies rarely allocate people or resources to respond to a high volume of applicants. You're better off if you don't expect a response.

With so many strikes against responding to help wanted ads, it's a wonder that their popularity as a channel to the job market continues. As long as they look like a sure, quick way to get through a job search, the interest will be remain . . . like buying a lottery ticket. Sometimes you win. For those ads that look especially promising, and for which you meet at least 60 percent of the qualifications (or else you will be screened out), go ahead and respond. But use the two-tiered response: answer the ad and tell your network of your interest. If you want to increase your odds, send your résumé to the actual decision maker as well. Your network or some research can help you determine who this is. If you actually get an interview and it starts getting serious, before you accept the job, make sure it has more going for it than being highly visible in a help wanted ad and taking you off the job market quickly. Test it against the template you developed for the top side of your marketing circle to make sure you'll flourish.

## Search Firms

Search firms are widely considered to be a good place to learn about job openings, but are they? Are search firms any more help than help wanted ads? I have heard literally hundreds of professionals say, "I've let the search firms know that I'm out here. They have the level of opening that I want, and they carry real, ready-to-be-filled jobs. I'll see what happens." Search firms sound like they're out there to help you, to match your skills with jobs that they have in their inventory. They're not. If you're thinking that search firms will help you shortcut your search, you're going to be disappointed.

Follow the money (what's on the bottom side of their marketing circle). Who pays the search firms? Companies filling openings pay search firms to find *exactly* what they are looking for. That means that search firms are working for the *companies*, not the job seeker. The search firm considers the company that hired it a client and you're a candidate. Retained firms operate at the higher ends of the salary scale and are paid regardless of a search's outcome. Contingency firms work at the lower end of the salary scale and are paid only if the position is filled. Some firms may do both, in different divisions. Know which category any search firm that you might work with is in, as well as its reputation, because they are motivated differently and behave differently. Your response to them should be different too. There are books such as John Lucht's *Rites of Passage at $100,000 to $1 Million +* (Viceroy Press, 2000) that describe the categories in more detail. Just don't bother with the direct mailing to the search firms that some of these books talk about unless you have nothing else to do. You'd rather differentiate yourself by networking in than by being a cold call that comes in a mail (or email) bag along with the junk mail.

Retained firms will do whatever it can to meet client expectations, and to meet them quickly. If you're not an exact match for position specifications, a major search firm typically will not consider you. It's not being discriminatory or unfair or mean, it just doesn't get paid for going "out of spec," or presenting candidates (you) who don't exactly match the client's specifications. If the company asks for a yellow duck with an orange bill, and you are a white duck with an orange bill, you may still make the right noises and have webbed feet, but their client won't be happy.

If you are changing functions or industries, a search firm will have a hard time presenting you to a company. Your network is a better bet in these cases. Rather than wasting energy on the unfairness of search firms not helping with functional or industry changes, understand for whom they are working. They aren't rejecting or ignoring you. They're anticipating and meeting customer needs as quickly as possible, which explains why they don't get back to you a lot of times.

Including search firms as part of your strategy is fine. Since 10 to 15 percent of professionals find their jobs through search firms, you don't want to ignore them. You also don't want to spend 60 to 70 percent of your time on them. The following process is a great way to start identifying and building relationships with search firms that you'll want to keep for the long term.

> **If you are changing functions or industries, a search firm will have a hard time presenting you to a company.**

Identify firms that may be appropriate to your search. Kennedy Information's *Directory of Executive Recruiters* (current edition) is one resource. Search by industry and function. You may find that the best recruiter for your industry is on the other side of the United States (for example, you may live in California and work in the oil industry, but you may use a search firm in Texas for jobs back in California).

The Big Five search firms, the five executive-level and international search firms that handle some of the most senior-level searches in the world, are:

---

- *Heidrick & Struggles, Inc., www.heidrick.com*
- *Korn/Ferry International, www.kornferry.com*
- *Russell Reynolds Associates, Inc., www.russellreynolds.com*
- *SpencerStuart, www.spencerstuart.com*
- *Egon Zehnder International, Inc., www.ezi.com*

---

These top firms typically manage searches for jobs with a compensation of $250,000 and above. The directories of search firms report that these companies require a minimum of $150,000 in compensation for candidates, but the search firm's partners spend most of their time (and interest) on the higher-level positions. Some have online services you can use if your compensation is approximately $100,000 and up. These firms are the hardest to penetrate on a cold-call basis because so many senior-level job seekers are after them. I've had partners from all five firms speak at the executive networking sessions that I run for ExecuNet (a great resource described in Strategy #4: Network As the Norm). All five partners emphasize the importance of building relationships with them. This is not a quick hit phone call when you want a job. They need to know you're on the A list before you're even looking for a job. Start now by thinking about what you could do that might help the partner who heads your industry specialty.

Find the names of the partners in the search firms you identified who handle your specialty. Their industry expertise is often listed on their company's website along with their bios. Add these names to the Hit List that you started developing as part of your homework in chapter three, listing companies and individuals that you'd like to learn more about.

Word of mouth is even better and faster than going through a directory for identifying search firms that fit with your background. You can either show someone your Hit List and gather feedback on both search firms and companies, or, if you're chatting informally with someone who has hired search firms before, you can say:

"Have you worked with any search firms that you've found particularly helpful?"

If the person answers "Yes," say, "They sound like they did a good job for you. Was there someone that you worked with in the firm who you would recommend?"

If he or she volunteers a name, say, "What I'd like to do is call that person, use your name, then see if we can talk. They may be conducting some other searches that would be a fit. Would that be okay?"

If you get the green light, say, "Thanks. I'll see whether I can help them with referrals for some of their other searches. (Better yet, "The company I used to be with is looking for a marketing VP, and I may be able to make an introduction." Or, "I was just talking to a company that is looking for a COO. I'll tell them about it.") I'll let you know what happens."

See how you just accomplished multiple goals at the same time? You:

- Moved from cold calling a search firm to networking into it.
- Got a referral from a client of the search firm ("Have you ever *worked with . . .*"). This makes a gigantic difference in how much attention the search firm will pay you when you call. They need to be nice to friends of clients.

- Took pressure off your networking contact. By offering to help the search firm with referrals or market information, you gave your friend a selling point to use if he or she is talking with the search firm about you. You're actually doing the firm a favor, using the bottom side of the marketing circle to level the playing field, so your friend feels good about putting you two together.
- Maintained control. You asked to use your friend's name and make the connection yourself. Now you can move at your own pace. You give up control when someone else makes the call for you (and may mean well but never gets around to it).

You can see that finding any response to or connections in help wanted ads or search firms often comes back to networking. Handshakes will move you from the "B" or "C" pile into the "A" group.

## *What Search Firms Want*

George Davis, the managing director for the Boston office of Egon Zehnder International, one of the five prestigious firms mentioned above, outlined in his presentation to ExecuNet exactly how senior-level job seekers should approach search firms. He recommended the following (parenthetical statements are mine):

*Don't depend on recruiters.* They are only one channel to the job market.
*Do your homework on search firms:*
- Is the company contingency or retained? (Does the company get paid to get someone in the slot, or does the long-term relationship matter?)
- Is the company a boutique, large, or a single shingle? (A boutique is a small firm that typically specializes in a particular industry or function. A large firm will have multiple offices, often international, and cover various industries and functions. A single shingle is a sole practitioner. Some in each category are very good, some aren't. Check them out.)
- Which partner and office should you contact? (Contact the one that handles your industry specialty in your geographic area of interest.)

*In your communications to recruiters:*
- Give them some context. Be precise. (Tell them what companies you've worked for. They need to know the scale of your responsibilities up front. Tell them your title and major responsibilities. Quantitative results are

appreciated. Don't ramble; you'll lose them. Your Elevator Story will work well here.)

- Don't be creative. Fact-based, chronological résumés are easier to digest.
- Sending résumés by email is fine now.
- Provide proof of your skills and relevant industry experience.
- Don't expect an invitation to a meeting after the first date. (They typically will meet with you only when they are screening you as a candidate for a current search.)
- Remember the golden rule: How can you help them? Be proactive. Do you have referrals for them? (Do you know other candidates that might fit their searches or other companies that might benefit by using a search firm?)
- Relationships take time. Touch base.

He's right. And these expectations apply to all of the major search firms.

Let's get started on some action steps and homework for help wanted ads and search firms, then we'll see how *not* looking for jobs will broaden your options.

---

### H O M E W O R K

### ☞ *Want Ads and Search Firms*

1. **Help Wanted Ads.** If you've responded to help wanted ads in the past several months, pull them out and see whether you can network into these companies. Interview some non-decision makers in the company to see what it's like to work there. Identify the person who would actually be doing the hiring for your level and area of expertise, and try to network into him or her. (We'll discuss this more in Strategy #4: Network as the Norm.) The job you responded to may still be open, the company may have additional needs, or the new hire may have some leads that she ended up turning down.

2. **Search Firms.** Pick out five to seven search firms that look interesting and relevant to your search. Word of mouth is a good way to find them. Identify the firm's specialist in your industry, then try to network into that person. How can you help him or her?

## The Birth of a Job

To give you more options than waiting for help wanted ads or search firms to surface, let's look at how jobs are created. This is truly the main course: how to find meaningful work by not looking for jobs, but by creating them. Remember when we talked about a job being an arbitrary package of work that needs to be done (chapter one)? A job's boundaries are artificial; they change all the time. How a company divides work in order to produce its products and services must shift continually because market needs, technology, and economic conditions can shift overnight, changing the demands on the company. You can take advantage of these changes to create the type of work that you'd like to do by tapping into the job formation process earlier and not waiting for approved, funded job openings to be appear.

Let's look at how jobs are created to see why getting involved earlier can give you more interesting choices. Jobs don't just exist when a company is started; they are born when there are problems or opportunities. Your company has just won a new contract; you have a deadline and aren't sure whether you can make it; you're not getting accurate, timely information for decision making; you don't have enough business. There are millions of problems every day in every operation, and good times can create them as well as bad times. These pressures may not lead to someone thinking, "I need to get some more help here" so much as "How in the world am I going to handle all of this?" Can you tell where I'm headed?

Traditionally, internal pressure mounts to a point where it is clear that additional help is needed. Then the manager, or a smart administrative assistant who plants the seed, realizes that it's time to get serious and start the formal, let's-hire-someone process. In order to actually hire someone, many steps are needed. Someone needs to take responsibility for shepherding the job through the system. Job descriptions, consensus with other employees, budgeting, approvals, and timing all need to be worked out. Once a job becomes official, it's often posted internally first. Then, and only in a small portion of cases, is it advertised publicly in a newspaper or trade magazine or through a search firm. If you were in human resources, would you really want to list a job in the paper? It costs a lot, brings in a lot of garbage, and gets people mad at you for not responding to them. Placing a large, expensive want ad in a newspaper is closer to an act of desperation than a standard operating procedure.

If a company does place an ad, it will now be culling through reams of paper. The employer will call some people in, but many times what looked good on paper is not impressive firsthand. Back to the pile. Eventually, he or she finds a candidate, checks references, and makes an offer. The offer will be negotiated and finally accepted. You've probably been on the company's side of the table before. It's a slow process because it's getting worked into someone's already full agenda. To the job seeker, it seems even slower.

A timeline of the hiring process would fall into a bell-shaped curve.

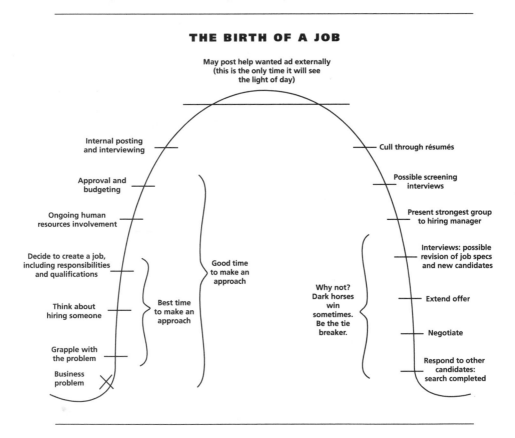

**THE BIRTH OF A JOB**

May post help wanted ad externally
(this is the only time it will see
the light of day)

Internal posting
and interviewing

Approval and
budgeting

Ongoing human
resources involvement

Decide to create a job,
including responsibilities
and qualifications

Think about
hiring someone

Grapple with
the problem

Business
problem

Best time
to make an
approach

Good time
to make an
approach

Why not?
Dark horses
win
sometimes.
Be the tie
breaker.

Cull through résumés

Possible screening
interviews

Present strongest group
to hiring manager

Interviews: possible
revision of job specs
and new candidates

Extend offer

Negotiate

Respond to other
candidates:
search completed

See how an approved job opening is visible to the world outside the company for just a small portion of time, if at all? Look at the slopes on either side of the curve: one leads up to the job's approval, funding, and advertisement, and the other side leads down to the final selection. *You can approach a job from either side of the bell curve.*

The right side of the slope leading to a candidate's selection is fairly straightforward. A company will be heavy into the interviewing mode after having collected as many reasonable applications as possible, both internally and externally. If you approach a decision maker at this stage, you might hear, "I'm sorry we didn't meet sooner. We're just in the process of selecting our finalists." Or, "We're not accepting any more applicants now." If you know he or she hasn't hired anyone yet, you don't have to quit trying entirely, however. Ever seen a house purchase fall through at the end? You might be the white knight that can break a deadlock or put the deal back together. You might rescue a company after another candidate's references didn't check out, after a candidate accepted another offer, or after a candidate's spouse couldn't relocate. The company really doesn't want to reread all those résumés again. I've conducted job searches and dreaded going back through the electronic or paper piles. You may have had to face the black hole of more résumé screening, too. Now, as a job seeker, you can provide a solution by helping the company get back to solving the problems that were creating the job in the first place.

> **Stop looking for jobs. Start looking for problems to be solved.**

## Look for the Pain

The left side of the slope leading from the birth of a job to the internal posting is fertile ground for creating meaningful work. Whether you want to grow within your current company or move to a new venue, this is the slope on which jobs are created. The point is to stop looking for a job and start looking for problems to be solved, then become the solution.

Jobs are finite. Problems are infinite. Why not go after the infinite pool? If you can identify where the pressure points are in a company and position yourself as someone with solutions, you've just created a new job for yourself. What's particularly fun is that you're choosing a problem that you find interesting, then shaping your response to it in concert with a potential boss. You may be able to influence the responsibilities and level of a job rather than fit yourself into an already established pigeonhole. You could be coming close to creating your ideal working conditions, or as ideal as they can get.

In addition to shaping a job to your satisfaction, do you know what else this strategy does? *It eliminates the competition.* That's a big deal. Since this isn't a formal, posted job opening, the company hasn't developed a profile of the ideal candidate. They haven't pulled in hundreds of résumés from people who can walk on water. They aren't thinking that you're a square peg trying to fit into their round hole because they haven't even bored the hole yet. You're solving their problems without wasting their time and money on an extensive (or expensive) search. Good for you. Maybe some portion of what you saved them will show up in your pocket, especially if you bring this up during negotiations.

Isn't this great? You're not sitting around anymore waiting for some semi-relevant help wanted ads to come out. You're taking the initiative, targeting companies and industries that are of interest, identifying their problems, then packaging yourself as a solution. This strategy gives you much more control over your career. Carol used this approach of looking for problems rather than job openings to test out three different companies before she selected the one she wanted.

Carol was a very successful product manager for a large, nationwide insurance firm when she was "restructured." Although angry about her fate, she didn't lose much time looking back. After identifying four target markets for potential employment that would fit with her experience, interests, and goals, she started researching the marketplace to determine its needs.

After doing her homework and learning which firms were growing, who still needed help, which decision makers she should meet, and what the potential was in her various markets, she narrowed the field. Two of her original four markets had the profile she wanted.

Using her network, she got the handshakes with the decision makers that she needed to meet in her chosen markets. Carol was always clear on Strategy #1: Take Control. She knew her value to other companies, and she could describe how she would make a company successful. Carol was, and is, passionate about her work, her products, and in developing a company (and herself, as a result). People loved this confidence and focus.

Within two months, Carol had landed three contract assignments with three different companies. She listened to their needs and carved out jobs ranging in content from improving a distribution network and product development to managing a start-up sales operation, all within time parameters that she specified.

Carol knew that this wasn't a long-term situation. She nearly killed herself working three jobs for a couple of months until she knew which companies to eliminate. They all offered her full-time jobs. She selected the best fit, and she is now the corporate vice president of a growing operation.

Carol is a great example of not looking for formal, approved jobs. She found a company's problems, then presented her skill set as the solution.

Important point: Don't say, "It sounds like you'll want to build strategic alliances to minimize your up-front costs in product development. Why don't we create a job here? I could take responsibility for it and be your first vice president of business development." This starts off fine, but the last two sentences are *totally on the top side of the marketing circle,* about your needs instead of the company's. Take the emphasis off of job creation, and talk about results. You'll be hard to resist.

Do say, "It sounds like you'll want to build strategic alliances to minimize your up-front costs in product development. I have some specific companies in mind that might be worth considering as alliance partners. Would you like to get started?"

They'll be salivating. You focused on the company's needs, the bottom side of the circle, and demonstrated that you can start solving its problems immediately, a minor investment considering the potential returns. Your objective is to treat the incidentals of creating a job as a minor sidebar to getting started on solving its problems and improving its results.

You also used a strategy I call dangling a carrot, based on the proverbial way to get a donkey to move forward. Tie a carrot to a long string, hang the string from one end of a long stick, then dangle the carrot in front of the donkey. In this case, corporate results are the carrot, and you want to keep the employer moving forward. The carrot you dangled was that you "have some specific companies in mind that might be worth considering as alliance partners," meaning you have names and relationships already in place. What you *didn't* do, however, was tell the employer all your ideas. *You aren't hired yet. Don't give all of your carrots away.*

There are plenty of unscrupulous, "cost-effective" employers who interview high-quality talent and sometimes ask consulting companies to invest a lot of time in proposals, then decide not to go through with the hiring or the project. Granted, there are often perfectly honest, acceptable reasons why they don't, but you shouldn't give them all of your ideas anyway. Reserve some of your inspirations, connections, and relationships until after you are hired. Remember the risk mentioned earlier, when the employer is wondering, "Why buy the cow when the milk is so cheap?"

You don't have to work three contracts simultaneously, as Carol did, to see which company is the best fit, but, like dating several people before getting married, she knew which management team and industry offered the most long-term potential before she settled down. It's sometimes hard to tell true chemistry by interviews alone, when everyone is on their best behavior. She learned chemistry by experiencing it.

## Find Their Needs

Determining a company's needs and then doing something about them will win you a lot of friends and opportunities, both in your current company and in new ones. Finding them early on is the challenge. "How do I know what the company's problems are?" you ask. Well, if you work there, you have insider information. Look for the problems in the departments where you want to work. Forget about specific job openings. Decide how you can help make your company more successful by solving problems. You'll expand your relationships, your reputation, and your skills in the process. If you want to move up in your operations job, for example, ask your boss if you could take a look at reducing average product cost. If you can develop a process that reduces costs without sacrificing quality, not only have you made a name for yourself within your company, but you have a notch in your belt that is a hook for other companies, should you decide to leave.

Sometimes a company's problems are obvious. A company may be all over the papers for its rapid growth rate (their systems are strained), a non-profit may need help fund-raising (some companies allow sabbaticals for community service), or a major change in the political or economic scene may demand attention. Governor Tom Ridge of Pennsylvania, who was tapped as Secretary of Homeland Security after the terrorist attacks on the United States in 2001, is a high-profile example of how a job is created to solve problems. He's also a great example of something else I'll bet you're working toward: building your reputation. As you become known, people will start coming to you for solutions; you won't need to seek others out as much.

If you're in transition, you'll want to identify the pain that potential employers have. If you want to change your industry or function, identifying needs and getting to know the people looking for solutions is essential. These searches need networking even more than your typical round hole-round peg searches (staying in the same industry and function), and both you and your network need to be able to explain that you can address those needs. As you become well versed in the latest problems of your new industry and function you can start to make yourself look like a round peg—a very important transformation. There are two ways to identify problems: asking about them and tracking trends.

### Ask, "Where Does It Hurt?"

Asking people what they see as the problems in various industries makes for fascinating conversation. You can do it as social chitchat, with your colleagues, with friends, with big cheeses. Anytime, anywhere. Everyone has an opinion. You're conducting informational interviews without people knowing it, and they'll have a receptive audience for their viewpoints. The following three types of questions are for use in general, social situations; refer to Strategy #4: Network as the Norm for more specific informational interviewing questions. Learning to ask the right questions is an important part of tracking trends and of learning to Network as the Norm. Refine your questions as you progress so you collect the information you need to keep on top of changes. Many times, I have heard executives blame other people for not being helpful. Upon examination, it was the questions they were asking that were at fault. They didn't bring out useful information.

These are types of questions that will start interesting conversations in a casual, conversational, social-type setting. They will elicit information about industry concerns. They focus on the other person's industry, and ideally overlap with your function (engineering, research, and investment management, in these examples).

---

**INDUSTRY PLUS ECONOMY**

- *"What's going to happen to microelectronics, given the recent economic changes?"* (This is very broad. Tailor your question to what's been happening in the economy.)

**RECENT ADVANCE PLUS INDUSTRY NEED**

- *"How is rapid throughput screening affecting your drug development pipeline?"*

**COMPETITIVE PRESSURE**

- *"I noticed that some other law firms are getting into investment management for their high, net-worth clients. Is this a good use of their time?"*

---

There are a couple of points to consider before you plunge in:

- *Don't press too far in a social situation.* If you've just met someone, or have run into a distant acquaintance on the soccer field or at church, it may not be appropriate to stay on a heavy topic for too long. Besides, you'd rather talk to him or her in a work setting where you can gather environmental networking and cultural information as well as learn about potential business problems. If things start to get interesting, ask whether he or she has a business card on them and if you can call at the office. In the meantime, switch back to a lighter topic, like the goal his or her daughter just made.

- *What do you do with the information once you have it?* Each person that you talk to about the mutual fund industry will have his or her own opinion. Helpful people will tell you exactly what's happening and what you should be doing. Take it all with a grain of salt. It's just like résumé feedback. If you base your actions on what each person tells you, you will be knee-jerking both your résumé and your analysis of problems and needs in your industries forever. Look for recurring themes.

The themes that you identify will not only outline a company's needs, or their BoSoC, as you talk to decision makers, they also will allow you to ask increasingly sophisticated questions about the nature of these problems. If you're changing functions or industries, start using the new vocabulary and ideas you're collecting to ask more penetrating questions. You're on your way to becoming a round peg.

## Track the Trends

Another way to identify a company's needs, or the early stages of them, is to scan the information that passes in front of you with a whole new perspective: "What's changing?" You're not jumping wildly into different areas of research; you're analyzing what is going on around you and how it is affecting your profession, industry, and organization. Look back at Farren's three levels in the Web of Work™ that interact to influence the stability of your job in the overall economy in Strategy #1: Take Control, and see what you jotted down for your own profession, industry, and organization. What changes are impacting each one? This is important work and makes for stimulating conversation with colleagues. You're doing market research. You're doing trend analysis.

## The Power of Trends

Why is tracking trends important? Your future lies there. If you want to direct your career instead of reacting to what other people plan for you, you'll need to stay informed about shifts in business in general and in your area in particular. You can't afford to ignore this. The engineering support people still working on drafting tables mentioned in chapter two were let go all at once because they were obsolete. If they had kept track of trends, they wouldn't have been caught flat-footed, without the right skills, in a competitive marketplace.

If you want to stay in control of your career, *don't expect your company to track trends for you.* Companies should track industry trends and the better ones do, but good career management means that you are making your own conclusions about how the trends affect you. Your manager is not tuning in to what works best for you as an individual. You can't afford to wait for him or her to take action. You have to know what's going on in your field to protect yourself. Staying well informed on an ongoing basis means knowing:

> **Don't expect your company to track trends for you.**

- What skills are important for the work you want to be doing?
- Who is the competition? What are they doing that's so good? That isn't so good?
- What's happening on a global basis and how will it affect your profession, industry, and company? This includes evolutions in technology.
- What's happening on a local basis with business trends, companies moving into town, promotions in other companies, contracts awarded, business restructurings, and so on.
- Who are the major thought leaders in your field, and what are they saying?

"But my company doesn't pay tuition for the skill upgrade I'm going to need." Or, "I'm out of work so I can't get to the professional association meeting." Sorry. No whining; get creative. Prioritize what is most important in keeping competitive, and go after it. Period. If you need a course on C++, and it's important for your future plans, you'll find a way. If you can't afford to pay tuition and your company isn't covering it, go for a scholarship, take it over the Web, trade skills with a friend who uses it in her company (use her BoSoC to motivate her). If you're self-conscious attending a professional meeting because you aren't affiliated with a company, see if you can trade registration fees for working for the group running the conference; this will give you an identity and get you inside. If you're creative and work the bottom side of the circle, trading needs with other people, miracles happen.

Is tracking trends giving you more work to do? I think of it as a necessity that can be enjoyable, like a wonderful meal. It's intellectually stimulating to be in front of the pack and be thinking not only about what problems are emerging, but about the best way to respond to them. You may be the one leading the charge.

## Where to Find Trends

What are your sources of information? Do you read daily newspapers, *The Wall Street Journal*, business magazines, websites (you can even request that updates from specific topics be sent to you every day), trade magazines, or professional association publications? TV and radio count too; along with the Web, they are the fastest-breaking sources of information. If you have a limited amount of time, pick out your favorite source within each of the following levels:

---

- *General news or business:* (*Business Week, The Wall Street Journal, The Economist*)
- *Your profession:* (*Banker and Tradesman, Lawyers Weekly USA, IEEE* publication)
- *Your industry:* (*JAMA, The Chronicle of Higher Education, Advertising Age*)

---

Evaluate the best way to stay informed so you can get what you need in a timely manner. Important: This is not a one-time assignment. Staying in touch with life outside your current or future company is an ongoing assignment. Heads up.

What are you looking for when you're gathering information? You're looking for change. Change creates opportunity. Even in disasters, someone is making money. When there is a bankruptcy, the lawyers, consultants, outplacement firms, auditors, and sometimes even the media are benefiting. The section about who's being promoted in the business section of your local paper will identify vacancies that have been created and the new hires who may be reorganizing their departments. When contracts or venture capital is awarded, you know that an influx of cash will need to be spent shortly. You can help with that (professionally, of course). Once you start looking for change instead of job openings, your horizons are unlimited. As one client said, "I can hardly get through reading the newspaper anymore. I'm seeing so many more leads than I used to."

## Identifying Company and Industry Hot Buttons

"How can I do this?" you're asking. "I just learned about the company recently. How can I know what their buttons are? How do I know the trends in the industry?" You're not going to have all of the answers up front. Knowing how to get them is a lifelong career skill, however. Continuing to stay on top of company and industry hot buttons is part of what makes you a desirable commodity for the long term. There are two main ways to learn what you need to know about emerging issues: ask people and do research.

To learn about a company's needs, ask questions of both insiders (people working within the company) and outsiders.

### ASK INSIDERS

- "What keeps you up at night?"
- "What are the two greatest issues that you'll be working on in the next couple of months?"
- "What one thing (in the company, in the division, in their work) would you like to change?"
- "What are the bottlenecks?"

### ASK OUTSIDERS

- "What do you know about Company X?"
- "Laura, you've been selling to Company X for a while. What are they like as a customer?" (Listen.) "Who should I talk to there?"
- "Ken, how do you compete against Company X when you're selling against them?"

- "Al, do I understand correctly that you've been a Company X customer for years? Has this worked well for you?" (Coming into a meeting with customer feedback is especially powerful. You may want to keep the names of the customers confidential, however.)
- You can identify a company's accounting and legal firms in directories such as *Standard and Poor's*. If you know the CPA or lawyer managing the account, you may get some feedback that is "public information."
- Show your Hit List of companies and their top officers to your contacts. Ask whether they know any of them.

Once you've asked questions of everyone who might have some ideas, do your own research on the company's needs.

- You should definitely go to a company's website and, once you have a meeting set up, read its annual report. Remember that you're only reading what it wants you to see, however.
- Use an Internet search engine, such as www.google.com, and type in the company's name. Skim through the responses.
- Read what the media is writing about your target company. Check the Internet, use InfoTrac at your library, or read the archives on a business magazine's website, such as *Fortune* or *Business Week*. This takes more time since you have to go to each individual site.
- Check out business websites, such as Hoover's (www.hoovers.com), Value Line (www.valueline.com), 1Jump (www.1jump.com), Business. com, Vault.com, and Dow Jones Interactive (www.dowjones.com). They can give you comparative research about competition and industry rankings.

To find out about industry trends, use the same two approaches: ask people and do research.

- "What do you think is going to be the most significant change in our industry in the next year?" (Stretch the time frame much past a year and people will get glassy-eyed.) A good follow-up statement is "I assume that you're going to need to respond to this fairly quickly."
- "How is the recent news (insert the latest economic challenge) going to affect how you do business?"

Once you've asked questions of your contacts, do your own trend research.

- Stay informed of world events as well as business events. The major ones will impact your work. Read both a weekly news magazine and a business magazine, and you'll cover a lot of the waterfront. It's not just knowing what's happening that's important. It's learning to project: "What does that event mean for us (in manufacturing, in financial services)?" You'll be considering some outcomes that other people aren't. You'll be keeping a broad perspective so you won't be blindsided when one industry (electronics) develops a product that wipes out another industry (slide rule manufacturers). You're in front of the wave.

- Ask different people the same question about how an event will affect your industry. If their thinking is headed in the same direction as yours, you may be on to something. Shape your ideas into trend questions when talking to decision makers.

- What are the professional associations in your industry? Read their journals. Go to their meetings. On a national level, what topics are on the program's agenda? Those are usually hot buttons.

- Read the publications for your industry. If you aren't sure what they are, ask senior-level people in your informational interviews, "Are there publications that you find particularly worthwhile?" You can also ask, "Are there professional associations that you find worthwhile?" at the same time.

- The Internet can be a great resource for tracking industry trends, but beware of the black hole that it can create, sucking in all your time. Use it for specific purposes. If you have defined topics that you're tracking (such as offshore chip manufacturing or consumer confidence index), search agents or Web crawlers can help collect the information. Ask your colleagues or reference librarians to suggest one they like.

## What to Do with a Trend Once You've Cornered One

Whether you've spotted an actual trend (a global slump in the chip-making industry) or a more localized market need (Staples opens up a distribution center in your area), you know that jobs are going to be created. And you're prepared to get in on that birth. What a great place to be.

Even in a slump, a different kind of trend, there will be action somewhere. Resellers will need to sell off inventory from companies that are having problems. Product manufacturers experience increased demand for field service when customers keep aging products instead of buying new ones. Bankruptcy lawyers, liquor distributors, bond traders, and many others do well in slumps. Track down the person who will be overseeing solutions to corporate challenges or the company that might benefit from someone else's problems, even if he or she is out of state. Show the person that you have some ideas that will help; he or she may have needs for you in the local office. You could even open up an office for the company, assuming you can demonstrate that it would be in its best interest.

When the headquarters of a new distribution center is elsewhere, for example, you start by identifying the decision maker. The Web, your friendly librarian in the reference section, or the operator at your targeted company can help. Place a call to the decision maker. I know this is no small feat, but ideas for making the connection will be in the next chapter, which covers Strategy #4: Network as the Norm. First, the conversation:

**You:** This is Carol Brown from Des Moines. I've been setting up warehouses and inventory centers for retail operations for years, and I see that you're going to be opening up a distribution center in the area. Welcome.

**VP:** *Thanks.*

**You:** I wondered whether you might be interested in hearing more about what's going to happen with your highway access once the cold weather moves in. I've run into some logistical nightmares in this area that I might be able to spare you if you want to sit down and go over some ideas before you get too far along.

**VP:** *Really. Why don't you talk with so and so . . .*

**You:** Great. I'd be happy to. Shall I just send them an email to set up a time to talk and copy you on it? Okay. Let me get those email addresses while I have you on the phone. I will let you know what happens.

See how you stayed on the bottom side of the marketing circle, meeting the VP's BoSoC the entire time? You also politely challenged him, as we talked about in Strategy #1: Take Control, by introducing some information you weren't sure the VP knew about, how winter weather will affect the company's transportation scheduling. Even if the VP has people working on this already, he shouldn't ignore ideas from an expert. That was the carrot you dangled, your expertise in a potential problem area for him. If he does ignore your offer, you can write him off with a clean conscience. He had his chance, and you learned what he'd be like to work with.

Finally, and most importantly, you stayed in control of the follow-up. Even though it would be preferable for the emails to come from the VP himself, the odds of his actually doing so diminish the minute you hang up the phone. The VP means well, but he's busy and will get distracted once you lose his attention. You volunteered to make the connections, you got the email addresses while you were on the phone, and you will copy the VP so the recipients can see you are for real; you are the one who will make things happen. Send off your emails that day and follow up.

Will anything come of this? You don't know. Might you volunteer your expertise with no job offer or compensation? Absolutely. That's a risk you run. But you're not giving them all your ideas or your time. If you actually end up doing some short-term work together you'll reserve some of your good ideas, because you still want them to "buy the cow." So the disadvantages of taking the initiative in starting a relationship are the risk of rejection and the potential waste of some time. Not bad tradeoffs for the possibility of getting into a good company that "isn't hiring" at the moment.

Look at the advantages of approaching the job market creatively. You're:

- Targeting where *you* want to go and taking the initiative, not waiting for help wanted ads or for other people to come up with ideas for you.
- Shaping work to take advantage of your area of expertise rather than jumping from function to function.
- Shaping work to fit your life. You might integrate discussions about why a company doesn't need to hire someone full-time to do the work if you don't want to work full-time or want to balance two jobs, for example. You're suggesting the time commitment *you* want, but presenting it in terms of *its* needs.

Even if you aren't compensated for your short-term work, as may happen with the distribution center example above, and it doesn't result in a long-term job, all is not lost. You've:

- Met some new people, all of whom have their own networks that might be helpful to you (and you to them).
- Worked inside a new, interesting company. If it's useful, you can add it to your résumé and your conversations. "What are you doing now?" "We'll, I'm doing some inventory control work for . . . , and I'm still keeping an eye on the marketplace for. . . ." (This is a much more impressive response than saying you're staying up to date on the soap operas.)
- Expanded your skill set, which may set you up for new opportunities.

- Extended your reputation. You're obviously going to do a great job, right?

Are you game?

---

**H O M E W O R K**

☞ *Track Your Trends*

List your three to four top target markets. You can transfer them from the ones you listed in Strategy #2: Market for Mutual Benefit. For each market, list trends that are happening either within it or within a specific company in that industry. Are there ways that you could take advantage of these trends to benefit your target companies?

---

## Package Your Time

What type of work do you want to create—full-time, part-time, consulting, or contract? You don't know yet. You have a preference, but that's a hidden agenda now because it's on the top side of the marketing circle. Your main priority now is to get employers to pay attention to you. Stay focused on results and outcomes. Once they're engaged, you can suggest new ways for packaging your time. You may use one work style to get into a company, then move to another once you're in and more firmly entrenched.

You'll find that there are more ways you can work with a company now than there were ten years ago. Although a full-time, on-site employee is still the norm, there are other, interesting models. In *The Age of Unreason* (Harvard Business School Press, 1990), Charles Handy foreshadowed this trend when he said, "Eighty percent of the value [of a company] is carried out by people who are not inside their organization. . . . All nonessential work, work which could be done by someone else, is therefore sensibly contracted out to people who make a specialty of it and who should, in theory, be able to do it better for less cost." What is your specialty? Once you have a decision maker talking about her needs, you'll know how to package your time and your specialty to meet her needs (and yours).

"The book you're working on sounds really interesting," a former editor of a medical journal told an author. "I'll bet that it's going to take a lot of time to research your topic." The editor liked doing research on a freelance basis, and she was open to full-time employment as well. See how she was leading the witness? If the author said, "No, I have most of it done already," it would remain an interesting, friendly conversation. If he said, "Yes, I'm swamped," she could ask, "Do you want me to free up some time for you? I might be able to give you a hand." The discussion would stay on his side of the circle. You leave a graceful exit for a "no" so neither one of you feels awkward, which is important for long-term relationships.

Because of the new ways to work with a company, you no longer have to wait for an approved, funded, full-time job offer to get started working. In fact, you may be more likely to end up with that full-time offer if you remove the immediate pressure of a hiring decision and just start getting the work done. Make sure that you're both clear on the scope and duration of your work before you plunge into some of these creative alternatives. These are some of the various models you'll see in the workplace:

- **Temp to Perm**
  You may start off in a temporary position then move to a permanent one (what a euphemism—who's permanent these days?). After a defined period as a temporary employee (possibly on a consulting or project basis; be clear about what you're signing on for), you may become a full-time employee. The trial period works both ways: you're evaluating them as much as they're evaluating you, a level playing field.

- **Full-Time for the Short Term**
  You may start off full-time—they're in a crunch and need a major quality initiative installed in manufacturing by the end of the year—then back off to consulting for them in the first or second quarter. The fact that you will cut back your time later should be clear up front. You may want to get some cash flow going while you're in transition, or you may prefer working in spurts. Your challenge will be to continue your campaign while someone else wants you 120 percent of the time. If you don't keep your campaign alive while consulting, you'll be starting from scratch at the end of the company's crunch.

- **Interim**
  Closely related to the above, variable-load structure is an interim arrangement. You'll see it frequently with CFOs. You're full-time for a specified duration, and then you're done. This could be until the company finds the next CFO (hence there'd be an "acting CFO" feel to it) or until they complete a specific transaction. Some professionals are interim executives for a living. If you can live with the marketing part of it,

the flexibility and financial rewards can make it worthwhile. IMCOR, www.imcor.com, does executive-level interim searches for companies, but beware, the supply of candidates always exceeds the demand.

- **Short-Term Consulting or Project Assignments**
  You may carve out projects or consulting assignments with no interest in regular employment. They should be well defined and have measurable outcomes. Otherwise they could drag on forever and the client could ask you to include additional assignments at no cost (known as "project creep"), without adding any value for you. Beware the lure of putting all your time into an assignment that's going to end shortly. Protect your time and yourself by continuing to stay in touch with the marketplace while you're delivering on the project.

  You may create a consulting arrangement because you like being self-employed and want to be a free agent, as Daniel H. Pink labeled independent consultants in *Free Agent Nation* (Warner Books, 2002). Marion McGovern even founded a company around brokering independent consultants called M$^2$, www.msquared.com. In *A New Brand of Expertise* (Butterworth Heinemann, 2001) Marion states, "When we ask our consultants why they decide to hang out a shingle and go into business for themselves, the overwhelming desire is for control. . . . Whether it is control over where they work, like Curtis [Flood, the major league baseball player who refused to be traded to Cleveland], their hours or their vacations, overwhelmingly, it is a desire to make work fit into their lives and not vice versa." Marion works with experts who choose consulting as their function rather than with professionals who consult between jobs. Her concepts feed into Handy's prediction that a company won't need to hire noncore employees, but will use outside specialists to cover these functions. Maybe you would like to be one.

  You may consult as part of a short-term strategy. Jack did this masterfully. An experienced president and general manager, he turned down a full-time offer from a company, but asked if he could work out something on a consulting basis. He offered to give the company 50 percent of his time so both sides could evaluate whether they had a long-term fit while he was relieving it of some short-term pressures. That was the message for the company, or the BoSoC. Jack wasn't sold yet on the management team's being the right fit for him. He managed two lucrative consulting assignments while he evaluated both management teams, and he kept his campaign going at a reduced rate. If and when he tells a company "no," he'll try to refer it to a potential replacement. This part of his professional behavior contributes to his reputation and continued referrals. Jack didn't want to be a consultant for the long term. He used it as a means to an end and as a way to buy time.

- **Part-Time**
  Beware of this title. Many part-time positions cover benefits. That's the good news. The bad news is that work under this heading typically pays a fraction of work called "consulting," even though the actual content may be similar. Part-time can also mean full-time for a finite period (more of a project-type assignment), or less than forty hours a week for an extended period. Many part-time jobs are repetitive, lower level work and pay on an hourly basis. That doesn't mean they are *bad* jobs; they're an essential part of a company's operation. Work part-time if you like the job content and the overall working arrangement. Just know what you're signing up for.

- **Create Your Own Combination**
  This is the fun part about the workplace now. There are so many work models, you can often negotiate what you want. If you're currently employed, you have the liberty of proposing different ways to deliver your work. Just stay on the bottom side of the marketing circle and focus on the needs of your boss and your company ("more cost effective," "free up some space," "research shows higher productivity with telecommuting").

*You're not discussing any of these options with potential employers yet.* Right now, you're just trying to engage the decision maker, to make him or her realize that you are *the* person they have to have. There are direct parallels with fly fishing. You have cast your fly into the stream by starting the conversation with the company. You are now "presenting the bait" by showing that you understand what they're doing and can make or save them money. You haven't decided if you're going to panfry or grill your catch yet; it's too early. Just get your target to nibble. Once the Big Fish accepts the bait and agrees that, yes, he really needs you to step in and get them through the end of the fiscal year, you feel the tug on the line. When the employer says something on the order of "Let's get started," you set the hook. "How would it work if we set this up as a consulting arrangement for the first ninety days? You'd have more flexibility, time to decide if we're a fit, and maybe even a little less paperwork up front so we can get to work faster." If they say no, be prepared to back down for now. The conversation will move to compensation soon after. We'll discuss that in Strategy #5: Negotiate in Round Rooms.

## "Volunteer" Opportunities

Creating a job by helping a company without a specific job opening in front of you has the sound of volunteer work, doesn't it? You don't need to introduce volunteering too early in the conversation, however, unless you want the work for the pure joy of it. We'll talk about establishing *value* first, because that's what you want to do. Establishing your value shows a company how you can make or save it money. The company is more likely to offer compensation if you can show that you're going to bring in more than you would cost. You're not going to use the "V" (volunteer) word too early because you value your time, but there are occasions when volunteering might be a good strategy. Here are some guidelines to use if you sense that a potential employer is happy to have your ideas, but doesn't have, or won't spend, the money to make you official.

- First, don't start creating a job just anywhere. Be selective. Approach the top three or four firms that look like they have potential, then narrow down your list as you gather feedback from the decision makers. You may be willing to volunteer some consulting time for your top choice, but don't overcommit your most limited resource—time. It's hard to do consulting work for more than one company at a time and still carry on the rest of your job search. Be choosy.

- There are only a handful of reasons for taking the risk of working pro bono. If the company name would brand you and you can use it to increase your credibility, if you would acquire a new skill for your campaign, if it restores your confidence, if it would let you make an industry jump that would be hard to do with a full-time job, if it would give you connections with some Important People in your field, then give away some of your time. Ten to fifteen hours per week is plenty for an additional commitment.

- Set a time limit. "I'll get you off the ground with this portion of the project, then we'll sit down in two months and evaluate where we are. Does that work for you?" You could be sucked into a volunteer's black hole otherwise.

- Create an agenda that describes what the company needs and how you can help in the future while working on your current project. Drop some hints. "Do you want to take a look at how you could set up that compensation program when I get done here? I see several ways that would avoid the high fixed overhead on these salaries. I'll put it on the agenda for us to go over." You're not inventing work; you're spotting needs and responding to them. By the time you get through with your project, you will have built a new job description.

## Grow within Your Work

You're already building your New Job Security. You know the importance of being clear about your direction, keeping on top of changes by doing trend tracking, and compiling materials (résumés, bio, Hit Lists, PARs) to market your accomplishments. You know how to increase your options by solving problems rather than concentrating on official job openings. It's time to identify a model for the long haul—one that sustains and grows you as you work—as well as the let's-get-the-next-job phase. Once we look at how you can continue to keep yourself in touch and competitive while you're working, we'll come back to look at how this "systems" approach sets you up for shorter transitions and the Job Pipeline.

Directing your own growth as a professional is the ongoing, fun challenge that drives your career throughout your entire working life. Continually learning and improving will keep your engine tuned for when you want to speed up, make fast maneuvers, or, eventually, slow down. *You* decide how you will grow. The four main ways are to:

---

- *Develop Yourself*
- *Reshape Your Current Job*
- *Uncover Job Openings*
- *Create Jobs*

---

These methods all exist within your current company. You can start planning ways to develop yourself right now. When you leave your company, only the second concept, reshaping your current job, goes away. The other three ways to grow are not only available to you, they are essential. Using all these pistons simultaneously will give you greater power and more choices. Let's talk about how to develop yourself, reshape your current job, uncover job openings, and create jobs within your current company first. If you're currently in transition, look for a boss and a corporate culture that will support this growth.

## *Develop Yourself*

If you are satisfied with your current position, but are not doing anything to challenge yourself, you could be getting a little stale around the edges. Complacency can creep in quietly, so congratulate yourself for recognizing it and responding. Don't wait for your company to take care of you. Decide what will keep you at the forefront of your function and profession and what you truly enjoy doing, then go get it. This might mean coursework, learning new software, selecting a mentor, leading a project—you decide what actual behaviors will move you toward mastery of your field, will build your reputation, and will benefit your company at the same time. If you can persuade your boss that attending the annual meeting of your professional association will improve your performance, let you collect some competitive information, and raise the profile of your company, you've just used his BoSoC to present a win-win proposal. Maybe he'll pay for the trip. If not, do it on your own time. It's like showing up for your first visit to your new health club. You've thought about getting in shape for a long time. Now you're actually going to invest in yourself and follow through. New behaviors will start changing your outcomes. Some of your plans could overlap with reshaping your current job.

## *Reshape Your Current Job*

If you basically like your work, your boss, and your organization but feel like you've reached a dead end, reshaping your current job may be worth consideration. Maybe you find that the same stack of papers sits forever on your desk, or the same items are perpetually on your To Do list, or you avoid going to certain meetings because they take you away from something you would rather be doing. Face it. You don't like doing those things you're putting off. Is there a way, *in the company's best interest,* that you could shift your job content so it would be more meaningful for you? You might even do better work if you were more excited about it. In the following example, Iris shifts her job content while building external relationships to increase her alternatives.

Iris was the Director for Distance Learning at a large, West Coast university. With a doctorate in educational technology and extensive experience in a field that was just taking off, Iris was in demand. Her current job, however, was proving unbearable. With a combination of multiple administrative duties running a rapidly growing program and teaching responsibilities that kept her constantly online (that's how distance learning works), she rarely came up for air. When she did, she would find that her less-busy colleagues were undermining her success, working on taking over some of her responsibilities or claiming her progress as theirs. Not a pretty scene. Was there jealousy? Perhaps. Iris didn't have time to figure it out.

Iris had been with her university for many years and had multiple supporters. If there was ever a time to start reshaping her work to get rid of some of her day-to-day responsibilities and to set herself up doing the type of work she loved, this was it. She found funding for some administrative help that relieved her of some of the routine chores, started using email more to save time, then headed straight for developing her professional skills and reputation. The two reinforce one another. She did some consulting work with schools to train teachers in technology. She was a guest speaker at a national professional association meeting, and she lectured in other countries. As she grew, so did her reputation and outside connections. The internal squabbles faded as she moved beyond the reach of her colleagues, both by shifting her job description to get rid of some of the more repetitive work and by increasing external validation that muted some internal politics.

Iris not only reshaped her current job, she opened up many more possibilities for herself. She was spending more time on the creative, thought-provoking work that she loved and was also attracting outside attention that reignited her university's appreciation of her.

Iris's career management machine is purring. She's positioned herself internally and externally so she has options and is constantly enhancing her competitive strengths. You don't have to be looking for an outside job to develop this momentum. The expertise and reputation that you need to be considered a hot commodity benefits you whether you want to grow in your current organization or another one, so start now. You might be so pleased with your redesigned position that you decide to keep it.

Gaining the world's recognition of your competence doesn't need to mean moving up the ladder. You may not want to climb it. Growth can mean increasing your expertise within your function and profession, including mentoring others in your area. Some companies have dual career tracks so you don't have to move up into management to continue your professional or financial growth. Technical expertise is critical to a company's maintaining its competitive edge and should be nurtured in all respects. As Beverly Kaye, a noted organizational consultant, says, "Up is not the only way." If you want to reshape your job to encompass more of your passion, consider how you're going to help make the company more profitable by doing so and your boss just might listen.

Before restructuring your current job, you need to anticipate any possible objections. How could you change your job so it would be a win-win? What portion of your job could you give to someone else, or outsource, so you would have more time to concentrate on what's important to both you and the company? Caela Farren, CEO of MasteryWorks, the organizational career management consulting firm, suggests that you give the 20 percent of the work that you don't like to someone else who would see it as a developmental opportunity. "What's gravy for the goose. . . ." How will this benefit the company? Will they save money? Develop bench strength? Make better use of staff time because duplication of work is being eliminated? Determine what will motivate the decision makers, and you'll often get your way. Their motivation usually centers around profitability. (Surprise, surprise.)

You may have a shot at restructuring your current job because you are proposing to give away some of your work in order to take on a Killer Opportunity for the company. Stepping into an acting position, managing a project or transaction, or turning around a crisis are all finite jobs that you could take on for a change of pace, after you've proposed how your current job will be covered. You'll need to decide up front whether you'll want your old (or upgraded) job back so that can be part of your planning and negotiations. With a finite job, you can build skills that support your career direction, you won't be getting stale, and you will promote your reputation by taking risks and succeeding. Just make sure that you have a path back out of the project. Avoid getting caught in this great-job-but-what-am-I-going-to-do-now trap. Plan early.

## Uncover Job Openings

If you can't grow any further within your current job, it may be time to look around. Maybe your boss doesn't encourage change, maybe your division is being spun off or closed, or maybe you have acquired and practiced all the skills that you need for the next level and the next level just isn't open and isn't going to be in the foreseeable future. Is there any work within the company that you'd like to tackle before you consider leaving? An additional path to Growing within Your Work when you're employed is to uncover a current or emerging opening in a different department or division. You can network into a position or volunteer to help a new group on a minor project so they see your talents firsthand. You'll know how to handle your current boss . . . explain how it meets his needs or BoSoC. A good boss will support employees who go after more responsible positions outside their current area or who lend a hand on a project; an employee's continued success reflects well on the boss's reputation. If your boss doesn't support your efforts outside his area, keep a lower profile strategy so you can get to know others while still doing your job back home. You're not going to go far with that boss anyway.

People often stay with their current company even when they don't like it, usually for economic or security reasons. Ideally, you're with a company that has a mission you believe in, that has a logical long-range vision of how it will compete and grow in its industry and the overall economy, and has a management team that you would follow into battle. (You do, daily.) If this is the case, you'll undoubtedly be able to grow within your company, even though your present department or function may not give you the options you seek.

## Create Jobs

We've already discussed the fourth way to grow professionally—to create jobs. It's the process of spotting needs and addressing them. Combine all four methods of professional development—develop yourself, reshape your current job, uncover existing jobs, and create jobs—and you see a continuum, not a binary system. It's not Work versus No Work; it's what-do-I-need-to-continue-to-grow-and-how-do-I-get-it-so-everyone-benefits?

**Working on creating new jobs at the same time that you are applying for existing jobs yields the fastest results.**

Growing within Your Work is the engine that moves your career forward. You'll want to maintain that engine on an ongoing basis. Most of the time, you'll be expanding your skills within the context of your current job, keeping yourself competitive when you're employed rather than waiting until you're in transition to start making yourself marketable. Sooner or later, however, odds are you will be in transition, whether it's your choice or the company's. So what's next?

What's next is to create jobs and uncover existing jobs to maximize your alternatives. You know how to do both. You know how to identify needs to create jobs and to use ads, search firms, and networking to uncover existing ones. You can do this confidentially, while you're still employed, or openly, when you're in transition. You can do this within your company and within your target markets. The efforts should be *simultaneous* rather than sequential. "Wow," you say. "How can I find interesting job openings and create jobs at the same time? Isn't that a giant time commitment?" Well, which takes longer: applying for existing jobs and either finding out you didn't get them or are being ignored for much longer than you thought humanly possible and then having to start over on the next round of job openings, or having a process that gives you the initiative to create something that you enjoy doing without competition, while spending 3 to 5 percent of your time (the response rate for ads) on applying for existing jobs?

Creating jobs and uncovering existing ones are mutually reinforcing activities, too. You'll find out both about existing jobs and about needs and connections within companies during your ongoing career networking (see Strategy #4: Network As the Norm).

## The Job Pipeline

Have you ever seen an annual report of a biotech company? Many times, there will be a picture of a pipeline in it. It's a common metaphor in biotech because those who fund the companies are well aware of the importance of having drugs in all stages of development, from initial discovery to the final stages of clinical trials. If a biotech company doesn't have multiple drugs in different stages simultaneously, the elimination of one drug due to unpromising results, which happens frequently, can cause the company and its investors significant financial trouble. A giant hole has been created in revenues. I've been there to do the outplacement after this happens. Also, if drug development is all clumped in the same stage, for example all work is in the initial discovery phase, then resources—time, talent, and facilities—are pushed past the breaking point. The gap until revenues are generated is too great for the company to tolerate. The concept of a pipeline will work for your search as well. You can analyze where the gaps in your campaign are and shift your activity, just as a company can. To give you a visual idea of how creating a job and applying for an existing job can work together, take a look at the Job Pipeline.

The goal is to keep your Job Pipeline filled. Activity within your Job Pipeline has the potential of developing into real jobs. You're working through the phases of gaining an employer's interest, setting your hooks, and negotiating offers. Things are happening. It takes some work to move inside of it, however. Let's see how the Job Pipeline can give structure to your job campaign.

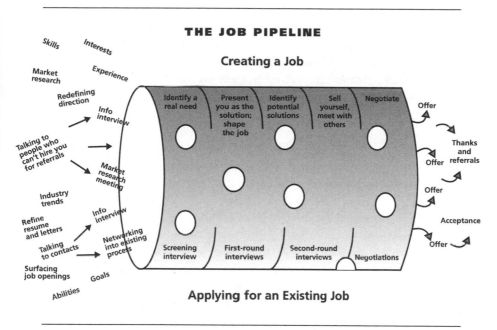

**THE JOB PIPELINE**

Creating a Job

Applying for an Existing Job

## Using the Job Pipeline

Early in your job campaign, you're outside the Job Pipeline because you're not ready to approach potential employers yet. You're defining your goals, defining who needs what you have to offer, then communicating your value and skills to others through your résumé and conversations. This is part of Strategy #1: Take Control. You want to be the one who decides where you're headed after doing your research. Start gathering information as we talked about in Strategy #1: Take Control and Strategy #2: Market for Mutual Benefit, then move toward the major decision makers as your clarity and connections start to gel.

Once your direction and message are clear, you're ready to set up meetings with decision makers. When applying for an existing job, it's fairly straightforward. You have uncovered a job opening and moved to the beginning of the Job Pipeline.

When creating a job, you may not know if you are generating interest until you actually see sparks of life from the listener. You will be meeting with people frequently as you gather information. How do you know which meeting will click? Often you don't, except that one may have more potential because of the *level* of the person you're meeting and your *interest* in the company. Go prepared, as if there were a real job opening, being conversant in the company's issues and market challenges. Assume that you will identify actual needs in the meeting and will position yourself as an experienced problem solver. That should definitely move you into the pipeline.

Your objective at the end of an initial meeting is to land the next meeting, not to get a job offer. Just move forward in the Job Pipeline. At the end of the first meeting, questions like, "Do you want to pencil in some time next week to get together? I can have some ideas together for you by then. What's your schedule like?" work well. It's a soft sell. "Pencil in" is nonthreatening, but it gets you on the calendar.

The middle stage of the Job Pipeline, both for creating a job and applying for an existing job, is to get the employer committed to you. This does not involve hard selling on your part. I often see professionals who want a job so much that they spend their precious time with the decision maker *talking*—about themselves, about how many exciting things they've done, about their last company. That's a hard sell. By the way, the best percentage for talking versus listening in an interview is 40 percent talking versus 60 percent listening. Surprised? Sales professionals working with potential customers use even higher standards: spend 70 percent of your time listening. The natural tendency when you truly want something is to push the product (you). Just the opposite approach is more effective, especially at senior levels. Let the decision makers have center stage. Not only is it a stroke to their egos to have their opinions solicited, but most decision makers think interviews go better when they do most of the talking! The real reason you want them to do most of the talking, however, is to garner the information in their heads and to learn how to best present yourself. If you can get them to talk about their needs before you go into your own background, you can customize your presentation. Otherwise you're firing your cannon before you know where the target is. You could spend a lot of time telling them how you've brilliantly integrated an acquisition, when that is the furthest thing from their mind. You just made yourself a square peg, regardless of how relevant the rest of your skills are. Listen and ask first; talk later.

The middle stage, therefore, involves asking open-ended questions (more about this in the chapter on Strategy #4: Network as the Norm), pinpointing needs, throwing in some quick examples of how you've addressed these issues before, and then steering the conversation into concepts rather than detail. Asking, "How are you going to respond to the new Dell product introduction?" will engage your decision maker in something he enjoys thinking about. It lets him see that you know what's going on with the competition, and sets you up for a quick antidote about how you dead-ended someone else's new product with a superior one of your own. This approach is much better than "How many days a week would I be on the road?" That question belongs at the end of the Job Pipeline, when they're committed to you. In the middle stage of the Job Pipeline, you're setting the chemistry for your relationship and showing that you not only have a grasp of their issues, but know solutions to their problems.

When you reach the final stage of the Job Pipeline, you should subtly start to make your presence felt. If you're applying for an existing job, you may still have competition at this point, so you want to be helpful rather than presumptive. Ask to meet with the people you'd be supervising, provide unsolicited testimonials, volunteer to contribute to a project they're working on or to go on a sales call with one of their people. You're increasing your presence in the company and increasing the number of people you know, "broadening your base in the account," as salespeople would say. Did you see the *Seinfeld* episode when everyone in one company thought Kramer worked there because he kept showing up? Becoming more involved during the final stage of the Job Pipeline shows people firsthand that you're the best choice.

### Evenly Distribute Your Job Pipeline

When you first start looking for a new job, you're delighted with *anything* that goes into your Job Pipeline. "Yes!! A meeting that might actually lead to something! Hurray!" You're right to give yourself a pat on the back, but don't relax yet. Keep doing your research, keep initiating conversations with new companies, and keep adding relationships to your Job Pipeline. The strongest job campaigns have activity in all phases of the Job Pipeline—the beginning, middle, and end—to ensure that you have *options* coming out of it.

As your campaign progresses, map the stages you're in with different companies, and see where you need to increase activity. Remember to give yourself a break when you're first starting to research companies. You're not going to have anything in the Job Pipeline yet. The Job Pipeline below reflects approximately three months' worth of work for Richard, an environmental services professional.

---

## THE JOB PIPELINE: TRACKING YOUR PROGRESS

### Creating a Job

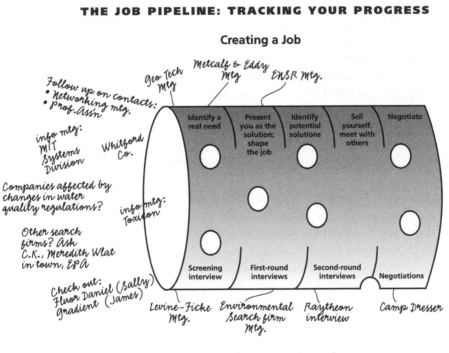

### Applying for an Existing Job

---

Where would you say that Richard needs to shore up his campaign? You can see that he has a lot going on outside of his Job Pipeline, he is doing well with initial interviews, and he has one initiative that is in the final stages. You can also see that Richard is running into some challenges converting initial meetings into second- and third-round interviews. The Job Pipeline is also a diagnostic tool that shows you where you may need to tweak your approach or redistribute your time.

## The Job Pipeline Has Holes in It

Notice how this is a sieved pipeline, with holes all along its surface? You already know what's coming out of those holes, don't you? Some companies that you've been considering. It happens. You're going to eliminate them some of the time, and they'll eliminate you too. That's the main reason that you need to make sure that your Job Pipeline is always being fed, even when you think it's full. Things have a way of disappearing, and you want to make sure that some results are coming out of the other end. Analyze companies that have slipped out of the Job Pipeline, then put them in your tickler file to revisit in a month, when the dust has settled. Are they still a viable option? Or have they had their funding cut and moved onto something else? Remember when you were on the other side of the desk, how finding a new person was important but not a raging fire that you had to stomp out right away? If you haven't experienced an outright rejection from an interesting company, circle back around later. In the meantime, keep your Job Pipeline filled so you have choices when you want them.

## It Ain't Over Until It's Over

When things get serious with a company, when you're actually into negotiations about your terms of employment, what is your reaction to starting any new initiatives? Frequently I hear, "I'm not going to follow up on this lead yet because my interviews with Global are going well. I want to see if this one plays out before I start anything new." Red alert. It may save you some psychic energy now not to start anything new, but you've just increased the amount of pain you'll feel and the length of time you'll spend searching on the other side should Global not come through, not to mention decreased your lack of leverage in negotiations with them due to your lack of alternatives.

Deals have been known to fall apart at the end. Some of the most awkward cases I've seen are people being told on their first days of work that something happened and their offer is being rescinded (no funding, the company was acquired, an internal executive is moving back from Kuala Lumpur). So sorry. Thanks anyway. Now you have to restart your campaign. Some companies hire zealously, then have to stave off starting dates for new employees when business drops. They ask new hires not to come to work for them right away, but to spend six to twelve months doing something else, often with financial incentives attached. Some companies offer partial pay for doing community service work in the interim. Talk about the land of the living dead. A year off might be personally fulfilling, but you will have lost professional momentum.

The point is to keep priming the Job Pipeline until you're starting your job. Do you have to keep plugging new companies in at the same rate as before you started negotiations with a good company? You can slow down the rate if you are in negotiations with several companies, but not just one. Those mid-pipeline companies that haven't quite made up their minds become increasingly important, too. They are your safety net if your first choices don't materialize. Don't neglect nurturing them in the heat of negotiations. You want to have more than one company competing for your attention at the end of the Job Pipeline. This serves multiple purposes, primarily clarifying your choice and providing leverage for increasing your compensation. The challenge is to get the offers to come out at the same time. Strategy #5: Negotiate in Round Rooms will give you ideas about how to get your offers on the table simultaneously while still maintaining good relationships with the companies that you'll eventually turn down (one of your better problems).

## Wrap-Up

Wow. Look at how far you've come in this chapter alone. You're really in the thick of things now, into creating your own New Job Security. You've seen that the easily visible jobs, from help wanted ads and search firms, are not under your control and the yield isn't great. That doesn't mean to ignore them, but to keep them in perspective. You've tracked how jobs are born out of need, out of problems waiting to be solved, and you know that you can go upstream from help wanted ads and create a lot more opportunities for yourself. You also know how to find a company's needs, by asking people and by tracking trends. And regardless of whether you or your company decide that reshaping your current job or moving within the company is an option, you will be growing professionally, which will continue to develop your options externally or internally. If you're constantly tracking trends, listening for needs, developing your skills, and seeing how you can help others, you'll be as nimble as a sports car on the autobahn.

STRATEGY #4

# Network as the Norm

*Our lives are connected*
*Like waves upon a shore*
*Sometimes with a whisper*
*Sometimes with a roar*
*Sometimes we think we leave no trace*
*But sometimes less is more. . . .*

"Facets of the Jewel"
by PAUL STOOKEY of Peter, Paul, and Mary

"I'd like to network with you."

How does it make you feel when someone says that to you? I've asked this question of hundreds of professionals in my networking seminars, and the reactions are much the same: they cringe. People don't like the concept of "being networked with." Why? The word "networking" has a bad reputation, although the activity itself does not. The word brings out feelings of being used or of using, of asking others for help when you have always been the one *giving* help, of looking less than knowledgeable on a subject when you've always been the expert, of taking advantage of others, and of embarrassing yourself. Well, we're about to change all that.

I probably don't need to convince you of the value of the activity. You know firsthand that networking is important. When was the last time you found a baby-sitter out of the Yellow Pages? A doctor? You may have already landed a job after networking, and you may have read about senior-level professionals who depend on it for work success more than any other distribution channel. It's true. The odds are with you. Outplacement and

Alumni Career Services surveys report that 65 to 85 percent of job seekers find their jobs through networking. Look at your own efforts to find the right job and see whether they reflect that same percentage.

If you have a tendency toward shyness, are an "I" on the extroversion/introversion preference of the Myers-Briggs Type Indicator, or gravitate toward working with ideas more than people, these percentages may look daunting to you. You're more likely to prefer doing in-depth computer research on companies before you approach them, sending out direct mail, posting your résumé on job boards, or using search firms to find the opportunities for you. Unstructured socializing, multiple phone calls, and approaching people that you haven't met before are not your idea of a good time. Not to worry. There are plenty of presidents and CEOs just like you, but you'll have to consciously go against a few of your natural inclinations during your transition to new work. Very few people pull down great jobs strictly through research. Picking up the phone and shutting down the computer earlier (unless it's to use email to set up a meeting), doing less planning, and getting in front of new people frequently with a good Elevator Story will head you toward that 65 to 85 percent range.

Networking is not just for between jobs any longer. That's changed. That's the focus of Strategy #4: Network as the Norm. We'll talk about the "norm" part of networking once we've set some other ideas in place. First, let's look at the history of networking; there are some lessons that you won't want to repeat in today's marketplace as well as some new permutations that will make your networking more powerful.

## Not Your Grandfather's Networking

The concept of networking evolved from work on informational interviewing created by John Crystal and Richard N. Bolles, two brilliant career theorists. They described the advantages of talking to someone who is doing the type of work that looks interesting to you, not to that person's superior but to the actual person who is doing the work that you're considering. In order to interview this person, you would ask someone whom you both knew for an introduction. Voilà! A network is born.

If you'd like to tap into the research that is evolving on the relationships between networks and job change, start with Mark Granovetter's *Getting a Job: A Study of Contacts and Careers* (2nd edition, The University of Chicago Press, 1995), in which he defines that initial contact you just made as "some intermediary known personally to the respondent, with whom he *originally* became acquainted in some context *unrelated* to a search for job information." In other words, a friend gave you the name. There is some fascinating social psychology beneath what you're doing, but we'll come back to that later.

The original insightful idea of purposely building a network for information morphed over time and has been abused. People started asking potential superiors for informational interviews, promising that "I'm not looking for a job. I'm just looking for information." Guess what? Everybody knew that that wasn't the truth, so the people who had been kind enough to grant the interviews felt mistreated. The idea of interviewing people about their expertise was so good, however, that the demand from job seekers continued to build until some companies set up policies that employees weren't allowed to give informational interviews due to time constraints. That brings us to irritated companies and overloaded, abused interview givers. Not a pretty place to start, is it?

One easy solution, before we get into more complex ones, is to change your vocabulary. Don't tell someone that you want to network with him or her. Don't ask for an informational interview. Always be honest. Say, "I don't expect you to know of any openings just because I'm calling." This is true, and it takes the pressure off the listener, but it makes it clear that you have an agenda other than pressing for names and openings. And you do. To set up the meeting, you can say, "Can we get together for a cup of coffee?" Or, "Can I pick your brain about how you think deregulation is going to affect us?" Or, "Can we trade ideas on hot, small cap companies?" You haven't asked to network or to have an informational interview. You haven't triggered any knee-jerk reactions, you don't sound like you're taking up too much time, and you are more likely to earn a receptive audience. If you need to refer to the meeting with others, call it a "market research meeting" since it's accurate and doesn't raise hackles. When you see the terms "networking meeting" and "informational interview" in this book, know that they're shorthand we can use among ourselves, but when you're out in the field setting up your conversations, take off the pressure by changing your vocabulary.

## The New Networking

The new networking includes the concept of gathering information, which Bolles and Crystal introduced, but emphasizes the relationship and the reciprocity between the two parties more than the information. My definition, which takes out much of the sting that senior-level professionals feel when contemplating networking, calls the new networking a barter system based on the exchange of mutually valuable information.

You and the person to whom you'd like to speak both have areas of expertise. You're equal partners in the conversation, regardless of the organizational levels between you. You can be of help to this person. Your challenge is to figure out how. Remember your Market for Mutual Benefit homework? Spend some time thinking about the needs of the company or individual you're approaching before you make the initial contact. Before I pick up the phone to call one of my clients, I always consider, "What can I do to help this person?" You get a more positive reception, and you are creating a relationship rather than a sales call.

> **The new networking is a barter system based on the exchange of mutually valuable information.**

Thinking of what you can do to help other people, leading with their needs and staying there, not only drives the marketing circle so you can get your own needs met, it also shifts the power balance inherent in the earlier style of networking. This shift makes networking much more palatable than it used to be because you're still the expert; you're still the person who is helping others. A senior executive can practice the new networking and keep his dignity intact. A mid-level professional can get the attention of someone at the top of an organization because he has ideas to make her more successful. You may be giving more help than you're getting at this point. That's okay. You're building a relationship.

In the earlier style of networking, you, the person seeking information, would approach a Learned One asking for names and referrals. They had the power; you were the supplicant. Now you approach them as a colleague, on a level playing field regardless of the number of levels between your title and theirs, because they need your information just as much as you need theirs. Let's talk about what you have to offer that will be of value.

## Catching Your Value Wave

It's always amazing to me how many incredibly talented people aren't aware of what they have to offer when they first start networking. Your assets are often more obvious to others than they are to you. You should have an idea of your competencies and strengths from doing your homework in Strategy #1: Take Control. Additional strengths will surface over time as you continue to get feedback from others, review old performance appraisals, and analyze help wanted ads. "I have everything they're looking for," you'll say after reading some ads. Your strengths are right there in black and white. Pick out your top five favorite strengths, and we'll use these in the Value Wave in just a minute.

Strengths alone don't win you the beauty contest though, do they? After figuring out what you have to offer, you need to integrate your talents with a company's needs in order to catch their attention. You are (or are becoming) familiar with company needs having done your research on target markets in chapter three. Company needs are the second part of your Value Wave. Remember, the more you keep the conversation about increasing a company's profitability in your discussions, the closer you'll be to their needs.

There's another wave, a larger force behind company needs that you may catch even before the decision makers in a company do. It's the trends that are hitting an industry. Needing to be profitable is a constant, but market trends will shape *how* a company is going to be profitable. Your secret weapon: Know what's happening in an industry, and you can predict the needs of companies in that industry. Your agenda for informational interviews will not change dramatically for companies within an industry, and your up-front research for each company will be lessened. You did your *industry* research and learned to track trends in chapter four. These insights ensure that you come across as a visionary leader who can actually make a difference.

Now that you have a sense of industry trends, a company's needs, and your strengths, you're ready to navigate these three waves to more powerful conversations in your networking meetings.

---

- ***Overlaying industry trends:*** *"Would you like to talk about ways the strategic alliance that you're pursuing could be used to develop markets for your filtration instrumentation in some new sectors? It looks like there is going to be a growing demand in defense and government labs, and I have some ideas about how you could go after that."*
- ***Building in company needs:*** *"It sounds like you're in the process of developing some strategic alliances that will broaden your product offerings. I have some experience with that."*
- ***Your strengths:*** *"I have strong marketing skills."*

---

Take a look at one person's Value Wave to see how the conversation becomes increasingly powerful as industry trends overlay company needs and an individual's strengths. You're subtly opening up the possibility of creating a job.

---

## CATCH YOUR VALUE WAVE

**Industry: Instrumentation**

**Function: Senior operations management**

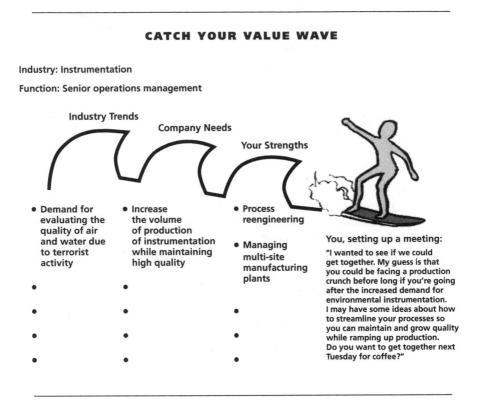

Industry Trends

Company Needs

Your Strengths

- Demand for evaluating the quality of air and water due to terrorist activity

- Increase the volume of production of instrumentation while maintaining high quality

- Process reengineering

- Managing multi-site manufacturing plants

You, setting up a meeting:

"I wanted to see if we could get together. My guess is that you could be facing a production crunch before long if you're going after the increased demand for environmental instrumentation. I may have some ideas about how to streamline your processes so you can maintain and grow quality while ramping up production. Do you want to get together next Tuesday for coffee?"

---

Hopefully, you now have some ideas of how to keep on top of changes in companies and industries of interest to you. I don't want the research to sound like a big deal or you'll be tempted to put it off. Researching trends can be interesting, fun, and manageable, something you can do informally, bit by bit, all the time. Ask someone at a party how the Federal Reserve interest rate hike is affecting his work. Subscribe to the *Wall Street Journal* and skim what you can. Go to a professional association meeting. You'll likely meet people in your field who can tell you what's happening at their companies, you learn what's happening in your profession, and you can take on leadership roles to develop your reputation. Think of information gathering as sharpening your saw, that is, investing in yourself; build in some minor routines to your everyday functioning that will pay off in major league ways.

The question at the end of the Value Wave and the conversations it can open up are your payoffs. It's worth spending some time creating a thought-provoking question as you'll be able to use this same question, or a similar one, with other companies in the same industry.

Now for your own Value Wave. Fill out the three columns in the blank "Catch Your Value Wave" in Appendix G, then convert them into questions that you can use with decision makers. They'll be wondering where you've been all of their lives.

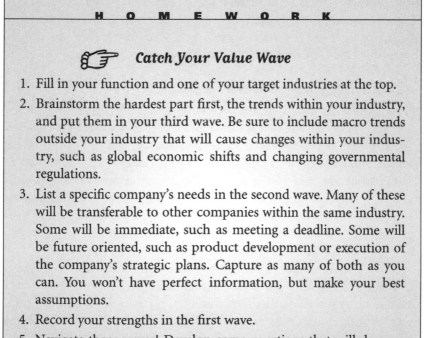

**H O M E W O R K**

☞ *Catch Your Value Wave*

1. Fill in your function and one of your target industries at the top.
2. Brainstorm the hardest part first, the trends within your industry, and put them in your third wave. Be sure to include macro trends outside your industry that will cause changes within your industry, such as global economic shifts and changing governmental regulations.
3. List a specific company's needs in the second wave. Many of these will be transferable to other companies within the same industry. Some will be immediate, such as meeting a deadline. Some will be future oriented, such as product development or execution of the company's strategic plans. Capture as many of both as you can. You won't have perfect information, but make your best assumptions.
4. Record your strengths in the first wave.
5. Navigate those waves! Develop some questions that will demonstrate your value to decision makers as they position their company to capture opportunities. You just happen to have some ideas about how to do it.

You may want to chart a separate "Catch Your Value Wave" for each industry that you've decided to approach. Your message may need to change. Not only will industry needs vary, but company needs and the strengths you showcase may shift as well. There is a blank copy of this form in Appendix G.

# What Network?

Now that you're armed with the concept of networking as a successful bartering system and you see the value you can add to a company by anticipating and responding to trends, what are you going to do next? You're all dressed up with no place to go. It's time to start networking.

But where is this infamous network? Do you feel that other people have stronger networks than you (network envy) or that yours is somewhere between weak and nonexistent? "I don't have a network," or "I've used up my network," or "I've recently moved to town and have to start a completely new network" are frequent regrets that I hear from professionals, regrets that are reversible and within your control. Be assured, you *do* have a network. However, you may need to uncover it, like King Arthur's parting the mists to see the Lady of the Lake's stronghold.

## *Structuring Your Network*

To bring your network to life, let's start with the "how," then we'll plug in the "who." How will you manage the names in your network? Picking out a system now that you like for tracking information will save you time and improve your work results for the rest of your career. A tall claim? Not really. Software can help you remember details, come up with names you'd forgotten, and remind you to do things that might otherwise fall between the cracks. Although paper-based systems work, they're more cumbersome and can't cross-reference the name of the administrative assistant and everyone else you've met in a company as quickly as a computer.

You may have contact management software already. These programs are databases that keep track of the names, contact information, events, and tasks that you feed into them. Initially, they were used by sales professionals to keep track of customers. You'll basically be doing the same thing. You can also use them to keep track of your personal relationships, from holiday card mailings to soccer team memberships. You'll really be on top of things. A president of one company can't believe that I remember her birthday every year. I don't. The reminder function in my software does.

Outlook is one contact manager program that many people already have on their computers without knowing it because it is bundled with Microsoft Office along with Word, PowerPoint, and Excel. Check under your "Programs" listing to see if it's there. Or you may want to investigate other contact managers. ACT! is another popular choice. If you want to sync up with a Palm Pilot or personal digital assistant (PDA) at some point, make sure the software you select will be compatible.

---

H O M E W O R K

### ☞ Tracking Your Contacts

Pick out a system to use for tracking your contacts. Guard against spending too much time analyzing which one is perfect because it will slow you down. You can always switch if you need to. Just start entering a couple of names to get the process started.

---

## Okay, So I Have a System

Now to the "who" part of network development. It's time to start entering names into your database. Which names? Begin with the professional contacts that you're in touch with fairly frequently. Start a new card in your contact manager for each person, and enter what you know about them.

### SAMPLE ENTRY

**Full Name:**  Mike Mayfield
**Last Name:**  Mayfield
**First Name:**  Mike
**Job Title:**  Director of Product Development
**Company:**  Field Systems, Inc.
**Business Address:**  124 West Street
                      Longview, TX 12354
**Business Phone:**  (765) 432-9876
**Business Fax:**  (765) 432-9825
**Email:**  mike@fieldsystems.com

Talked to on 1/8. Said to call in 2 weeks.
Admin: Leslie Howe, 765-432-9873. Talked to on 12/5.
   Is going to Colorado for holidays.
Mike's thinking about acquiring some new drilling
   technology. Follow up.

If you spend time filling out every little blank on a card, it will take forever. Start with a person's name, phone number, and email address. Capture what's readily available for each person and keep going. "Wait a minute," you say. "I have hundreds of people in my Rolodex and stacks of business cards. Isn't this going to take a lot of time?" Absolutely. You may want to hire a secretary on an hourly basis to feed in a lot of the backlog to get you started. If not, just enter recurring professional contacts and add others, when you have the time. This is a lifetime reference book you're building, so getting information into it is important.

Most programs have a really handy function: an empty field where you can make notes. You can record the dates of meetings with the contact, the name of the person who introduced you, their expertise, and so on. This is your cheat sheet. If you can't remember a person's name, search on a key word and it will come up. However, your contact system is only as good as what you feed into it. You may hire someone for several hours a month to help you update your contacts as they change. It will become less time intensive once you're up and running.

If you don't think you have a lot of contacts, and your list fizzles out once you have ten names, don't be discouraged. Don't screen too tightly when you're entering people. They don't all have to be a big cheese to warrant an entry, nor do they need to live locally or be close friends. Just go back to your Rolodex, your business cards, or your calendar and capture data. More names will continue to pop into your mind. The art is to record the names before you forget them entirely.

If you want an additional stimulus, try the following Networking Brain Stimulator (a blank copy can be found in Appendix H). The important vendor-competitor-customer Referral Triangle that we discussed in chapter three is another group of relevant connections. Brainstorm who you sold to, bought from, and competed against at your various companies. List your buddies from school and the alumni who live in your area (even if you don't know them). Your alumni office can help. Your database should now be growing by leaps and bounds.

## NETWORKING BRAIN STIMULATOR

Once you have begun the process of identifying your personal contacts, you will want to develop a system to organize and track them efficiently. Keep adding people to your network and remember to give something helpful back so your networking moves forward on an ongoing basis.

Colleagues in most recent job (including bosses and staff):

Colleagues in former jobs (including bosses and staff):

Vendors:

Customers:

Competitors:

Social friends and neighbors:

Relatives:

Clubs:

College alumni:

Bankers, consultants, lawyers, accountants, stockbrokers:

Professional associations:

Sports:

Church or clergy:

_____

_____

Volunteer, common interest, political, or civic groups:

_____

_____

Doctors:

_____

_____

Other:

_____

_____

Whether you feel like you have too many contacts to enter them now or not enough to sneeze at, don't worry about "finishing" your database soon. It's never finished. It's a work in progress, and it will continually provide support for your career growth. Get a good start on it now, then add to it as you can. It's time for you to start talking to some of these people rather than spending all of your time in front of a computer screen.

## Working through Your Network's Layers

Randomly talking to important people may be hazardous to your career. I've often seen recently laid-off people, who want a quick fix, approach the biggest "ace" in their contact network first to see if they can be hired ASAP. The emotion is totally understandable. The strategy isn't. It's like a rebound after breaking up with a significant other; filling the gap would be nice, but you may not be in your best shape. When you approach your aces, you want to be clear about what you can and can't do, what the bottom side of the marketing circle means for them, and where you can add value. You may have one trip to the well, and you want to be prepared.

You prepare yourself by working through the layers of your contacts. Now that you have identified some of your contacts in your contact manager, sit back and take a look at them. You'll see that your network is stratified into three layers. The comparison of these layers to the rings in a target has been used for years to explain how the different levels of your network function.

**NETWORKING LAYERS**

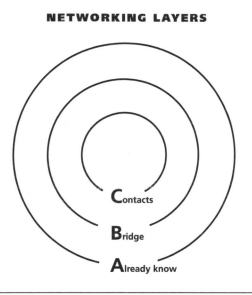

- **A Level**

  The outside ring is the people you *Already* know. These are people that you can go back to many times. You can ask them dumb questions, be undecided or unclear about what you want, pick their brains, and listen to their opinions. What do you want from them? You're investigating what's hot and what's not in various companies and industries and where there may be potential growth, and they may have some ideas. If you can visit them at their office to talk about possible recommendations and contact names, you'll typically get more detailed information than you would on the golf course. You might start a conversation with an A-level contact in an informal place, then follow up with a more formal one where you can practice your informational interviewing skills. These people are important; they're your main support during your job transition, so think of their needs, too.

- **B Level**

  The middle ring are people who create a *Bridge* for you. These people work in organizations of interest to you, but they aren't in a position to make decisions about you. You may have been referred to them by A-level people. You need two things from B-level people: names and needs. "Who should I be talking to, and what keeps him or her up at night?" Of course, you're not going to get helpful information if you don't establish a relationship first, so treat this as an informational interview, which it is. Anyone from the chief financial officer to the shipping and receiving clerk has opinions about how the company and the CEO are doing. Take all their input with a grain of salt, but build their trust; you have just developed a new relationship.

The job seekers in highest demand are often those who have spent some time with and learned from various B-level people. You have learned about the industry's problems from a variety of perspectives. You often know more about the competition than the company does . . . a damning statement, but true. You're not giving away trade secrets, but you can talk generically about how trends are playing out and about creative approaches to problems.

- **C Level**

  The inside ring: *Contact.* You've hit the decision-maker level. This is the person you've been waiting to meet, often introduced to you by a B-level person. These are typically tough people to break through to without connections. Your objective with these people is to form relationships, ideally through brief meetings, where you can ask some leading questions about challenges they're facing, then dangle carrots—your ideas for potential solutions. When you were setting up the meetings, you probably promised that you didn't expect them to know about jobs just because you're calling, so stay on the subjects of market research and problem solving. Don't worry. They'll bring up any appropriate openings if they think you're a match. In the meantime, your job is to try to create enough interest in your ideas about addressing their needs that they'll want to set up another meeting. You didn't think you were going to get a job offer in one meeting, did you?

Seeing the layers in your network should make it easier to identify who you can start talking to now. Warning: The boundaries between the three rings are permeable. Think carefully about the order in which you want to approach people. A-level people, ones that you already know, may be C-level, or decision makers, as well. B-level people may be C-level people in disguise. Timing is everything. As you refine your information and improve your presentation, you'll get better. You'll know when you're ready for prime time.

## *Whose Handshake?*

The flip side of working your way into and up the corporate food chain is making sure that you're perceived at an appropriate professional level. Executives often share a concern that doesn't get voiced because it's an awkward subject. "Whose handshake do I need to get the C-level person to pay attention to me?" In other words, to get an introduction, should you use the name of the B-level person you visited who is five levels away from the CEO, but who knows the CEO somewhat from a committee where they crossed paths? "It depends on your options," is the answer. If you meet a CEO through a friend that she made while sitting on another board, odds are that you will be trusted and accepted faster. Gather insider information from all your B-level people in that company to get an accurate representation of the company. Get the highest level introduction you can, then tune in to see how these senior-level people value the referrals of their employees. It speaks to the culture of the organization you're considering.

## Breaking Through: Catching the Uncatchable Person

It's time to set up a meeting with a B-level person you don't know yet. This is where building a network can break down because people often shy away from the one (or two)-handshake-removed connection. According to Robert S. Gardella in *The Harvard Business School Guide to Finding Your Next Job* (Harvard Business Reference, 2000), "Most job seekers do not break this barrier because they feel they do not 'know' the [next level of] people they contact, and thus greatly curtail the speed at which they could be expanding their network." Are you with me so far on the benefits of an active, helpful network that can plug you into new leads and opportunities? Great. Now you need to move beyond the people that you already know. They won't have all of the information you'll need.

The right mind-set can help make this jump into the unknown a little easier. Do you honestly believe that you have something to offer the company you're approaching that they could develop and exploit—benefiting the company, its customers, and maybe even its stockholders? This belief will help you whether the company is growing or needs turning around. If they don't take you up on your ideas, it's their loss. Seriously. Their competition may be interested in what you have to say. This is not some sort of head game. If you've been doing your homework so far, you will know more than many companies about the trends that are impacting their industry. You're also going to be further along than most companies in competitive analysis. After all, you're out there talking to people and getting current information. People have been bought for less. Go get 'em.

## The Phone Approach

You have a target that you'd like to meet. You have the name of someone who referred you. You have two Sharp Skills in mind (which you identified in chapter two) that will be close to your target's heart. You're set. Pick up the phone. Don't worry about being perfect. Just do it. If you get the person's voice mail, here's what you need to cover:

- Give your name, clearly.
- Give your referral's name (with quip, if appropriate).
- State the purpose of your call in relation to your Sharp Skills.
- Propose a meeting.
- Provide your contact information (always and slowly) and hang up.

It goes like this:

> "Hi, Cary. This is Pat Doe. Leslie Smith said that you're the world's greatest expert in mutual fund advertising [insert the specialty of theirs that overlaps with your interest]. I wanted to see if we could get together briefly. I've had some success reaching financial advisors at brokerage houses and building a lot of new business, and I know this is a target group for you. I have some ideas that may be of help. And you may have some suggestions for me about trends in your marketing work and at your company. Would you be able to grab a cup of coffee next Wednesday or Thursday morning? If these dates don't work, let me know what does. I'm at 321-654-0987 or patdoe@aol.com. I look forward to seeing you."

That isn't too painful, is it? A few points about your message:

- You kept it short. With only thirty seconds available to you, you can't ramble.
- You used a "double-hook" strategy. One hook was mentioning Leslie Smith's name, and one was suggesting that you might be able to help Cary be more profitable by giving him ideas on increasing business. The first hook lowered his defenses. The second hook made him interested in seeing you. Two hooks always work better than one.

- You used humor. The "world's greatest expert" line gets people chuckling every time, but use whatever works best for you. Giving people a laugh near the beginning of the conversation relaxes them and lowers the barriers a little.

- You went for the close. The close here was to set up a meeting. Suggesting specific dates, such as Wednesday or Thursday morning, sometimes forces people to action. Proposing explicit dates is much stronger than "Can we get together sometime?" and is more likely to work.

- You left your phone number (and email, if you choose). This is a pet peeve of mine. The harder you make it for someone to return a phone call, the less likely they are to do so. Don't ask your target to find the time and energy to look up your number. Odds are they won't bother. Leave it slowly and clearly at the end of each message. If they're retrieving your message while driving down the highway, they're more likely to remember the phone number if it's the last thing they hear rather than the first.

You can script your message ahead of time. Write out what you want to say, including the names and special skills you're going to mention. You don't have to actually read the script, but it can serve as a security blanket while you're recording, assuring you that you're being succinct and hitting the important points.

What if the real person answers? That's a nice problem. Use the same approach. Listen well and maybe throw in one more accomplishment, but keep the call short. It's easier for them to screen you out over the phone than in person, the telemarketer-at-dinner syndrome, so don't bury them with information now. Just dangle your carrots and aim for a meeting.

What if they try to brush you off over the phone? Your target won't be rude because you came in via a referral name. Regardless, he or she may decline a meeting. If it truly sounds like a refusal to meet instead of a temporarily crunchy time, here's your response: "I understand. That's not a problem. While I have you on the phone, however, may I ask two questions? First, what do you predict will happen with the demand for commercial retail real estate [insert their area of expertise that overlaps with your interest] in the next two quarters? (Listen) Second, what companies, besides your own, do you think are in a position to benefit from your prediction?" Worst case, you've added to your store of market information, and you may decide to target the companies that were mentioned. If your target really warms up, you can try a third question. "It sounds like Trampled Crow is well positioned. Is there anyone you can recommend that I should talk to about growing their retail side?" It's worth a shot. You might get the name of an ace target.

## The Email Approach

Contacting a target by email is sometimes easier than phoning them. There are fewer screens, so you might get to the big cheese without going through a secretary or switchboard. If you don't know the person's email address, either find an address for someone else in the company and use the same format, or send your target an email with an address that looks logical and see what bounces back. If several attempts bounce back, call the company. "The email I'm sending to Larry Ellison keeps bouncing back. I must have a character wrong. Is *lellison* correct?" It doesn't sound like a cold call with that approach, and you're more likely to get some help.

Your email should follow the same format as a phone call. Once again, it has to be brief. People have no more tolerance for long emails than they do for long phone messages. Mention your referring contact and your skills. Don't attach your résumé. You're swapping ideas, coming in at a collegial level. A sales call might scare him or her off, and a résumé looks like you're selling. If he or she asks for your résumé, send it then.

What you use for the subject line of your email address is critical. Your email may never be opened if you're one of eighty in the inbox and the subject line doesn't look interesting. "Leslie Smith's recommendation" should work; in other words, mention the person who referred you.

## Integrating Approaches for the Capture

There will be plenty of times when people don't return your calls. They don't respond to your emails. They don't follow up after a great meeting when you left on a high and they promised to get right back to you. It's not fair, but get used to it. Don't assume that you're going to hear back from anyone, and you'll be in better psychological and strategic shape. Most of the time, it's not about you, even though you feel it is. Whether it is an "erosion of etiquette," as a senior marketing executive in transition described the phenomenon, or simply overload, the results are the same: no news. Your job is not to hold your breath waiting for the promised follow-up, but to have an action plan in place and to have other initiatives you're pursuing simultaneously.

Getting a decision maker to take the next step, whether it is setting up the first meeting or negotiating the final clause in a contract, is both an art and a science. Brendan knew how to do both.

Brendan really wanted to work at SymmCo, the industry leader in data storage. He had left his director of regional sales job at an international health-care products manufacturer with sparks flying on both his side and management's side. To move up in that company, he would have had to relocate to corporate headquarters, a long way from his family, which meant it was time to look for another job, regardless.

His new target, SymmCo, was not lacking for applicants. Its products had a strong reputation, and its employees had been making a lot of money on stock growth. They were hiring, but what did Brendan know about data storage? His industry background wasn't a fit at all. His functional background, sales and marketing, was of interest to SymmCo, but they wanted salespeople who knew their products and their customers, ideally someone from the competition with current customers in tow. This did not describe Brendan. He would be a tough sell.

Brendan was good in sales for a reason, though. He was professionally persistent, didn't take things personally, and consistently focused on the bottom side of the marketing circle, helping others. People liked him. He started penetrating SymmCo by talking to A-level contacts, people he already knew, learning the names of B-level people, and setting up meetings with them. Everyone was fairly responsive in the first round because of the strength of his referrals' relationships with them. The hard part didn't come until later.

Brendan's first meetings went extremely well. He found company and industry needs and showed them how he could help. Had they looked at the health-care market? Had they thought about the giant opportunity it would be for SymmCo? The data storage requirements for the health care industry are enormous, and Brendan had been selling to a lot of people who might need it. (Notice how he switched products but played up the same customers?) He might have some ideas for them.

People were biting. SymmCo is a large company, so there were multiple places that Brendan might fit. His Bridge-level people referred him on to other people. He didn't want to narrow his options by pursuing only one opportunity early in his relationship with SymmCo. He wasn't sure where he was best suited in the company, plus he wanted to keep a little competitive pressure going. He pursued the next round of meetings, and things kept going well.

He began homing in on three separate opportunities: he was creating two, and one was a new opening in a growing department. The two he was creating would be at higher levels with more challenging work than the official opening. No surprise there. His favorite choice was a marketing opportunity to start up a health care vertical; his second choice, still interesting, was in channel management. The problem was that the decision makers weren't getting back to him; the marketing people were promising action but not delivering and his second-choice group was pursuing him. Turning down a potential channel management job could be risky because the marketing position might never materialize. This is where the strategy for breaking through to the right person comes in handy.

Brendan left a phone message for his potential marketing boss. "Hi, John. This is Brendan Span. I was calling to check on the status of my application for hire. I know this can be time consuming and might not be within your individual control. I was wondering if there was anything I could do to help the process along. Also, I am interested in another opportunity within SymmCo in the channel sales area, plus there's another department that has expressed some interest in me. Since I'm most interested in what you're doing, however, I want to finalize things with you first before I pursue any other options. I could really use your insight on this. Could we set up a time to get together next week, maybe Tuesday morning?"

Brendan was open and honest about talking to others within the company, but he also used it as leverage to get his first choice to move faster. As a result, Brendan wound up with several offers. Not only did he land the marketing work that he wanted, he negotiated for additional stock options and a more favorable base and bonus package. His rationale was that he was making a long-term career commitment and wanted to yoke his success with that of the company. He broke through the foot dragging and got the attention he wanted by finding ways to motivate people. You can do the same.

Brendan's story demonstrates the advantages of the "multiple warhead missile" strategy. Instead of depending on one relationship and one series of meetings to generate an offer, Brendan pursued multiple approaches simultaneously. Not only did he prime the Job Pipeline outside of SymmCo in case his efforts there imploded, he also primed it with several initiatives within one company to build internal competitive pressures. You can build a buzz about yourself and your name will get around, which is just what you want. The art is to keep the buzz positive. You should avoid playing off one side against another, sharing information that might not be appropriate or, conversely, withholding information that should be shared. "John, Arthur made me an offer today that I'm going to accept. I wanted you to be the first to know because your opportunity sounded like a lot of fun, and I appreciate the time you spent with me. I may have some names of other candidates for you." You're being up-front, you're ensuring that one of your champions hears the news directly from you, and you're still volunteering to help. It wouldn't hurt to ask John out to lunch shortly after you've started your new job to keep your network broad and engaged.

Additional strategies for breaking through to your C-level person include the following:

- Vary your approaches, alternating phone and email messages. If you really need to get through to someone, use both phone and email. Think through what you want to leave on a voice mail message before you even pick up the phone. Dangle carrots, propose a time for a meeting, then leave your phone number. You'll need to wait a couple of days to see if anything happens. Since you're realistic, you're not assuming that they will return your first call.

   About three days later, send an email saying approximately the same thing that your voice mail did. If you want, start it off with "Sorry that I missed you by phone the other day. Maybe email is an easier way to communicate."

- If you still don't hear back in a couple of days, try the "catch 'em" strategy. When are most people in their offices? Call before office hours, after office hours, and ten minutes before the hour. Meetings typically start on the hour, so call them ten minutes before. *Don't leave any more messages* until at least seven to ten days have passed. Call sporadically until you catch the person. When you finally get the person, do not vent your frustration. Making someone feel guilty will backfire. Move right to your future. "Glad I caught you. Let me tell you what I'm calling about."

- Use "deadlines" to put on a little pressure. If you say in an initial phone message, "I'm going to be in your area next Wednesday or Thursday and want to see if we could grab a cup of coffee," you're imposing a preferred time constraint. Leave eight other companies in that geographic area the same message and work out the times later. You now have an excuse to touch base with the admin support person (don't call someone a "secretary" until you know the correct title) to see whether your suggested time to catch the boss is going to work out. "I sent Susan an email last week about getting together tomorrow, but I don't know if that's going to work with her schedule. Do you know whether it will work, or should we find a different time?"

- Having to leave town (don't say it's for Disneyworld), attend an upcoming meeting with a client or a potential client, or meet with an influential person or someone in the media can all be used for leverage as deadlines. "Tom, I'm going to be meeting with Ford next week. I know that you've been talking to them about your new sensors. I can't guarantee that we'll discuss them, but if you want to get together ahead of time, I'd like to hear what you're working on." Once again, you want to be forthright, but if you really think this company has great sensors and that Ford would benefit from learning about them, your meeting definitely will catch the attention of the person you are calling.

- Befriend the assistant. An assistant can be your ally. Often a decision maker's voice mail message will refer you to that person. Sometimes, the operator will give you his or her name. Treat the assistant with humor and respect, something he or she will surely appreciate. "Jo, is it true that you're the real reason Nancy is walking through brick walls these days?" Making this person chuckle scores on both sides of the marketing circle. You're meeting his or her needs by acknowledging their legitimate importance, and you're building your reputation as a result. Having the administrative staff support you demonstrates that you're smart and a team player. They're often the Keepers of the Schedule and they're hidden persuaders, so you want them in your corner. If you pass their screen, you may land either an in-person meeting or a telephone appointment. Not bad.

- Don't leave a lot of messages. As Paul of Peter, Paul, and Mary said in his song at the beginning of the chapter, "Sometimes less is more." You're a professional. You're not desperate. Leave too many messages and you risk becoming an in-house joke. You'll know when to back off. If you try the above approaches and you still haven't hooked your C-level person, she truly is uncatchable. Don't take it personally. She probably isn't tuning in to her mother either. Keep moving.

On the plus side is that the number of people you actually can connect with will go up as will your number of meetings. You can use voice mail and email to move your career forward, leaving messages with questions or suggested action steps. You can establish interest and set up times to meet with people without ever seeing or talking to each other directly. It's faster and more efficient than playing telephone tag forever. You'll still have the human touch if the relationships gets serious.

## Framing the First Market Research Meeting

Congratulations. You've broken through to the decision maker, dangled some carrots, and set up an appointment. Victory comes in small steps, so pat yourself on the back with each one. It's time to start preparing for the meeting, but don't drop everything else. Your Job Pipeline is still hungry and needs ongoing initiatives to feed it as you move some of these earlier relationships further down the line.

### Who's in Control?

You asked for the meeting, right? That means that you're the one in control. If you've asked to go out for breakfast, lunch, or coffee (stay away from dinner or drinks; that may be too large of a time commitment), that means that you're supposed to pick up the tab. It also means that you're the one with the agenda and the questions.

You can develop your meeting agenda now. What questions do you truly want to ask this person you'll be interviewing? "Do you have a job for me?" is not one of them, by the way. Most of your questions will be conceptual questions, which are intellectually engaging and fun to consider. Your questions can subtly demonstrate that you know the challenges of the industry and the company. About 60 percent of your questions can be used in meetings with other companies. You have comparative data about trends, issues, and needs in your industries. (What a great springboard for writing articles!) The remaining 40 percent of your questions will be tailored to the specific company.

## *Prepare Your Funnel*

Now is the time to do some in-depth research on the company that you'll be visiting. You'll need to do a little research to even get the meeting, but if you sink a lot of time into researching a specific company and then can't land a meeting, you've just wasted your time, which is a valuable and finite resource. Do most of your research after the meeting is set up. When you were researching trends, we talked about sources such as your library, professional associations, the Internet, and colleagues, so plunge in. The stakes have just gone up.

Use these same resources to look up the person (people) with whom you'll be meeting. Finding common links with this person will get you further in these initial meetings than knowing everything on the balance sheet. Word of mouth is a great resource, and you can be creative about how you use it. Find a bio of your target through the Internet, and note where he did his undergraduate and graduate work. Do you know anyone who graduated from SMU around 1982? Do you know someone who worked at a former company of your target's? Can you find any hometown info? The possibilities are endless. But don't scare the decision maker in an initial meeting by sharing everything you may have learned about him. The idea is to lower his defenses with a common connection rather bring in the Identity Theft Police.

As you're doing your corporate and individual research, specific questions will start emerging for your agenda. The questions will vary depending on your function and industry, but remember, this is not a job interview. Questions that put on the pressure to hire you will backfire. This is all about relationships, helping others, and gathering information about their needs. You don't know if this is a frog that you'll be kissing or the actual prince(ss), but you'll walk away with a new friend regardless, warts and all.

Think of the order in which you want to ask your questions in your meeting (formerly known as an informational interview). You'll want to break the ice first, to relax the person with whom you're speaking. That's right. It's your job to relax her since you asked for this meeting and she has a million other things to do. If you can start someone talking about herself, insert a little humor, or find some common interest or connection that you share, you're off to a good start. Plan some icebreaker questions at the beginning of your agenda.

Think big when building your agenda. What are some conceptual questions you could ask about her industry? Here is where you mentally engage the person and show your grasp of her challenges. You then proceed to narrow down the topics into company-related questions, such as where the bottlenecks and major time sinks are (inoffensive ways to ask for her problems).

The agenda you're designing works like a funnel. It starts with a broad opening and narrows down to specifics. In the middle part of the funnel, you're poking around to determine company and industry needs. If there is no expressed need, you won't be able to create a job right away. Your fall-back objective is to acquire names. Names of further contacts and market-place information are the most typical outcomes from your initial meeting, though an occasional golden nugget—a problem just waiting for you to solve it—slips through.

It's time to start writing down agenda questions for your market re-search meetings. The questions you develop will provide you with a valu-able comparison base, helping you to decide which company attracts you the most. You might also gather some useful research data to publish an article for one of your professional associations. What questions would you like to ask in your meetings?

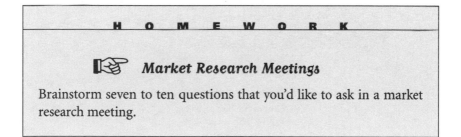

### H O M E W O R K

### 👉 *Market Research Meetings*

Brainstorm seven to ten questions that you'd like to ask in a market research meeting.

It's harder than it sounds, isn't it? Below, you'll find some ideas, but I asked you to think of your own questions first for a reason. Your questions should target your industry, the company you're visiting, changes going on in the economy, and the individual you're interviewing. Any list of sample questions could sound canned, so be sure to customize yours.

## Sample Questions for a Market Research Meeting

*Put into your own words.*

**Ice Breakers**
"Have you been at ___ for a long time?" Use clues in the environment. Bring up your mutual friend.

**Industry**
Projections for the industry: is it growing, stable, declining? Short- and long-term projections?
Are they cyclical? What new development do you see coming that could affect the success of
the field? What are the biggest challenges this industry will be facing in the future?

**Company**
What companies do you predict will do well or poorly over the next five years? How
do you see your company as a place to work? Who are your toughest competitors
and why? How did you get started?

**Area of Interest**
What type of background is typical of a successful _____ [your area
of interest] in your company? What are the four most important skills
that someone in this position could have? Would my background
be appropriate? What type of job titles would be used to
describe this type of work? What sort of salary and
career-growth opportunities exist in this area? Will
this type of work be in demand in the future?

**Needs**
What are the two to three issues that you'll be
facing in the next year? What type of skills
will it take to address these issues?

**Recommendations**
What is the best approach to be
considered as a serious candidate
for ___ [your area of interest]
positions? Are there other
fields or types of jobs that
I should be considering
that use the same skills?
Are there search firms
that you use that you
think are particularly
helpful? Which com-
panies have the high-
est likelihood of
needing some-
one with my
background?

**Names**

Does this list give you additional ideas for your agenda? Capture your ideas while they're still warm. Add them to the previous homework section as potential questions to ask. Your agenda is well on its way.

In addition to your agenda, you want to have completed your earlier assignments. This is where the market research meeting and interviewing overlap. What if you actually stumble on some problems that you could solve or an actual job opening that might be of interest to you? Eureka! You don't want to be caught unprepared to demonstrate your strengths, so before the meeting, have:

- Your Elevator Story.
- Five reasons why the company you're visiting needs you (or your best shot at it, given your research). The point is to think from their side of the circle, why *they* need *you.*
- Five brief stories (PARs in Appendix B) to demonstrate that you can deliver on these five reasons for hiring you.

With these tools in your tool kit, combined with the research you've done on the company, you'll be prepared for most interviews as well as market research meetings. You know your product (you), and you know your consumer. You'll be prepared for everything from "Tell me about yourself" (your Elevator Story) to "Why should we hire you?" (the three most compelling reasons of the five for hiring you, followed by asking if that's the type of background they're looking for). You won't be caught flat-footed. The process of moving from A-level people who you already know to B-level people who you don't know yet just got easier.

## The Meeting: The Birth of a New Relationship

The main reason to prepare well before a meeting is so you can demonstrate your competence, of course, but also so you can relax. You want to start a new relationship, not flog someone to deliver three names and then leave. It's the informal party model: you're deciding whether that person is someone you'd like to have a long-term relationship with, and in the meantime you're talking casually, helping the person with his or her goals just as he or she is helping you with yours.

Three main points will help you optimize your return on this investment: your opening, the shaping of a job, and your closing. It's all about meeting some new people, being genuinely curious about their work, listening for their needs, and seeing what you can do to assist. Piece of cake, right?

## *The Opening: Your Two Leading Questions*

A lot of these ideas will carry over to a job interview, not surprising since the mind-set that works best for both is one of curiosity and openness, that of a potential investor instead of a job supplicant. I won't present the mechanics here. ("Groom the receptionist. Go to the restroom ahead of time and make sure you look presentable. Dress conservatively. Get a real grip when shaking hands, not just the fingers.") There are interviewing books like *Knock 'Em Dead* by Martin Yate (Bob Adams, Inc., current edition) if you want more details. There's just one operational recommendation that I can't resist mentioning, however: take a pad with you. Have you seen those pads with leather binders that are fairly unobtrusive? They work well because you can have your agenda on the top page of the pad, and your résumé and Hit List on the bottom of the pad, where they stay unbent and out of sight until you want them. Just make sure that these documents aren't attached to each other so your Hit List of interesting companies doesn't fall out when you're telling Company A that you've never wanted to work for anyone else.

The first question is the what-do-I-say-when-we-first-meet one. Whether it is when you are presented at the door of her office or walking back to the office together, you need to be prepared with some icebreaking questions. Think fast: what is your mutual topic? You've got it, the person you know in common. Start by asking, "How is Jack doing?" or something related to Jack that would be of interest. If you don't have a personal connection, you can decide while you're waiting in the lobby what type of question would work for starters. (The weather? Their stock price? Traffic? Something in the news?) Go with your instincts and keep it informal.

The second question is the what-information-can-I-pick-up-from-the-office-environment one. You'll probably see pictures of the kids (a good lead-in), awards, memorabilia that will tell you more about this person as an individual. Did you hear the story of the interviewer who had a giant, mounted fishtail hanging on his wall? Anyone who didn't ask about the fishtail was immediately disqualified from further interviews. The executive decided that if such a major trophy was ignored, the candidate would not be inquisitive enough to fit in with the company's culture. People *have* been hired because of similar interests, whether it be fishing, aviation, golf, or military service. Forget whether or not it's fair; it's common ground.

## Shaping a Job

You may have promised that you'd take only twenty minutes of this person's time, so you're moving quickly by the middle part of your conversation. You have your agenda, and you're choosing the questions that seem most relevant. You're listening well. When the person you're interviewing seems engaged in the conversation, ask questions that will uncover the problems that could be fodder for job creation:

- What are your bottlenecks?
- What keeps you up at night?
- What are the two biggest time sinks for you in the next couple of months?

What you've just done is found three separate ways to say, "What sort of problems are you having?" If, however, you ask directly about problems, the temperature may chill. Companies, or people, rarely like to openly admit to problems. The sample questions are less threatening. Invent your own using your own wording and sprinkle them throughout the conversation.

As needs or problems emerge, ask questions that help you sense whether or not you might have a shot at creating a job:

- "It sounds like you have your hands full with that."
- If you're feeling especially intuitive and have some insights that the target may not, try out an observation. "It sounds like political issues are keeping you from meeting your deadlines."
- If you're getting agreement, that's a green light. Proceed with "I've had some similar experiences turning over political roadblocks to get back on track. Tell me about what you've done so far."
- You can follow with a story (PAR), but make sure that it's short, relevant, and uses the vocabulary of the company you're talking to.
- If he or she is still with you, ask, "Would you like me to get some ideas together for you about different ways that you could meet those deadlines?"
- "Why don't we touch base early next week since time is of the essence. I could make the meeting a little more relevant if I incorporated some ideas from your CFO (Chief Financial Officer) and CIO (Chief Information Officer) before we sit down. Would that make sense?" If it does: "Could I get you to send them an email to tell them I'm coming and cc me on it? I'll know that I can go ahead and contact them as soon as I see your email."

These leading questions mid-meeting with your suggestion of another meeting will give you a good reading on whether or not there is any prayer of creating work within this person's area. Notice that you did not mention a job or pay, or the idea of employment or consulting yet. Right now, you're just trying to help them. If the next meeting goes well, then you can start talking about how to structure the work. Get your hooks set first.

As mentioned in the chapter on Strategy #3: Stop Looking for Jobs, you're taking a risk when offering to give away some of your time. Don't throw the offer around lightly because your time is precious. Only use this strategy with your favorite companies, and ones that don't have The Right Job staring you in the face. The other risk you run is the "why buy the cow when the milk is so cheap?" one. If you give them all your solutions in subsequent meetings before you have set up any agreement, you undercut your value. On top of that, telling a company the "right" way to solve its problems in your first meeting is dangerous. You don't know all its history or what it has attempted so far. Saying, "This is what you need to do" in a first meeting could sound superficial. Doctors always ask questions, listen, and find out histories before they diagnose.

If you actually spark your contact's interest in creating a potential job, you don't need to settle all of the details in the first discussion. Pace yourself. Another one or two meetings after the initial one should be plenty of time to decide on the scope of the work. As you're reaching an agreement, tell him or her you'll draft a plan (things will go faster if you take the initiative) so you all can keep moving. Note that you just stressed the bottom side of his or her circle—moving quickly—to help keep him or her motivated. It's a good idea to include a review period in your agreement, after three to six months out. Ask your friends in human resources, employment law, or professional consulting to help you structure an agreement.

You won't explore developing a job in most of your market research meetings, however. You'll most often be with B-level people to gather information. Your goal now is to head for referrals to C-level people in target companies.

Referrals must be requested with a light touch. They're based on trust. They're like a letter of recommendation, reflecting the judgment of the referring party. Your contact will only recommend you to his or her colleagues if you are competent and helpful and won't waste their time. To push too hard for leads, "I need to leave here with three names," is to run the risk of looking like a machine that is using other people rather than helping. People will back off. There will be times when your networking connection genuinely doesn't know anyone in your target areas, so don't assume home runs with all of your meetings. One base at a time with some walks and doubles will get you to home plate just as well.

There are two ways to ask for referrals: through your general conversation about companies and by referring to your Hit List. Let's say that you're talking about what companies are hot, why, and where the opportunities are going to be emerging. Maybe some contact names within these companies have been volunteered. If not, try, "It sounds like an interesting company. If you know someone there who it makes sense for me to talk to, I'd appreciate a connection." Now stop talking and see what happens. This question should flush out leads if there are any to be had. You may need to reassure your contact that you don't expect people to have jobs just because you're calling but that you might actually be in a position to offer some helpful ideas.

Your ace in the hole is your Hit List. Reach for it and say, "I'm particularly interested in two companies that you mentioned. I'm going to follow up with them. Let me share with you the types of companies that I've been thinking about so far and see whether you have any opinions about them." (A sample Hit List is in Appendix D.) Decide before the meeting whether the company you're meeting with should be on the list.

Give the person time to review your list. It's amazing how well this works. Imagine someone giving you a list of thirty companies and twenty names that you could skim easily instead of asking you for suggestions of where there might be work for someone with his or her skills. The Hit List shows that you're not depending on other people to define your interests. It also helps them help you because your list encourages them to brainstorm networking connections quickly and easily. When deciding on individuals to add to your list, choose some executives from each of your favorite companies who could influence your selection, whether it be board members, top officers, vice presidents, or directors. Why have names of individuals on your list as well as company names? How many times have you gotten to know people at soccer games, church, or dinner parties and haven't tuned into their professional affiliations as much as their personal ones? Your contact is as likely to make an association with an individual's name as he is with a company's. "Susan? Oh sure, I know her. Is that where she works? Our kids play soccer together. Let me give her a call."

## *Classy Closings*

Keep track of your time. Note when you're within three to four minutes of the time that you promised the meeting would end. You'll look less professional if you run over your boundaries without acknowledging them. "Anne, I asked for twenty minutes of your time when I set up the meeting, and we're nearly there. How are we doing with your schedule?" Let her choose whether to wrap up or continue, which is much better than having her silently resent your eating away their time.

At the end of a market research meeting, you'll want to do two things: review the action steps and clarify how you can return the favor. In the heat of a meeting, your contact may be magnanimous about volunteering to undertake various initiatives for you. After the meeting is over, however, the best intentions are often not fulfilled. This is nothing personal. Don't expect him to really call you as planned or make calls on your behalf. Jot a note on your calendar to email him three to four days after he said he was going to call. Take as much initiative as you can to help the person deliver. "Thanks for your willingness to give Bill a call on my behalf. I hate to give you more things to do, however, so would it be easier on you to get his contact info now, then I'll follow up directly with him next week and use your name? You won't have to think of it again." Note: You focused on the bottom side of the marketing circle by emphasizing how you will save her time, plus you waited to hear her response to make sure this was comfortable with her. It might not hurt to send your contact a reminder email just before you email Bill. If she forgot to tell Bill about you, she has a second chance to do so.

Clarifying how you can return the favor of someone's sharing his or her time and information with you is a classy step. You're separating yourself from the rest of the pack right here. You may hit on something before or during the meeting where you can be of help. After all, you're becoming a lightning rod of marketplace information and decision makers. You may pick up on a need that you could pass along to a third party. "Oh, you're renegotiating your insurance coverage? I know someone who does a great job with risk management if you're looking for ways to limit your liability. Would you like me to have Bob give you a call?" That's a win-win-win. If you don't have any helpful ideas to offer by the end of the meeting, ask. "Now, what can I do to help you?" This simple question will totally disarm your contact because he or she is accustomed to being asked for help rather than being the recipient of it. If he or she can't think of anything right away, you continue to try. Just spreading his or her name around in a complimentary way helps to build his or her reputation . . . and yours.

### Follow Up

"I've given hundreds of informational interviews, yet I rarely get a thank-you note," a president of an advertising firm lamented. "Giving an informational interview is actually more of a favor than giving a job interview, but I get less appreciation for them." Writing a note after a meeting, just like asking what you can do to help, makes you a little classier than the average person. Some heavyweight paper and a few handwritten lines are all you need. Include an email address or a phone number that you promised, then your note will be saved for a while, a visual reminder of you.

Whether or not to stay in touch after the meeting is your call. Make the decision consciously. There will be some contacts—with valuable networks, spheres of influence, and perspectives—that you definitely want to stay in touch with not only during transition, but throughout your career. More on this below. Some relationships will end with your thank-you note. If you say, "I'll keep you posted," at the end of your meeting, it's a nice idea to actually do so, especially after you call or meet with one of their referrals.

Now, you know the structure behind a meeting. The next step is to actually schedule real ones, if you haven't already done so. Just pick up the phone. Start with people who you do *not* anticipate will be major players in your career plans. The objective is to practice your skills. You'll get better with these meetings as you do more of them. The skills from these meetings will roll over into your day-to-day life as well. The questions you're asking should not be reserved for job transitions. You need to ask them on an ongoing basis to make career management part of your daily routine. The conclusions you reach and actions you take will become part of your New Job Security.

## The "Norm" Part of Networking

Finally. The fourth strategy of managing your career is Network as the Norm, and you're just now getting to the norm part of it. Why? It's important to learn the correct networking approach before plunging in. Without knowing the right moves, you could burn up or wear out your network, not to mention thwart opportunities to expand it. Like meeting with a trainer when you first start using a gym, you learn the right form and the right exercises so you can accomplish your goals correctly. Consider yourself trained. You know how to arrange meetings; you know how to ask questions informally to gather information; and you know to help people, without any guarantees of return. Now for the workout.

## What: Network as the Norm

Let's look at the what, why, who, and how of Network as the Norm. The "what" part, defining what it means to Network as the Norm, won't take long. You already know that it means staying in touch with a network on an ongoing basis throughout your career, not just while you're in transition. You know that maintaining it as an ongoing resource is critical. How many times have I heard from professionals who recently started new jobs, "I've learned the hard way. I will never, ever let go of my network again." Relationships come neither quickly nor easily. To hope you can turn on the tap only when you need it and have relationships and connections flow out is to be sadly disappointed. These same professionals who swore their allegiance to keeping their networks alive are often the same ones who, a year later, are bemoaning their lack of time to stay on top of their new jobs and their old networks. There are ways to do both, however. We'll cover them in the "Who" and "How" sections that follow. You don't want to give up what you've gained.

## Why: Your Survival Life Jacket

Why do you want to continue networking for the long term? It's your survival life jacket for your ongoing journey to the New Job Security. Replacing the paternalistic job security that one company used to provide you is an intersecting grid of information and connections that keep you on top of market conditions and expectations. You just moved from a single lifeline to a net. Research demonstrates that your net will most likely lead to your next job and it provides perspective about what's going on in the marketplace. If you don't take the initiative to stay in touch with your network while you're employed, you slowly, silently become out of touch and obsolete. Your network maintenance skills determine your future.

If you're still hesitant about embracing the new networking, be reassured that your tendencies are rooted in tradition. In *Achieving Success through Social Capital* by Wayne Baker (Jossey-Bass Inc., 2000), it says that "[A myth] prevalent in this culture is the fiction that success is an individual matter. To suggest that one's fate depends on relationships runs counter to one of the dearest American values: individualism. [Instead,] pay, promotion, and accomplishments are largely determined by the structure and composition of one's personal and business networks. . . . It is our ethical duty to deliberately manage relationships—and that anyone who doesn't is unethical." Strong words. The point is that you have relationships. You can either choose to consciously manage your relationships, like you do every time you find someone you enjoy talking to and plan to get together again, or you can manage relationships by ignoring him or her. Which would you prefer? Consciously managing your relationships is not only the more fun of the two, it keeps information flowing and provides continual opportunities for you to help others, which keeps your network there for you when you need it.

## Who: Double Low Density

Not to worry. Keeping your network alive doesn't have to be overly time consuming. As with the professionals above who were feeling overwhelmed with managing their new jobs and maintaining their networks, you just need some realistic strategies. There is fascinating research going on in academic institutions right now about just what you're doing: building and sustaining networks for work success. Ideas issuing from this research provide a system that will allow you to access people more efficiently, and thus minimize your time commitment.

Professor Herminia Ibarra of Harvard Business School and INSEAD writes about the importance of consciously building your influence through effective networks in her classes and research in "Network Assessment Exercise, Teaching Note" (#5-497-001; Harvard Business School Publishing; April 11, 1997; p. 5): "Effective networks provide *links to multiple networks,* serving as ports of entry to social and organizational groups to which one does not have direct access. To be 'well connected' in this regard is to position oneself on the boundary of many nonintersecting networks. . . . Density refers to the extent to which people within one's network know each other . . . a high level of density may signal a 'redundant' or 'inbred' network that will not afford them access to new ideas, information and opportunities. . . . Managers with sparse networks advance more rapidly in their careers."

In other words, a sparse or "low-density" network is your goal for career networking. A low-density network includes people in different areas of your life who do not know each other. Part of your value to them is the unique information and connections from different groups that you can share. Dr. Ibarra made a startling statement in an ExecuNet presentation that she gave at a networking meeting I hosted. "You're more likely to receive job assistance from someone you do not know very well than you are from a close friend." Surprising? Her point was that you're already likely to know a lot of the same information as your close associates, but people further removed will have access to ideas and connections that you don't typically run across. She is building on Mark Granovetter's work in *Getting a Job* (Harvard University Press, 1974) and on Ron Burt's work on structural holes in "The Network Structure of Social Capital" (*Research in Organizational Behavior*, JAI Press, 2000), demonstrating that weak ties are more useful than strong ties for people who are searching for jobs. Food for thought.

Dr. Monica Higgins, an associate professor at Harvard Business School doing social network research, furthers the work on the structure of relationships in an article called "Changing Careers: The Effects of Social Context" in the *Journal of Organizational Behavior* (Volume 22, No. 6; September 2001; pp. 595–618). She describes what would happen if you only refer to a group of advisors who are "high density," hence are well connected with each other. "Advisors who already know each other may be thought of as different 'doors' to the same 'room,' while advisors who do not know each other represent access to different 'rooms.'" You'll want the "different room" option as you decide who to actively keep in touch with over the long term. She describes network groups in terms of their diversity. High diversity is better.

In structuring your career network, first think of "constellations," or groups of relationships that may include work, family, and friends, as described in K. E. Kram's *Mentoring at Work: Developmental Relationships in Organizational Life* (Scott, Foresman, Glenview, 1985). Which groups are your highest priority? Regarding work, think of colleagues, bosses, and subordinates from your most recent job as well as from earlier companies. Professional associations can be very helpful because they take a horizontal cut across a large number of companies for their memberships. Relationships with officers in an active professional association will connect you with their contacts also.

# DIVERSITY RANGE

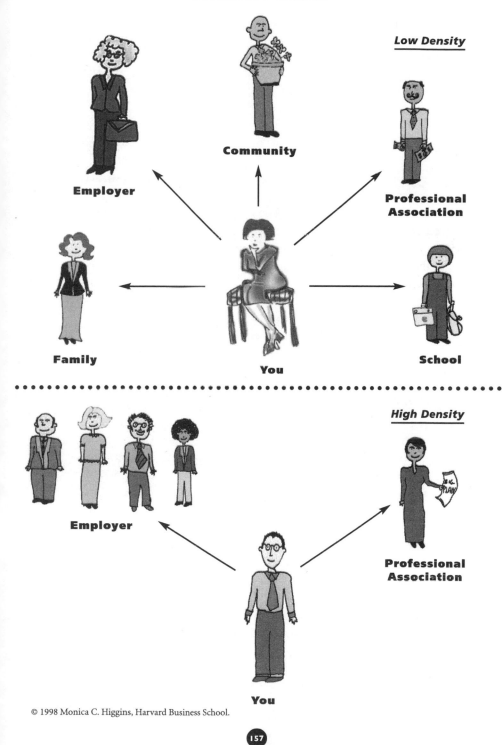

Low Density

Employer

Community

Professional
Association

Family

You

School

High Density

Employer

Professional
Association

You

Family is always an important part of your network. Slice and dice their categories in whatever way is most helpful to you, from the types of work they do to geographic or lineage associations. They're clearly a group you can go back to over and over again.

Friends outside work can be organized in various categories, from people you went to school with (an important group because you already trust each other), to friends that you know through sports, clubs, religious activities, children, the neighborhood, and common interests. Some of these categories will have surfaced when you first started entering your network into a system earlier in this chapter. Now you can decide which are your top categories to nurture, your low-density groups. Since they won't know each other, to use Dr. Higgin's analogy, you'll be walking into different "rooms" of information as you keep in touch.

Use the following chart to identify the top groups of people that you want to connect with over time, then identify a key player within each group that you will help and share resources with. Who should you select? Look for three characteristics: someone who is relevant to your work life, someone who is available and receptive (that would eliminate Bill Gates–type people unless you have direct relationships), and someone who is a low-density networker in his or her own right. In other words, if your selection is involved with unrelated groups of people also, she will have nonredundant information to share with you—more insights, more leads, and more connections that you would not have been able to access on your own. You now have a *double* low-density network since both you and your key players have low-density networks, and you are becoming increasingly valuable as a contact because of it. Drop the term, "double low-density network" at your next party, and you'll be the center of attention (sort of like "double secret probation" from the movie *Animal House*).

Now you're ready to select a finite number of groups, with a key player in each one, so you can have a manageable career network. Your objective is to surface five to seven names. You don't need high volume here; you just need different groups represented by well-connected people. You may also want to include a maverick who isn't in a target group, but who would be a great source of information. Your friend who is a consultant for McKinsey might count because he's inside major companies all of the time. Your CPA, someone you know on several boards, or your thesis advisor might not be in targeted categories, but might be a connection with low-density networks. Keep them in mind as you're selecting your top five to seven key players.

---

**H O M E W O R K**

👉 *Your Key Players*

| Group | Top five | Key Player contact info | How can you be helpful | Next follow-up |
|---|---|---|---|---|
| Example: Former employer, Motorola | Yes | Former boss: Dan Jones (djones@aol.com) | Tell him that I have heard a potential customer is unhappy with its current vendor. | March 5 |

---

You may not be able to complete the chart on your first pass. Work with the chart for a while, then come back to it a couple of days later. Your top names will fall into place shortly. However, you don't want to announce to this select group that they've won your contest. Like telling someone, "Guess what! I've decided that you're going to be my best friend!" it might make him or her nervous. You'll also want the flexibility of changing the key players in your network as your needs change, something you can do more easily if their initial selection is known only to you. It's your behavior that will change the relationship, and that brings us to the "how" of career networking.

## How: Pelicans and Dragonflies

Before we plunge into process, I want to clearly state the values behind career networking. Wayne Baker, in his book, *Achieving Success through Social Capital* (Jossey-Bass, Inc., 2000), could not have said it better. "If we create networks with the sole intention of *getting something*, we won't succeed. We can't *pursue* the benefits of networks; the benefits *ensue* from investments in meaningful activities and relationships." Networking is never about using people. Rookies or people you don't want to hang around may take that approach, but your approach is more honorable: you're taking the risk of helping first, without a guarantee of any return. Since you can't help everyone in the world equally, you have to decide where to spend your time, just like you do when you're developing any friendship.

First, let's actually identify ways you can jump-start your career network so people in it can hardly wait for your calls. Next we'll then talk about structured networking meetings, groups pulled together specifically for the purpose of lead generation, that will help you broaden your exposure and your support. These categories, your hand-selected key players group and your structured networking meetings, are examples of the two categories of relationships you'll use in your networking. Some will be more in-depth and others more tactical. In her article titled "Managerial Networks" (#9-495-039; Harvard Business School Publishing 1996; p. 3), Dr. Ibarra defines these two categories as:

- *Long-term, high-reciprocity ties: Close bonds and reciprocal relationships ensure reliability under conditions of uncertainty. These include peer alliances that function by exchange of favors, ties of trust and loyalty, and so on.*
- *Short-term, instrumental ties: Many important network ties serve highly circumscribed job-related functions. They are often dissolved when the relationship has served its purpose. Networks that consist exclusively of close, "important" relationships usually have important gaps from a task-related standpoint.*

You'll want both types of ties in your career network. Your key players should be in the long-term, high-reciprocity category and others may move in and out of it over time. Think of yourself as a pelican with this group. Have you ever seen a pelican flying over the surface of the water searching for its next meal? When it spots its target, bam! This bird intuitively makes an immediate nosedive (or is it a beakdive?) into the water. It dives deeply, disappearing quickly. Just as you think it's going to drown, the pelican surfaces with a giant fish in its bill. Mission accomplished. You'll want to be a pelican with many parts of your network. You'll want to dive deeply, immersing yourself in your element. Delving deeply into your profession or industry to learn from the experts enables you to become and stay an expert also. The depth of knowledge and connections that come from these long-term, high-reciprocity ties are part of your New Job Security.

Contrast the pelican's style with the dragonfly. The dragonfly rarely slows down. It constantly skims over the water's surface, touching down briefly, then off again, moving continually from reed to water to a piece of driftwood then away. Staying on the surface when you're building a net-work gives you a sense of momentum. You start setting up meetings with a number of people, generating activity and some leads. "I didn't know net-working could be so much fun," newly laid-off professionals report. "If I could just get paid for this, I'd be happy." These short-term, instrumental ties are perfect at the beginning of a job campaign and are essential, to a more limited extent, as your campaign continues and during your long-term career networking. How else do you find out that shipments aren't going out of a certain company's loading dock like they were last quarter? How else do you know that another company is going to outsource the payroll work that you'd like to bid on? Short-term, instrumental ties can feed you ongoing, real-time information.

Don't neglect the pelican's approach, though, if you find that being a dragonfly is seductive. If you're high on the "E" or extroversion scale of the Myers-Briggs, or gravitate naturally to meeting new people, the dragonfly approach may feel very comfortable. Stick exclusively to the dragonfly ap-proach and you will start wondering after a while why nothing is moving forward; there's a lot of action but no results. Although keeping that wide-angle view of what's going on in the marketplace is valuable, you also need the in-depth knowledge of your targeted industries and your profession. Use your networking abilities to network *down and into* your specialties as well as across the marketplace in general. If you stay too broad, you won't have the expertise in any one to two areas that people are looking for. Tar-geted industry insights will sell you and build your reputation. You'll know what the needs are, which companies are hot, who the movers and shakers are, what the right vocabulary is if you're changing industries, and maybe even the names of some potential customers for them. You've come up with the big fish.

## PELICANS

Let's look at some tactics for approaching your high-reciprocity group. They're similar to some of the ideas in Strategy #2: Market for Mutual Ben-efit and Strategy #3: Stop Looking for Jobs. No surprise, huh? The care and feeding of your key players does not need to be exhausting. It's like keeping in touch with your friends. Sometimes you email them, sometimes you phone them, sometimes you get together. You see and hear things that may remind you of your friend, so you tell him or her about the scat you're not going to be able to use at an upcoming event in case he or she is interested. With your key players, the content will be slanted more toward common professional interests, but the process is the same; you're thinking about the bottom side of their marketing circle, then following through.

Here are some ideas to get you started:

- Tell them about an emerging business opportunity they might pursue (a perennial top-of-the-list favorite because it relates to increasing profitability).
- Email them a magazine article of interest.
- Send them a book.
- Tell them about a meeting or speaker that they might enjoy.
- Offer to help with a crunch they may be facing.
- Ask them whether they're going to a professional association meeting. Set up a time to get together at the meeting.
- Pass along a compliment you heard about them.
- Say something complimentary about them to others.
- Suggest names or connections for a project they're working on.
- Give their name to a reporter as an expert to interview.
- Help their kid.
- Give them a gift subscription to a relevant magazine.
- Invite them to do something outside of work that's appropriate, such as golf, squash, or dinner with the spouses.

Here are some things you should *not* do with your key players:

- Don't put them on email joke distribution lists.
- Don't put them on *any* email lists where they look like one in a crowd.
- Don't contact them constantly.
- Don't do anything that is too familiar or not politically correct. You probably don't know their values or boundaries yet.
- Don't give them expensive gifts.
- Don't call or email just to chat. Have a clear purpose; then you can chat, if desired.

Maintaining a career network of five to seven people doesn't sound so bad after all, does it? It doesn't take too much time and the methods are unlimited. It's fun to be creative about how you can help someone.

What do you do with a key player once you have one? Now that you're doing all of these good works, just what is on the top side of the marketing circle for you? These are the people who can help you stay competitive. You need them while you are employed as much as when you are in transition. When you are employed, you are likely to get caught up in the day-to-day details and lose touch with the skills and competencies expected by the outside world, not to mention the shifts in companies and players in the marketplace. Your key players can keep you current on this. Don't let your contacts slip when you are busy at work; they're an important part of your New Job Security. By asking them questions similar to the ones you asked in your market research meetings, you will keep yourself sharp and updated with valuable information to trade with other key players (as long as it isn't confidential). Remember, these people don't know each other, so you have a unique cross section of perspectives. Go write an article, and quote your key players!

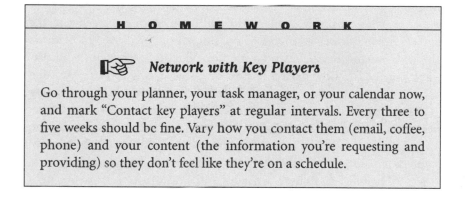

**H O M E W O R K**

☞ *Network with Key Players*

Go through your planner, your task manager, or your calendar now, and mark "Contact key players" at regular intervals. Every three to five weeks should be fine. Vary how you contact them (email, coffee, phone) and your content (the information you're requesting and providing) so they don't feel like they're on a schedule.

You'll find that you can delete some of your reminders when you come to them because you've just been with Anne at a trade show and just talked to Guy about the project he was working on. Great. It's working. Your reminders are simply a safety net so none of your key players are ignored.

## DRAGONFLIES

The short-term, instrumental tie group has obvious applications when you're in transition, but let's touch briefly on its advantages when you're employed first. These are task-related relationships that dissolve upon completion. Can you think of any dragonfly encounters you've already had serving on teams or projects? Job-related dragonfly encounters are no different. Even though you may not be grooming these people as you are your key players, I've seen ten-year-old connections reactivated when they were needed. "Phil, this is Emily Parker from Alpha Industries. We worked to-gether on a project for Beta Sites several years ago. You were setting up the systems architecture, and I was feeding you expectations from the end users. Remember? Can I catch you for a couple of minutes? You did a great job on the conversion, so you immediately came to mind when someone was asking me how we should integrate our information. I have a couple of questions." Later on, you can ask, "If there is some consulting work here, may I give them your name?" You established the connection, you compli-mented him, you asked your question, then you tried to reciprocate. That's all you need to do. Old and new connections with competent professionals can typically be activated with a simple, clear request. Be sure to add these people to your contact management database. You don't have to know everything in life because you have dragonfly connections to help you out.

When you're between jobs, short-term connections speed up your tran-sition. Just like a mutual fund broadens your risk of loss over investing in one stock, your dragonfly connections will broaden your exposure to the marketplace and lower your risk of missing an opportunity. "Individuals with wide-ranging social networks are more likely to learn about opportu-nities sooner than those having narrow ones," according to Peter Marsden and Elizabeth Gorman in an article titled "Social Networks, Job Changes and Recruitment," from the *Sourcebook on Labor Markets: Evolving Struc-tures and Processes* (2000, pp. 6–7). I constantly see proof that people who do not know each other well are still happy to be helpful, so don't be hesitant about asking. Just don't apply too much pressure, and be helpful in return.

Your dragonfly connections will supply the information that your peli-can group doesn't know. When one of your key players says, "I've heard ru-mors that the CFO position at Widget may turn over," you research the names of the top decision makers and board members at Widget, then email them to a group of dragonfly contacts to see whether they have any contacts with this group. Use the bcc (blind carbon copy) line for your list of names to give them privacy and so it doesn't look like you're mass mail-ing. A similar approach works well for a small number of help wanted ads that look particularly promising. Go ahead and respond, but put out an all points bulletin to your network at the same time, listing all the officers and decision makers for the job. This gives you a good chance of finding a mutual contact. Responding to the designated person in the ad will get you into the proper queue. Networking in at the top will get you into a more power-ful group. All you're asking of your network in either case is "There may be something coming up at Widget that I'd like to pursue. Do you know anything about this company or these people?" Be conscious of how frequently you "go to the well" with questions for your contacts, however. You don't want to wear them out. Either lump together several inquiries in one communication, or couple them with something that is helpful to your contact. You'll want both pelicans and dragonflies to look forward to your messages.

Where do you find your short-term, instrumental tie group? They're all around you. All those people in your contact manager database or Rolodex that didn't make it to your key players group are in it. Anyone you meet socially, through family, or through work or professional connections is in it. You can even start an entirely new set of short-term connections that you meet through networking meetings. Networking meetings designed for the purpose of sharing leads are everywhere. The business section of your local newspaper should have a calendar section that lists some. Employment divisions in your state government should have networking group lists. The government frequently funds One Stop Career Centers that will have information on networking groups as well as additional career resources for you. Professional associations and local churches often host such groups. People have figured out that networking is the way to find jobs, so events abound.

I need to make a disclaimer. I'm highly biased toward a specific networking organization called ExecuNet that has been mentioned elsewhere in this book. It's a nationwide membership organization of career-savvy executives who earn over $100,000 in compensation. Even though you may not be at this level, you may want to learn about their process and start your own networking group where you define your own parameters (examples below). If you're well above this compensation level, their services are even more relevant. Finding senior-executive openings and appropriate career support gets tougher the higher up you get, and they provide both. I direct ExecuNet's New England Regional Networking Meetings and have become a total convert to their structured networking process and job listings. They get results. People get real-time market information. People get leads. People get jobs. Do 100 percent of the participants get jobs through ExecuNet? No, but those who learn how to work the system get connections that serve them well for the long term. Smart people. These meetings take place in metropolitan cities throughout the United States and some in Canada. You can plug into the meetings, job listings, and other resources at www.execunet.com.

Dave Opton, the visionary founder and executive director of ExecuNet, created an integrated model to help professionals search for their next job and manage their careers in 1988 that combines job listings, career education, networking, and giving back. Since it's the largest and oldest executive career management site in the country, search and human resource professionals know about it and use it for their listings. They get a higher quality applicant than they would with a job board because you, the potential candidate, need to be a qualified member to view and respond to the listings. Listing openings with ExecuNet is a good use of their time; reading them is a good use of yours.

ExecuNet regional networking meetings let people plug into underground information about what's happening locally. These are *not* chitchat, cocktail-type parties where it's random luck whether or not you get leads. At these meetings, you sit with eight professionals at a table with a proscribed amount of time per person. You state your background briefly, ask the people at your table a specific question, then get the benefit of their knowledge and connections. This is a good place to test your Elevator Story and your Hit List. They give you any help they can, from names, to leads, to actual openings, to feedback on your presentation. They will be direct and tell you things other people won't, for better or worse. You get new information and a list of attendees for continued networking outside the meetings. If you don't know many people, are moving into a new area, or just want to keep in touch with what's happening with the market in general as well as companies in your area, check them out.

If the above types of networking organizations and events don't meet your needs, then start your own.

James was general manager and vice president of an international instrumentation company prior to its leveraged buyout. He reported that his network outside the company was nearly nonexistent since he had focused all his energies on the company and traveling to his offices throughout the Far East. "How will I connect locally?" he wondered. "I'd really like to have a group of peers who I could share resources with as I go through this transition." He wanted something small and personal, with a constant group of members at his level. Be careful what you wish for!

We defined a group with these characteristics, which were also in James's broader industry of manufacturing, from ExecuNet attendees and our own dragonfly connections. We made phone calls and invited them to an initial, pay-for-yourself breakfast at a nice, centrally located hotel. It worked. James chaired a breakfast of twelve people the first time, where each person briefly presented to and received feedback from the entire group. They continued to meet, developed an email distribution list, gave themselves a name, TBG (The Breakfast Group), shared information and leads between meetings, and grew. It became so large that James's original vision of a small, ongoing advisory group was diluted. The coordinating role passed on to other people over time, and the group continues to evolve independently of its founders.

James, in the meantime, had clearly mastered the job of networking. He tested multiple professional association and industry groups to determine the best use of his time. He then became involved with those of greatest interest to him. He joined a newly formed, small networking group that was close to his original goals, a functional group (a CEO group), and several groups that cut across his industry (turnaround, corporate growth, and corporate director foci). He balanced his networking time between those who were in transition (they typically know where the action is) and those who were employed (the ones creating the action). James is now seen as a resource by companies and individuals as the guy with connections. His Palm Pilot is golden.

Another newly formed networking group that James joined had a different model. John, a senior vice president of human resources with extensive international corporate experience, formed Hilltop Group. His mission was to have an ongoing group of very senior-level professionals with international experience who were committed to remaining in the group when employed. The group has a constant membership of the same ten people, and they meet in one another's homes once a month on a Saturday afternoon. They stay in frequent communication through the website that one member designed. They all know the importance of staying connected and of giving back. James has a "board of directors" for his career management for the long term. What a good idea.

There are two main points from James's story that may be of use in your career networking. One is that you can create your own networking group instead of, or in addition to, attending already-established groups. You decide whether you want a short-term group that dissolves as people get jobs or a long-term group that people stay in when they're employed. Ask people to attend a pilot meeting to see whether there is a need, and, and, poof, you may have just created something. The second point is the balance between pelican and dragonfly concepts. James has some of both and you can, too. The proportions may vary from times of transition to employment, but the combination will give you both breadth and depth. You're on top of things now. Not much can get past you.

## The Sixty-Second Career Networker

If you're currently employed and feeling that your outside connections are slipping away, congratulate yourself for noticing. You're showing that you're taking control of your career management. You need a quick fix to stay in touch. No problem. You already have the four easy pieces.

1. Make sure you've completed the "Your Key Players" chart earlier in this chapter.
2. Make sure you've completed your "Network with Key Players" homework in this chapter. You now have a three- to five-week schedule for contacting your key players. You've just set up your structure.
3. Here comes the sixty-second part. When the reminders pop up for your first follow-up, do something that's quick and easy. Passing on a lead, forwarding an article, ordering a book, or recommending them as a speaker doesn't take long.
4. Many of your follow-up contacts can be coupled with a networking question. Your email might say:

```
Lydia,

I just took the liberty of giving your name to Tom
Richards, who sets up the program for the ACA confer-
ence. I thought you'd make a great speaker. If you
don't hear from him soon, give me a call.

    Besides the ACA, do you have any favorite profes-
sional associations? I'm looking for the most senior-
level ones in our industry, and I bet you have some
inside information. Thanks. I hope you're doing well.
```

A subsequent email could invite Lydia to join you at an association meeting.

That isn't so bad, is it? As you continue to develop your relationships, you can insert your side of the marketing circle in your conversations. Discussing what companies, skills, ideas, and trends are hot should be interesting to your listener as well as to you. You can share a fun, thought-provoking discussion that is informal, essential to your ongoing career management, and fairly brief.

## Wrap-Up

You've come a long way in this chapter from defining how networking has evolved, to setting up a system for your own network, to actually breaking through and meeting with new people who can provide you with information. You know how to structure a long-term, career network that keeps you connected with the outside world, with a limited time commitment, while you're employed. When you're in transition, your network is like an accordion. It can expand rapidly. Sounds like you've mastered this career networking thing, doesn't it? That's a Big Deal.

STRATEGY #5

# Negotiate in Round Rooms

*Money is better than poverty,*
*if only for financial reasons.*

WOODY ALLEN

Negotiating is like spinach. We know it's good for us, but we avoid it. When I give negotiating seminars, I ask a room full of executives to raise their hands if they've ever negotiated their salaries. No more than 20 percent will raise their hands. I then ask them to raise their hands if they've ever negotiated a contract before. Nearly 90 percent will raise their hands this time. Why the disconnect? Why is there extensive experience and comfort in working out terms for products, services, and even whole company acquisitions and divestitures, but not in working out terms for personal compensation? You would prefer negotiating a deal for your company than a deal for yourself, right? If you feel that negotiating your compensation is too close and personal, and that you'd just like to get through it and on to the job, you're not alone. This discomfort has existed since Adam failed to negotiate a counteroffer with Eve. You could be missing out on more than apples, however. Your income, clout, and reputation are at stake, so let's increase your comfort level with pricing the product (you're the product, remember?).

In this chapter, we're going to focus negotiating an incoming compensation package because that's when you have the greatest leverage with a company. Some ideas about pricing your services if you're creating a job are at the end. Just because these examples are at the early stage of your relationship with a company, however, doesn't mean that you put your negotiating skills on the shelf once you enter the door. Negotiating, as you will see in the following examples, is omnipresent in daily life. Read Deborah M. Kolb and Judith Williams's book, *The Shadow Negotiation* (Simon & Schuster, 2000), for additional ideas about handling the constant negotiations you experience when employed (it's targeted toward women, but the strategies are universal). Consciously develop negotiating as one of your career management skills using win-win outcomes, and your satisfaction will grow as much as your income.

Now, back to pricing the product—perhaps an easier way to think about yourself because it's so objective. An initial step in accepting the merits of negotiating for yourself is to recognize that you're already an expert. Can you think of times when you've met the *Random House Dictionary*'s standards for negotiating because you have "arranged for or brought about by discussion a settlement of terms?" You're actually negotiating all the time and may not have credited yourself with doing so. Have you ever bought a car? A house? Raised a teenager? A two-year-old? On the job front, whenever you worked on teams or projects, or with customers, vendors, or bosses, you have negotiated. Closing contracts with other companies, labor unions, or funding sources is more obviously negotiating. You are making trade-offs with people, time, space, resources, money, and responsibilities to reach your goals and the company's goals. Your own compensation package deserves at least the same amount of energy.

A second point that may encourage you to negotiate more frequently is that companies expect you to do so. If you're working on a salaried basis, especially if you are at a senior level, negotiating your package is more the norm than the exception. After Bob finished his compensation negotiations with his new boss, he stopped by the human resource director's office to tell her about the deal. Bob reflected his mild surprise that the CEO had responded so quickly to Bob's wish for a higher base. "We already had the money in the budget," the HR person said. "We would have been disappointed in you if you hadn't asked for anything more."

You're establishing your competence and your reputation by asking about other compensation options before signing. You have value, the company will benefit by hiring you, and *you're not going to lose the offer* if you explore alternatives to the first proposal. That is the most common fear: "I'll lose the job if I ask for more." Au contraire. Ask for more correctly, and you just may get it, along with a little more respect. After all, if you're going to be representing this company and its best interests, don't you need to demonstrate that you can represent your own interests in a professional manner?

## So What Are Round Rooms?

Round rooms don't have corners you can paint yourself into or straight lines that intersect at only one point. You want the same conditions for your negotiating: lots of options and ways that you can intersect, or reach agreement, on compensation so both you and your new employer are satisfied.

Broadening the base of your negotiating—getting away from a narrow focus such as, "I made X dollars in my last job, and I need to earn a minimum of that amount in my next job"—will actually help you to achieve your goals. (That specific concern will be addressed later in the chapter.) The point is that if you're relaxed and open as you discuss your compensation, seeing it as a business deal, then you may come to an agreement that serves you better than the original offer. Stating a specific salary requirement, for example, could cost you a higher offer. Stay loose at the beginning of your financial discussions; listen to what other people have to say first. The main characteristic of broad-based negotiating is that there is more than one possible outcome to the negotiating process that could satisfy both you and the company.

You will be broadening your scope in three different capacities as you negotiate:

> **There is more than one possible outcome to the negotiating process that could satisfy both you and the company.**

---

- *Broaden what you're asking for: It's usually more than the money.*
- *Broaden how you talk about your compensation if you're quoting past salary history or future expectations.*
- *Broaden the number of ways an employer can say "Yes."*

---

Like a triangle resting on its broadest base, you will have more stability and a greater chance of success if you and the decision maker have multiple choices and options during negotiating. A triangle balancing on one point, a "we have to do it this way or I'm walking" attitude, will topple. Your goal is to secure a job offer, and you're more likely to do that by keeping your presentation broad and flexible until the numbers start getting fairly specific.

# Prework: It Pays

Before you even get close to talking about money with a company, you'll want to develop three pieces of prework: your marketing circle, your timing, and your compensation figures. Your financial results will be closer to what you had in mind if you're prepared. Let's look at your marketing circle first.

## *Your Marketing Circle*

You thought through the marketing circle for your target company (see chapter three) prior to crossing its threshold for the first time, right? Your needs are represented on the top side of the circle. You know what is important to you in addition to being compensated fairly. This information will help you test whether a job is truly a fit for you and where you might have some flexibility in your negotiations if you need to make trade-offs.

It's the bottom side of the marketing circle, however, that has probably gotten you where you are today, entering negotiations with a good company. Responding to a company's needs is even more important when it comes to negotiating. If you want the company to offer you more, do your homework on how you can contribute toward making the company more profitable or successful. A salary is rarely increased just because you want it to be, or because you made more at your last company, or because you have two college tuitions to pay. Those are on the top side of the circle. Plan how you're going to help pay for yourself—with your breakthrough research skills that will let them finally get their products to market, with your project management skills that will motivate teams to do more with fewer resources, with your treasury skills that will ensure that the funding will be there when it's needed. You just moved to the bottom side of the circle. Figuring out why you're worth more is part of your preparation. You need to be able to verbally express your value and not assume, "Surely they knew that." Don't expect the company to wonder if you're worth more than it offered you. That's your job, and you'll want a defensible position.

## *Jack Benny Timing*

Did you ever see Jack Benny, the famous comedian, perform? He was a master of timing. His key to success was his pauses. He would stand there, on stage, with his arms crossed waiting for the audience to get the punch line before he said it.

**Holdup man:** *Quit stalling—I said your money or your life.*
**Jack Benny:** I'm thinking it over!

They roared. You can consciously time your statements about money as well. The "when" and "who" of timing money conversations will have a direct result on the "how much." When do you want to talk about money with a company? Take a page from Jack Benny's book. Pause. The answer is "as late as possible." Putting off discussions about money will increase your chances of getting more of it. Why? You haven't set your hooks yet. Early on, the employer doesn't know that you're the answer to his or her prayers, so you're easy to discard. If you quote your current salary in response to a compensation question in your first interview or over the phone, you've just given him or her a reason to eliminate you. Your answer will to be too high or too low, period. If it's exactly what he or she was going to offer, you just positioned yourself too low. If your former salary is too high, he or she will decide that the company can't afford you. If your salary is low, rather than thinking that they would be getting a good deal, employers often feel like they're getting someone too junior or inexperienced. Talking about money early on, therefore, is *not* to your advantage. It pigeonholes you. Should you need any further inducement to hold off on monetary discussions, ask yourself, "Have I ever seen employers find additional money for someone who they really wanted to hire?" My surveys show a resounding "Yes" to that question. Employers don't go rooting around for additional money after just one meeting, however. They'll wait until they are convinced that you are indispensable and that the investment would be well worth it. That commitment develops toward the end of the hiring process, not at the beginning. You've moved from being a commodity to a necessity.

Who should first bring up money? This is part of your timing strategy also. The answer is "Not you." You have nothing to gain by introducing a loaded topic early on. You might even give them reasons to exclude you. They'll get around to the topic if they're serious, so bide your time. There's an old adage in negotiating: Whoever mentions numbers first loses. It's true. Ralph knew the rule. He was talking to a Fortune 500 firm about the presidency of one of their divisions, and salary wasn't brought up during the first four rounds of interviews. By the time the company introduced the topic, guess how many other people the company was interviewing? Zero. Guess how much leverage Ralph had now? A lot. The decision makers really didn't want to go back through a pile of résumés and start all over again. They wanted their problems solved, and finding a cheap group president wasn't one of them. Ralph knew that the conceptual sale had to be closed first—they had to see him as their solution—then the compensation discussions would be fairly easy. He did well.

Although all of this makes sense, you're still asking, "Aren't I wasting my time if I don't find out from a company early on whether we're in the same ballpark?" The answer you probably already see coming is, "No." If you think a company and its management team have some potential, talk to them without bringing up money. You're not wasting your time. Worst case, they become good practice for you, what I call "garbage interviews." As you proceed, you'll find that some companies aren't good fits for you, but you can still try to help them and refer a candidate if you can. Not only will you build your reputation, but you'll build your interviewing and negotiating skills so you're ready for prime time when the right company emerges. You get better with practice. The best case is that the company can actually afford you and you continue interviewing, or, if it can't afford you, the company refers you to an emerging internal position in another division or to one with another company. I've frequently seen people referred to more appropriate, higher-level positions within the company that weren't advertised externally. You never would have had this inside connection if you hadn't accepted the interview.

The next question is, "With whom do I negotiate?" You don't want to get into deep discussions about your compensation with someone who has no authority to make those decisions, such as search firms or human resources staff (unless you're reporting to them). Your superior who is making the hiring decision is typically the right person. See the section titled Advanced Negotiating Plays for Catching Curve Balls later in this chapter for more details.

To sum up, you want to wait until the hiring manager brings up the subject of compensation in at least the second round of interviews, if not later, to proceed with negotiations. Let them be the first ones to quote actual numbers.

### Four Sets of Necessary Numbers

Determining your salary requirements is the third component of your prework.

*Calculate Your Lowest and Highest Figures.* For your lowest figure, decide what your absolute minimum salary is. This is the amount that you need just for your ongoing expenses. This is not something that you'll use in a discussion. It's your private safety net. Determining this figure now will help you make wise decisions in the heat of the moment, when you're being wooed for a start-up venture where you eat air for the first year with the promise of back-end rewards or for other limited cash flow opportunities.

For your highest figure, think of the highest salary you have ever made. Add in any bonus you earned there. If you received one every year, choose one of your better years. Add in a modest allowance for your benefits. I recommend a modest allowance instead of the actual dollar amount because these figures can get really large, which can skew the grand total you're calculating. Human resources professionals report that salaried employees typically receive 30 percent plus of their salaries in benefits such as 401(k) plans, health insurance, life insurance, vacations, and stock programs. An average number is fine here because you might sound too expensive otherwise. Add them all together and see what comes out.

The following sample works with salaries from $25,000 to $1 million. Insert your own figures.

| | |
|---|---|
| *Best salary* | *$88,800* |
| *Bonus* | *$ 8,800* |
| *Benefits* | *$ 7,000* |
| **Total** | **$104,600** |

The next step is to take this approximate number and round it off. You can present the above package, for example, as being in the "low six figures" or "low one hundreds." Both statements are honest, accurate, and not too detailed. This is exactly what you're looking for with broad-based negotiating. These figures reflect your previous compensation package or your overall compensation and will be correct if you need to get into past history in your discussions. Notice that we haven't added any stock options that you may have. I love stock options because they're so vague. They're hard to quantify quickly, and that will work to your advantage. The examples coming up shortly will give you some other ways to present your earnings, but remember that you only want to get into this subject if it works to your advantage, not as a base from which to plan your next salary.

*Establish Your Market Value.* What are you worth? If you don't know the going rate for your services, other than your most recent salary, you're a victim-in-waiting. You'll be basing your new salary expectations on your old salary, and who's to say that that is accurate? If you're changing functions or industries or if you're doing some consulting, your old salary will not be relevant. Time to do some homework.

Standard economic theory on pricing a product (you) is "what the market will bear." As long as a willing buyer and a willing seller agree on a price (typically at a point of some discomfort for both), they have a deal. Learning what the market is paying for your competition is a good place to start. This doesn't mean that you can't price yourself higher or lower than your competition, but you need to be aware that you're doing so and with good reasons. If you're just starting in a field, you may lower the going rate a little. If you have an extensive background, you may decide to exceed the going rate. The company gets what it pays for, and you can explain what that added value is.

How do you find out what you're worth? As you track the skills you need to stay competitive, the companies that are hot, and the trends in your industry, the value of your worth is but a question or a website away. You should determine your going rate now, then check it occasionally while you're employed to track any changes.

Ways to quantify your market value:

- Ask colleagues. As you're gathering information from people who will *not* be hiring you, ask them for the going rate for your type of work (or for the work that you'd like to be doing). *Going rate* is a nonthreatening, noninvasive term since you're not asking about their salary. These are not people you will be negotiating with later on and they'll be helpful because you already have a relationship with them.

- Check out websites and job boards. Some job listings, like the senior-level postings on ExecuNet.com or CareerJournal.com, will include salaries. Ignore geography during this research. You know that San Francisco listings may pay a little more and Austin, Texas, positions may pay less due to differing costs of living, but you're looking for trends rather than specifics.

- Contact the national office or website of your professional association. They often do salary surveys.

- If you have a contact, ask a consulting firm that has a compensation and benefits practice, such as Mercer, Watson Wyatt, or Towers Perrin. They often do salary surveys for their clients so companies can benchmark their salaries against the norms. This will take some networking because it isn't public information, but you might get some insider information from either the consulting side or the client side.

- Ask reference librarians in business libraries (including universities) for their favorite salary sources.

- If you're considering consulting, talk to other consultants about how they would charge if you did some work together. This has to be legitimate! I know what my competition charges because of the many referrals I've sent to them and received from them. You already know not to give away their confidential numbers to others, however.

- Look at business publications. If you're at the highest level of a company, business publications, such as *Fortune, Business Week,* or the *Wall Street Journal* will often report "What CEOs Make." Read the articles for background information, but take them with a grain of salt.

- Ask search firms. They won't typically talk with you unless they're screening you for a specific job, but if things are slow or you can network in, they will know real-time market information for your geographic area. If they're screening you for a job, don't pull out your market research questions. You need to sound focused on their opening. It's when neither of you is trying to sell the other on anything that you get more useful salary norms.

- Set up informational meetings and job interviews. Once you start getting out into the marketplace, you will receive direct feedback on what you're worth. You'll learn the salary ranges for jobs that you're interviewing for.

Does this give you some idea of how to collect your data? In that case, you're ready to go to work. Start thinking about your market value *now,* before someone catches you off guard with a salary question. You don't want to miss an opportunity.

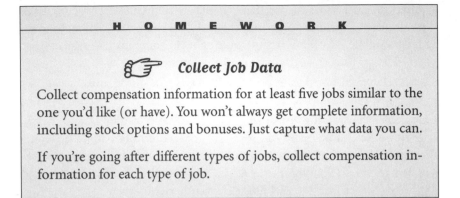

**H O M E W O R K**

☞ *Collect Job Data*

Collect compensation information for at least five jobs similar to the one you'd like (or have). You won't always get complete information, including stock options and bonuses. Just capture what data you can.

If you're going after different types of jobs, collect compensation information for each type of job.

Now that you have a feeling for the going rate for your work, you'll have a feeling about how you should price yourself in your negotiations. People typically make their biggest leaps in salaries when they change jobs, not when they stay employed with the same company and get the same 3.5 percent increase that everyone else does. You won't know whether you can make a big salary leap until you do your homework and maybe even get out and do some job interviewing. Using the old "I have to match what I was making" argument is narrow thinking. It's history and it's on the top side of your marketing circle. Saying, "The other opportunities I'm looking at are in the X range" is much more persuasive. It's market based, honest, and says that there may be some competition for you.

*Get Insider Information.* If you can find any information about the compensation norms at a company you're going to be negotiating with, you'll have a better idea about how much flexibility to expect. If your target is a publicly held company, you can find the salaries of the top officers on the proxy statement in the company's annual report. It's in the Security and Exchange Commission's Edgar database (www.sec.gov/edgar.shtml). This will tell you how to position yourself in relation to the top salary earners.

In addition to the general market norms mentioned above, search firms are another resource of information on specific companies, especially large ones that are more likely to use their services. When I was connecting some great employees with search firms after a company layoff, I learned that the company having the layoff was known for paying its people really well. That's helpful information for your negotiating strategy. Search firm people also know which companies don't pay well and which ones go through boom-bust cycles. Connecting with these people will take some networking, but you know how to do that. Don't forget your double low-density network, either, for learning the word on the street about compensation norms in your target companies.

Former employees are a third resource you can tap prior to a specific negotiation. Just ask them what the "going rate" or "norms" are for salaries in your area at their former company, then keep their feedback low profile and confidential. Integrate this information with the other sources of insider information you've gathered and you'll know what sort of flexibility a company is likely to have.

*Define Your BATNA.* Roger Fisher and William Ury's advice in the classic negotiating book, *Getting to Yes* (Houghton Mifflin, 1981), about knowing your BATNA, is still right on the money. "The reason you negotiate is to produce something better than the results you can obtain without negotiating. . . . What is your BATNA—your Best Alternative to a Negotiated Agreement? . . . If you have not thought carefully about what you will do if you fail to reach agreement, you are negotiating with your eyes closed." In other words, pinning all your hopes on one company is psychologically and professionally risky. This is the point of keeping your Job Pipeline filled, so your alternatives emerge at approximately the same time, giving you some leverage in negotiating (not to mention job choice). If other companies aren't getting serious, what are your alternatives? Continuing your search is an obvious one; doing some contract or consulting work, or maybe starting something of your own are also choices. Maybe being semi-retired or volunteering is your BATNA. Money isn't everything. Regardless, thinking about actual courses of action *other* than the one you're starting to negotiate will increase your confidence and comfort. You don't want to risk making an unfavorable agreement because you have no fallback options. If you are negotiating salaries at several companies, so much the better for your decision making.

## The Language of Negotiating: Saying the Right Thing at the Right Time

Now that you have done your prework, let's look at a standard compensation structure and at a standard process for negotiating, then we'll look at some exceptions. As you may already know, most medium to large companies have compensation systems in place. Similar jobs are grouped together into similar salary ranges to make sure people are paid consistently for similar levels of expertise and responsibility. When there is an official job opening, it is slotted into a specific band with a salary range attached. Now here's the trick question.

---

*When you're interviewing for a job, if you're quoted a salary range that goes with the job, which of the following are you being told?*
   ***a.*** *The whole range*
   ***b.*** *A portion of the range that corresponds to your experience and previous salary*
   ***c.*** *The bottom quartile*
   ***d.*** *A range that reflects their interest in you*

---

Roll of drums, the answer is "c." In most companies, if the interviewer quotes you a salary range at all, it's typically in the lowest quarter of the whole range. Is this deceitful? Not at all. People already in that range expect their compensation to grow with their experience, and that's what the top of the range is reserved for. If you come in at the top of the range, there is no room for an increase later. Yes, you might be able to upgrade your salary range, but it isn't an easy thing to do. Job content has to meet certain criteria to merit a range change. Aiming for a higher-level job is usually faster and easier. Be aware of salary structures prior to negotiating; there is usually more money in the overall band than what you are being quoted. A manager can't typically fork it all over, but if you want a shot at getting any of it, you'll have to ask.

Now for the standard negotiating approach. We're going to assume that it's the right time, at least toward the end of a second-round interview if not later, and you're talking to the right person, your potential employer.

**Employer:** Pat, it looks like you have the type of background that we're looking for. What would it take to get you?

(There are only two types of questions an employer will ask about your current salary, "What have you been making?"—your history, or, "What do you want to make?"—your future. Everything else is a variation on these two themes. These are predictable questions, so practice your answers ahead of time.)

**You:** The money is important, obviously, but it's getting this product to market and getting to work with this team that have me particularly interested. I'm seeing a wide range of compensation packages in the marketplace, so maybe we can start with you. What did you have in mind?

(You put the money into perspective, showing that it isn't your only driver. You implied that there might be some competition for you by knowing about other compensation packages, then you ducked, trying to get them to break the ice by quoting numbers.)

**Employer:** *Well, the range is $78,000 to $83,000 plus benefits and bonus. Is that what you had in mind?*

(It's amazing how many people will give you the range if you just ask.)

**You:** (Pause.) I'm sure we can work out something. I was hoping for a little more. What sort of flexibility do you have?

(There are three key phrases to keep in your tool kit: "Do you have any flexibility?" "Is that in your ballpark?" and "Can you see your way clear to . . . ?" You see "flexibility" here, but practice using all three of them. They are three nonconfrontational ways to stay open and ask about numbers without committing yourself.)

**Employer:** *Not much. What did you have in mind?*

**You:** I was expecting a base in the low to mid $90s. Is that in your ballpark?

(You can go 10 percent over the top of someone's range without blowing them out of the water. He or she is probably quoting you the bottom part of the overall salary range for your level anyway. You can then round up a little from the 10 percent and put your number into a broader band so you don't commit yourself to exactly what you would accept yet. Asking a question immediately after you quote a figure is an important strategy; you get feedback on whether or not they're going to play at your level. If you don't know your market value yet, you can fall back on your old salary that was in the mid $90s if you have to, as long as it's true. It's just a weaker position than "I'm interviewing for jobs in the low to mid $90s. Is that in your ballpark?" By the way, once you say "low to mid" anything, the employer will only hear the lower of the two.)

**Employer:** *I doubt it. I can look into it. I can do $83,000, however, and I might be able to do a little more on the bonus.*

**You:** Tell me more about the bonus.

(Notice that you haven't agreed on the base salary yet, but at least you got the employer to the top of the range. What's emerging is lower than you want, so table that discussion and find out whether there are other ways to close the gap. Always talk about your salary first rather than jumping into benefits. You will have to live on the base salary that you're setting now, so get it as high as you can before bringing in distractions.)

## From Salary to Benefits and Back Again

Now it's time to begin a relaxed discussion about benefits and variable pay. Benefits could include anything from retirement plan contributions to flexible working hours to medical insurance to stock options. Human Resources can tell you about the standard benefits. Your boss is the one to ask for any exceptions. Decide on your top benefits priorities ahead of time. You may have the time and energy to discuss up to three benefits, depending on their complexity, but don't wear down the new relationship by fighting for the country club membership unless it is integral to your success.

Ian knew he had already maxed out on his salary negotiation. A major university had extended a job offer for the chief marketing position and Ian wanted to close the deal. The position had been newly created and the organization knew the job was important to its future growth. The search committee had already upgraded the position several times because the salary originally offered didn't bring in candidates with the experience necessary to work with their board of trustees. A higher salary level would bring in a different caliber of applicant, but now the budget was strained.

One of the major search firms was handling the search, so Ian got feedback from them during the early stages of his negotiation. He asked for several thousand dollars over the university's quoted salary and they agreed. He knew they were jumping through hoops to deliver this, so he dropped salary as a topic. Next he brought up benefits. Now that he was in his late fifties, Ian was interested in moving out of the for-profit world to achieve some of the intangible benefits a nonprofit organization could offer.

"I'd like to talk with you about the vacation time that is allowed with this position," Ian said, as they started getting into the details of the package. "I already have a family commitment for this fall, and I need to honor it." (He and his wife had made plans to go to Europe, but Ian didn't need to get into the details.) "Is there a way that I can work out an extra week's vacation in October? I'll make sure everything is covered before I go."

"Sure, we can handle that informally," his new boss reassured him.

If you don't ask, you'll never receive. Ian ended up doubling his vacation time and, in addition, his relocation package. During his benefits discussion, he went for things that were either nonrecurring expenses or that didn't cost the organization much but meant a lot to him. Smart guy.

Ian talked about his salary first, then moved to a discussion about benefits. If you're talking with a for-profit organization, however, you may want to bring up variable pay options such as bonuses, incentives, and profit sharing, between the salary and benefits discussions. Variable pay options are additional ways to add to your overall cash compensation that companies aren't obligated to pay unless they're doing well financially, and they may be a higher priority to you than some of the benefits. You may ask for a larger percentage of the group performance bonus, for example, to close the gap between what a company is willing to pay in salary and what you were expecting. They may be more likely to grant your request because they'll only need to pay the bonus when they're doing well. Columnist Diane Lewis quoted a Watson Wyatt report in the *Boston Globe* (December 2, 2001), saying, "Many employers have well-designed rewards programs in place with variable pay options that fluctuate according to business performance, especially for higher-level executives." You'll want to know what these expansion clauses are. Just remember that there is a finite amount of energy you and your future employer are going to spend negotiating, so spend that energy on the most important points first. Once you have the variable pay and benefits roughed out, you can circle back to the salary discussion.

**You:** I appreciate your pushing up the percentage on the bonus and the 401(k) plan contribution. It sounds like there are only two things still on the table: whether you can see your way clear to the $90,000 salary we discussed and the stock options. I would submit that the $7,000 difference between our numbers, and I'm going with the lower end of my range, is a drop in the bucket compared to what we're going to bring in as a result of the product rollout we've discussed. Can we work with the $90K?

(Even though you were discussing benefits at this point, note how you put the salary back on the table at the end of the meeting with a specific number attached. You chose the low end of your "low- to mid-$90s" expectation in return for bonus and retirement plan increases. You also pointed out how you were going to pay for yourself by doing a good job with the product rollout. This is a "show me the money" strategy that gives the employer an argument to use with others on your behalf. If she can't answer you right away, offer to get back to her in two days and find out if this gives her sufficient time to respond. You want to keep the momentum going at this point. When you call back, before you get into a conversation, ask, "Where are you now in your thinking about the salary and stock options?"

You've just finished most of the standard negotiating process at this point. If things move forward in your follow-up phone conversation, it's a nice touch to go back and finish the negotiations face to face. Use the same approach if you receive the offer in a letter. In both cases, there may be some odds and ends that you'll want to resolve with the company, and it's better to do so in person. It's much easier to tell you "no" over the phone than it is in person, isn't it?

## Advanced Negotiating Plays for Catching Curve Balls

You're bound to run into some curve balls when you're negotiating your compensation package. You can anticipate and prepare for most of them ahead of time.

### When They Want You to Propose a Figure First

There will be some occasions when your tactic of asking the employer to break the ice by quoting numbers first won't work. He will ask you to go first. He may be well trained or lucky. Regardless, if you've ducked once and it hasn't worked, it's time to be forthcoming. Just present your compensation so it works to your advantage. The dialogue below assumes that you are talking to the right person (your hiring manager) at the right time (second round or later).

**Employer:** *Susan, what sort of salary have you been making?*

**You:** I've had a good, but somewhat complicated, compensation package. Since your package will be structured differently and I'm sure you pay competitively, can we start with what you had in mind?

**Employer:** *We're open. You first.*

**You:** Okay. My package has been in the low six figures, with stock options on top of that. Is that in your ballpark?

**Employer:** *Could you be a little more specific? What is the base salary?*

**You:** My base was $100K, but I've been talking to several companies about jobs with base salaries from $110,000 to $125,000, depending on the variable pay. What range are you proposing?

In this scenario, you're gradually backing up. The normal response to "What salary are you making?" is to say, "$100,000 annually," and to say it quickly. You now know that immediate disclosure is not to your advantage and will pigeonhole you at your former salary, a number that will inevitably be too high or too low. You ducked in the first round by asking what they had in mind, but since they came back to the same question a second time with "You first," it's time to come clean. You don't want to look like you're hiding anything. The compromise is to give him a straight answer and then immediately show that you're worth more than that in the marketplace. Be sure to follow your salary revelation with the question, "What range are you proposing?" so you can see how he reacts.

This question at the end of the dialogue is particularly important. If you're in a corner because the employer wants you to quote numbers first, do so in a broad band (the "package in the low six figures" in this example), then *throw back a question immediately.* If you don't learn what he thinks of your request right then, while the topic is hot, you may unknowingly throw yourself out of the running. And you will miss an opportunity to renegotiate. If you ask, "Is that in your ballpark?" and the employer says, "Gee, Trey, I'm afraid we can't afford you," you know that you caught a rejection in the making. Try, "I don't know. Tell me what you had in mind, first, then we'll see if we can work out something." That will keep you in the running without looking desperate.

If you avoid quoting any figures the first time the question is asked, that may be about as far as you can go without looking like you're playing games. You can decide in the context of the interview. Notice that the second time Susan was asked, she answered generally with her whole package, but the third time she gave them the actual base and referred to competitive jobs. She hadn't closed on any other offers at that point, but mentioning them kept her honest and showed the company that she might have alternatives. Not bad. Susan's most recent salary was below what she was worth on the market. If she quoted her old salary alone, a company could have assumed that she didn't have experience at the level they needed, so she answered with her market value as well. It worked. After all, a company does have to compete for talent against the current market norms, so Susan's figures were in line with the other people it was interviewing.

If you run into someone who demands to know your most recent salary, and you know your salary is lower than her range, you can say:

> "Peter, if it's critical to our moving forward, I can share it with you. My company froze increases for several years, however. I am choosing to leave due to salary concerns, and I'm concerned that what I'm worth in the market, which is demonstrated by the jobs I'm interviewing for right now, will be lost with a piece of old information."

See what your interviewer does with that one. You can try it with search firms too.

Notice the room for continued negotiating all through this discussion. Susan did not paint herself into a corner once. She asked questions, she answered with ranges, she didn't make any specific salary demands. When the discussion moves to benefits, she can decide what other lifestyle decisions will be in her top priorities to negotiate, always presenting them from the employer's angle. "I've used some great video conferencing equipment that really cut down on our travel expenses and let us cover a more geographically diverse set of customers. Are you open to how much time I spend on the road if I can still improve customer service and cut travel budgets?" Don't forget to give your employer several ways to say "yes." Asking questions rather than demanding absolutes will identify the win-wins without pushing her too far. Propose two alternatives that are acceptable to you, then let her choose, for example, asking for more vacation time while accepting the salary proposal or a higher bonus percentage and a lower base salary. Does this remind you of asking your kids whether they'd rather clean up their room or do their homework before dinner?

## Too Early or the Wrong Person to Talk to about Salary

Companies need to eliminate candidates for jobs early in the hiring process, especially if they've run a help wanted ad and have hundreds of responses. Salary expectations are an easy way to screen applicants. You may get a phone call.

**Employer:** *Hi. This is Eric responding to your letter to Bolt 'Em. Your background looks interesting, and we'd like to ask you some more questions, but we want to be sure that you realize the salary for this job is $48,000. Is that in your range?*

**You:** Hi, Eric. Thanks for the call. I don't know if the salary is in my range. The work looks interesting and is certainly something that I've had a lot of experience with. Bolt 'Em has a great reputation, and I have some ideas about how to keep building it. What I'd like to do is set up a meeting with whoever is doing the hiring, and, if we have a fit, I'm sure we could work out the salary. Do you want to ask me your questions, then we could see if we should set up a time?

Eric has been making $63,000. Their figure of $48,000 is well below his salary range. It might be surmountable, but Eric doesn't know this yet. He did, however, follow two important rules in his response: he didn't try to negotiate with whoever called him on the phone, and he did attempt to get an interview since the company was of interest to him. It's not unusual to get entreé with a lower-level interview, then get referred to a higher-level, unadvertised opening once the employer sees how good you are. Eric did not have any leads that would help him come in at a higher level, but he liked Bolt 'Em, so he decided to go for the bird in the hand.

Not talking to just anyone about your compensation is a good rule of thumb. The person calling you on the phone to set up an appointment is rarely the one who will be deciding your compensation. Dodge their questions, and try the "I'm sure if we have a fit, we can work out something" response. Human Resources screeners' job is to eliminate people. The more material you give them, the more reasons they can find to eliminate. Don't let premature salary discussions be one of them.

If your first interview is with Human Resources, it isn't unusual for them to screen you and ask about salary history or ask you to fill out an application with salary questions on it. You want to be charming, but you don't need to cross all of the Ts on this one, either. For an interview question about your compensation by an HR professional, try, "I've had a good income. I'd rather hold off on salary discussions, if I could, until we get a little further along. Could you tell me a little more about . . . ?" as you redirect the conversation back to the job's content. You don't want to trigger a full-blown salary discussion this early in the relationship and with the wrong person, but you're getting the pressure off you by lobbing the ball back into his court. If he gives you the range, just nod and say something noncommittal, such as, "I'm sure we can work out something."

If he wants to play hard ball and says, "Eric, I need to know your salary expectations," you have to make a decision. In this case, you could say, "Look. I don't want to scare you off. I've been making a good income, and I don't want to run into any preconceptions if I come in higher than your range. You want the best person, and I want interesting work. Can we see whether we meet each other's expectations before we get into the details?" Another alternative is the above response Susan gave to Peter, which expressed her various concerns for not wanting to answer definitively because he would be operating from old information. Ultimately, you don't want to risk irritating a senior HR professional any more than you would a search firm executive. They're both doing their jobs by trying to get information out of you. You're doing your job by trying to keep your options open. Their responsibility is to screen out the less-qualified parties, and compensation is commonly used as a qualifier. You can tell if you need to give them your previous salary information, but remember to state it as positively as possible, mentioning variable pay and stock, and then ask for immediate feedback.

## Negotiating through Search Firms

The partners in the five largest international search firms described in Strategy #2: Market for Mutual Benefit are pros, as are many of the executives in the boutique firms. If you're negotiating with a search firm, they'll need to know your salary to present you to a company, so there isn't a lot of point in avoiding that discussion for too long.

If you have a very high compensation, your network contact might be able to use it to your advantage to introduce you to a search firm. "Bruce, I have a $400,000–$500,000 semiconductor company turnaround guy you should to talk to. Want to know more?" The people in your network would be better at doing this than you because you're not going to get the attention of the firms as easily as a mutual friend with good connections and it's a little too pushy for you to lead with your own salary. This should only be done with the highest-level firms that work with these salaries. You don't want a rookie who would love to work at your range using your name as a battering ram to get into companies. Whether you are making $50,000 or $500,000, if a search firm presents you for a search and it gets serious, their level of involvement in the negotiation may fade as you progress. Different firms work in different ways. Remember that your ultimate agreement is with your employer, and your boss is the preferable party with whom to negotiate. The employer has the authority to make exceptions in the proposed compensation package, and she is the one who will stand behind the terms. Negotiate directly with the decision makers whenever possible.

## Creative Ways to Close Salary Gaps

You've wrapped up the benefits phase of your negotiations and are now revisiting the salary base. The employer isn't going to budge from the original number, and you expected a little more. We have a gap. Before you walk away or accept less than you think you're worth, get creative about closing that gap. You may end up considering a different job or shaping a new job; remember Strategy #3: Stop Looking for Jobs. You also may find that negotiating more than money increases your potential job satisfaction. There is more than one way to skin the compensation cat.

Here are four creative approaches to consider if you would like to accept a job offer, but the salary isn't quite what you had in mind.

*Add Responsibilities.* You don't want to give up on your higher salary proposal yet, so you focus on the employer's needs and how you can help him or her.

**You:** Beth, I understand that $65,000 is the best you can do at this point and that you're facing some constraints due to internal equity and budgets. Since we're only $8,000 or $10,000 apart, I have an idea. You've been thinking about starting Six Sigma for a while now, but you don't have the necessary time to devote to it. What if I get that off the ground for you? You would see returns within the next twelve months that you wouldn't have been able to generate otherwise, and I will have more than paid for the salary differential. What do you think?

Sounds similar to an earlier tactic about raising your salary base, doesn't it? It is. This time, however, you're proposing that you take on additional work to warrant the increase. To use this strategy, look for trouble spots when you're interviewing such as bottlenecks or problems that the company doesn't have time to address. You're doing this anyway as you listen for its needs and consider how you might create a job (Strategy #3: Stop Looking for Jobs). You then present a solution to an issue that is important to the employer and interesting to you as a bargaining chip. Defining a task that is manageable in size and scope is essential, too, because you're just about ready to volunteer to take it on in addition to your new job. Notice how you actually "showed Beth the money" by suggesting how she could afford to cover your salary differential? Proposing to accept additional responsibilities may catch the employer off guard, and she may be surprised into mulling over your suggestion. You aren't looking for additional responsibilities, but you're willing to do it in return for the compensation. See what happens.

Your request attempted to unofficially upgrade the position into a higher salary range. You don't want to introduce new paperwork now, however; your objective is to close on a hiring decision. Next year, when you're in and have a good track record, you can request a formal position upgrade.

*Combine Jobs.* If both a lateral job and a lower-level job are open, why not save the company some trouble and make a proposal?

Ilene was smart. She was talking to a company about one job that looked interesting, but when they got to the salary discussion, she learned that the salary was about 60 percent of what she had been making, lower than she was willing to consider. She tried the standard negotiating process of trying to raise the salary, without sufficient results. Instead of ending the discussions, Ilene got creative. "In addition to the project management job we're talking about, I've noticed that you have a job opening for a team leader, something that I have extensive experience with and could do in my sleep. I have an idea. What if we combine the two jobs? It would increase my credibility as project manager when people see that I have hands-on experience as a team leader, and it would give me insider information on any kinks or personnel issues that might arise with any of the teams. Instead of paying two full salaries and sets of benefits, you could have a better qualified team leader plus a qualified project manager for 80 percent of their combined compensation. Would that work?

You've just saved the company the time of finding two people and the expense of two separate salaries and budgets. Bonus points for being creative.

*Reduce Your Time Commitment.* Lower value should equal less time. If you discover that the job isn't going to come close to what you're worth, you may have an opportunity on your hands. You've already gone through the standard negotiating process, so you both know of one another's salary ranges and that the twain are not going to meet. If you still like the company, make a proposal.

**You:** Tad, let me run an idea by you. This job has been open for a while now, and I'm sure you'd like to get the interviewing process over with and get back to work. For the salary range you're quoting, you're probably going to get someone with ten to twelve years of experience. I'd like the chance to work with you, but someone with over twenty years of experience won't need five days a week to do the work. If you have some flexibility about how you package this job, meaning the number of days per week I need to be on site, you can get a lot more experience and higher quality work for the same price. Are you interested?

If Tad bites, work out an arrangement for a part-time, professional job that is fair to both of you. The time-honored negotiating rule that you just observed when you proposed something less than a full-time commitment is to get something in return for what you're giving up. In this case, you're getting time in exchange for less pay. Telecommuting could be included in the negotiations. A tactic you want to avoid is lowering your price while receiving nothing in return.

Reducing a job's time commitment is a great strategy if you're considering an active retirement or part-time work. Two conditions will increase the likelihood that a company will consider repackaging a job: if you are overqualified for the position and if you have an inside connection. Being overqualified allows you to argue that you can do the same job in less time. If you're overqualified but don't know anyone inside, however, you may not make the interview cut. If the hiring manager screens you based on your résumé, she will be concerned that you'll get bored quickly, be too expensive, and quit once you have been trained. Get your connections talking you up so the company will meet with you and see how charming you are, not to mention what a valuable asset you would be to her firm.

*Ask for an Early Review Date.* You like the company. You want to accept its offer. You've pushed each other about as far as you're both willing to go. The only thing that is still bugging you is a $10,000 difference in salary that has not been resolved. Before you give your final "yes," suggest the following:

**You:** Thanks. I really do appreciate the offer, and I'm excited about the opportunity. I have one last question about the salary, if I may. If I forgo that additional $10,000 we talked about, can we sit down together in six months to review my compensation? If we're mutually satisfied with my performance, I'd like to see the $10,000 reconsidered at that point. Will that work?

Note the light touch. You made a proposal, then asked for a response. The worst that can happen is that your new employer will say "no," and you'll say, "Worth a try. Next year when we sit down, I plan on making that difference look like small change compared to our progress." If your new boss says "yes" to a six-month salary review, he hasn't made any guarantees that your salary will actually be increased. Start keeping a regular record of your accomplishments so six months from now you'll be able to demonstrate why you're worth the extra money.

Another point to keep in mind if your new boss says "yes" to your request for an early review: get it in writing. If you don't get this casually agreed-to six-month review in writing, it can vanish in the wind. Bosses leave, forget, get laid off, get promoted. One sentence in your offer letter that says something like "Bill's performance will be reviewed in June of (year) for a merit increase" will give you a more substantial standing than "He said so." It will be your job to track why you deserve the increase and to set up the appointment in the sixth month. Early review promises can fall into the cracks, so you take control.

Now that you have four ways to close the salary gaps in your negotiations, add your own variations—apply for a broader range of jobs, and negotiate creatively. Your goal is to get offers on the table so you can make the best choice; it is not to walk away from jobs that offer too little without attempting to turn them into something that will work well for both of you.

## The Offer

If the company doesn't automatically put the offer in writing, here's what you say when you have most of the compensation package worked out, but before giving them a final "yes." "Could I ask you to put what we've discussed into a letter for me? I want to make sure that I've understood everything clearly." See how you put the motivation for the request on your own shoulders? The company can hardly deny your desire to be clear. Requesting a letter is a great strategy because it serves several purposes: it gives you the only thing in writing about your terms of employment that you may ever see, plus it buys you time. You may need a little more time, as in the third response below, if you're negotiating other offers before you decide. You're slowing down the first company, and speeding up the others . . . all do-able. It's the end game in chess.

**Employer:** *Do we have a deal?*

**You** (choose one): Yes. Thanks for the offer. I'm looking forward to working with you.

> OR

I think so. It sounds great. Can I sleep on it overnight?

> OR

I'm really excited about the opportunity. Thanks for the offer. What I'd like to do, if it's okay with you, is to get back to you next week. I want to make a long-term commitment to you, and, as you know, I was talking to other companies in this transition process. Let me wrap up with them, and I'll get back to you next Wednesday. If you want, I can get started on some of those materials in the meantime. Does that work for you?

This last option shouldn't be a surprise to the interviewer because you have seeded earlier conversations with hints that you've been talking to other companies. If you're not sure, now is the time to evaluate whether you want to choose this option over your BATNA, or over any of your other options that were at least halfway down the Job Pipeline. Call any other companies that still may be high on your list and say, "I really enjoyed talking with you last month. I wanted to give you a heads-up that I have an offer that I need to respond to shortly (or you're in third-round discussions with a company if you don't want to wait until offer time). If we have anything further to talk about, I'd like to set up a time to meet. I really think we could do some interesting things together, and I want to touch base before I do anything rash."

Regardless of whether one offer or three offers emerge, that period between an offer being made and your responding is when you have maximum leverage. Congratulate yourself, but be careful of abusing your power.

You don't want to be perceived as someone who is using a company. Getting an alternative offer just to win a salary battle with your current employer is damaging a relationship that you might want later on, and it's not the reputation that you want on the street. Take advantage of the leverage if you want to motivate a preferred company to make a decision, but you don't have to mention the source of your offer if it isn't appropriate. It's normal to take some time to make your decision, but you'll want to treat the proposal with respect and enthusiasm.

If all else fails and you cannot reach satisfactory financial arrangements with a company, it's time to part company. Do so with grace, though. The people are probably feeling badly because they can't afford you; don't make them feel worse. "I'm afraid that it looks like we aren't going to have a match," you say. "You're doing some really interesting work, and I hope that we will cross paths at some point in the future. If you'd like me to keep my ears open for someone who might be a fit for the job, I'd be happy to see if I could be of help."

## Prenuptials: Contracts, Golden Parachutes, Change of Control Agreements, Stock Options

If you are negotiating for one of the top positions in a company, you will be considering benefits that other employees aren't dealing with—protection for the high-visibility, high-stakes risk that you are taking. These packages are very sophisticated, and you'll want to devise your own rather than read about how to do it in a book. Joe Rich, executive vice president of Clark/Bardes Consulting, the largest publicly traded executive compensation and benefits consulting firm in the United States, has some overall guidelines. He stresses that agreements are "really two-way streets. The general give and take is that the executive gets predefined severance benefits, and the firm gets a clean break. You forfeit the right to sue for wrongful termination." Your options (no pun intended) are so varied and are subject to so many shifting norms that it takes a specialist to stay up to date on all the regulations and valuation methods. It's a good idea to have one in your corner. "Read the company's proxy statement, and see what others typically get in a year," Rich suggests. Then talk to a confidential advisor. This could be an expert in executive compensation, such as you might find at a consulting firm specializing in this field, or an employment lawyer who has experience with contracts at your level, or both. Word-of-mouth referrals from your colleagues or senior-level search and outplacement professionals will help you find the right person.

I recommend that your advisor be confidential for a reason: to have a visible expert early in the negotiation process is a heavier tone than you want to set. It could be interpreted as adversarial. Companies often have a compensation specialist who advises the company and the board's compensation committee on equitable arrangements for linking your pay with performance and your wealth with shareholder wealth. The company may provide this person to advise you. Listen to this person's proposals, then refer back to your private counsel for advice that is not biased in the company's favor. If you need to bring up your expert, make clear to the company that you're using her in an advisory mode rather than an attack mode. Your private counsel may not want her name disclosed. Ask. The top professionals in these fields typically have companies for clients, not individuals, and want to keep their relationships and reputations beyond reproach.

## Pricing for Creating a Job

Now things are getting fun. If you've just created a new position—whether it's full-time, consulting, contract, or interim work—the compensation doesn't exist yet. That's the exciting part. Setting your price is like finding water with a divining rod; it is as much art as science. If you have the skills to listen for needs and shape a job, setting your compensation should be the easy part. Your approach will depend on the type of work you have defined. If it's full-time employment, it shouldn't be too tricky. The company will have norms in place, if not an actual compensation structure, and the process outlined above will work. Knowing your market value and BATNA is important so you aren't susceptible to off-the-wall proposals. From the initial "What did you have in mind?" to asking for a letter at the end, you're now negotiating as a potential employee.

In this book, we're approaching consulting as a means to an end (full-time employment) rather than as an end in itself. If you start having fun along the way and decide that you want to stay with consulting, go for it. Read books like *Flawless Consulting: A Guide to Getting Your Expertise Used* by Peter Block (John Wiley & Sons, Inc., 1999) and *Million Dollar Consulting: The Professional's Guide to Growing a Practice* by Alan Weiss (McGraw-Hill, 1997) to get more of a flavor for the function.

Here we're looking specifically at how to price yourself when you're between full-time jobs doing short-term consulting to create relationships, how to back into a company, build your skills, bring in some income, or stay in the flow. People will expect you to have standard rates and will also assume that they aren't your first consulting client. You'll want to respond with confidence, even if you don't reply with a specific figure right away. Before someone says, "What are your rates?" have an answer planned. "I don't know" doesn't count.

As you're thinking about your consulting rates, keep three things in mind: benefits aren't included; you don't get paid for days you don't work; and you're still looking for a full-time job. Your decisions about your rates and availability should reflect these variables.

To get some idea about the rates you should be charging, consider the following seven points.

- **Know Thyself**

  Even if you're just planning a one-time consulting project, you don't want to be too casual about your rates. You're stating your value and defining your reputation when you set your fees. Catherine priced her consulting work well in a temp-to-perm proposal. She took the annual salary she would be receiving should the job become permanent, and substantially rounded it up (remember the three things you're keeping in mind). She then divided it by the three months she would be working as a consultant, continuing to round up. The company responded with "We're excited about your ideas, but your consulting rates are more than we can afford. We've decided that we'd like to offer you the position as an employee now rather than in three months. Are you interested?" She was. After she received the initial offer, she priced herself to achieve her objectives.

  In addition to knowing your rates, you need to know what you are selling. Consultants have specific areas of expertise that people need. You may be an expert in strategy, accounting systems, lean manufacturing, or training. However, calling yourself a general business consultant won't do it. If you're positioning yourself as a management consultant, you're putting yourself in with a lot of people who aren't sure of their expertise and some killer sharks who work for the world's best-known consulting firms. Is that where you want to be? You'll discover that highlighting one or two of your skills will attract attention now and will eventually set you up for the type of full-time employment you want. Part of your challenge will be giving yourself credit for your areas of expertise. It will be easier to find work if you're specific about the areas of expertise in which you're willing to consult. It will be easier to price yourself, too.

- **Know Thy Competition**

  Just like knowing your market value when you're looking for employment, you'll want to know the going rate for consultants in your field.

You might underprice yourself otherwise. You may decide to charge a different rate than the norm (rarely lower!), but you should know what your differentiators are and why you are worth your price. You may be worth more than the average turnaround consultant, for example, if you have actually directed successful turnarounds as a line manager.

How do you find out what the competition charges, let alone what your rates should be? Do what you did with salaries: gather data. You can find information in the following ways:

*Refer to your own experience.* Have you ever hired consultants in your area of expertise? Do you know people who have hired them? Track down what they charged. Make sure that you're comparing apples to apples. Consultants who are part of a firm will typically charge by the project (often a hefty price) and will have overhead that you may not. It's good to know how the larger consulting firms as well as the independents set their rates. They are all part of your competition.

*Ask your double low-density network.* Combine your question about "the going rate for an IT consultant" with some information that would be of interest to your network, and send out an individualized-looking email asking for their pricing experience with consultants. Lumping together several questions in one email is a good strategy so you don't wear them down with a question-of-the-day.

*Get a proposal together.* If you're legitimately pulling together a team of consultants to submit a proposal for a consulting assignment, your subcontractors will tell you what they typically charge. You're now familiar with the going rates of your colleagues, some of whom may have skills similar to yours. Price yourself a little higher if you're the person managing them in this project.

*Ask consultants.* Ask professional consultants what the going rate is in your field. Saying "I don't have a clue what to charge" will bring out the mentoring side of many people. Professional associations of independent consultants, such as the Society of Professional Consultants and the Institute of Management Consultants, can provide additional information.

- **Define Your Pricing System**
  Consultants are paid in various ways—hourly, per diem, by project, or according to perceived value. Each method has some legitimacy, depending on the image you wish to set and the goals you wish to achieve.

## PRICING YOUR CONSULTING WORK

| Payment Type | Definition | Pros | Cons |
|---|---|---|---|
| Hourly | Hourly work is paid one hour at a time. You track your work and bill the client. The number of hours per week and the number of weeks may be set, or the work may be ongoing. | This method looks less expensive and more controllable to client. The client may be more likely to commit to you.<br><br>This work is usually open-ended (or is this a con?). Specific outcomes and a termination date typically are not defined, so the work may go on for a while.<br><br>You can end this work quickly if a preferable offer comes through. | This work is not relationship oriented. Client thinks twice before picking up the phone to discuss issues.<br><br>There is some paperwork: keeping track of your time.<br><br>Commuting and planning or design time are often not billable.<br><br>You need to keep your rates high to maintain your image.<br><br>The company can end this work abruptly.<br><br>The only way to make more money is to work more hours. |
| Per Diem | Per diem work is paid one day at a time. It works well for clearly defined, brief commitments, such as evaluating client needs, running seminars, or doing training workshops. This method can be used for work that is complex and long term, but irregular, such as valuing acquisitions or consulting throughout a project roll-out. | The net for one day is typically higher than for hourly work.<br><br>Companies are usually comfortable with per diem arrangements. They don't have to overcommit. | Commuting and planning or design time are often not billable.<br><br>You may complete a short assignment and find that the client forgets about you.<br><br>You are 100 percent on duty during the days for which you were hired, so keeping a job campaign going simultaneously becomes challenging.<br><br>The only way to make more money is to work more hours and days. |

## PRICING YOUR CONSULTING WORK (continued)

| Payment Type | Definition | Pros | Cons |
|---|---|---|---|
| Project | A project is a well-defined piece of work. It has a beginning and an end, with agreed-upon outcomes. Pricing is typically based on projections of estimated time involved and estimated costs, including subcontractors, materials, and operations (not travel), then a desired percentage of profit is added. | This method works well with a temp-to-perm relationship. You have a strong relationship with the client during the project. The client and others in the organization can call you whenever they choose for no additional charge. You control when and where you spend your time. You can spend more or less time on a project, as needed. You can carry on your job marketing campaign at the same time. The only billing paperwork is your invoice and reimbursable expenses. | A project can take longer and cost more than you estimated. Your success is easily evaluated. Did you reach the desired outcomes within the estimated time frame? Did you stay within your budget? You may need to submit a report with outcomes and recommendations. |
| Value | Value is based on the return on the client's investment. What is the problem, and what needs to be done? How much is the client currently losing because of the problem? How much can you save the client and how quickly? You quote a reasonable percentage beneath the savings to the company and well over your expenses. | This work has the highest income potential. You develop a strong, ongoing relationship with the client and others in the organization. You're a partner. The client and others in the organization can call you whenever they choose, for no additional charge. This builds trust and the relationship. You control when and where you spend your time. You can spend more or less time on a project, as needed. The only billing paperwork is your invoice and reimbursable expenses. | You will need more initial time with the client to assess issues related to the project and estimate related costs. Redundancy is easy to price; poor morale is not. You need to be sure the client is committed to working with you before quoting prices. Your success is easily evaluated. Did you reach the desired outcomes within the estimated time frame? Did you stay within your budget? You may need to submit a report with outcomes and recommendations. |

Although value pricing is the Holy Grail for professional consultants because of its margins, flexibility, and relationships, other methods of pricing may suit you better given that consulting is not your long-term goal. You may prefer pricing a three-month assignment as a project, which you hope will springboard you into a company you want to work for. Or you may bill hourly if you're a novice at a skill you need and want to develop it while consulting.

---

**H O M E W O R K**

👉 *Pricing Yourself*

1. What areas of expertise could you offer as a consultant?
2. What type of pricing would work best for you—hourly, per diem, project, or value?
3. What are three other consultants in your field charging?
4. What range of fees would make sense for you?

---

- **Hold Off on Quoting Rates**

  Remember the rule when negotiating salaries: whoever mentions numbers first loses? Well, you don't want to rush into quoting consulting fees too early, either. Although in this case you may be the one to reveal figures first, since you're bound to know what you charge as a consultant (right?), doing it too soon has two disadvantages. You probably haven't gathered enough information to accurately estimate the time and complexity of the work, and it makes you appear to be a commodity. If someone is comparing consulting rates over the phone or in a first meeting, you don't have to play his or her game. In his book, *Million Dollar Consulting* (McGraw-Hill, 1997), Alan Weiss, the guru for many professional consultants, recommends saying, "'I can answer that when I learn some more and have time to consider how we might help you,' in response to, 'How much?' But once you say, 'We charge $1,500 a day, plus expenses,' you've had it. From that point your fee can only decline and your margins erode." Wait until the relationship is solid and you know the scope of the work before you quote your fee, especially with project- or value-based consulting. You could end up losing money and looking less expert otherwise.

"Will I lose the opportunity if I don't quote them a price right away?" Ideally, you will be the only one talking to the company about the consulting work. Your goal is to shape one, or possibly two at most, consulting jobs so you can address some of a company's immediate needs that you have identified in your meetings with the managers. With no competition, there shouldn't be any risk of losing the work if you hold off on naming your fees for project- or value-based work. It's tougher to duck a discussion about hourly or per diem charges, but try to wait until a second meeting. When you do declare your rates, remember the rule from the salary section about what to do if you're the first one to break the ice: *Always follow up with a question so you can get immediate feedback.* "Are we in the same ballpark?" or "The rate I'm quoting you of $80,000 for the project will be a fraction of what you save within the first year after eliminating at least two redundant salaries and streamlining your processes. You'll then be set up to continue and improve upon these savings over the long term. Does that make sense to you?" Notice how you focused on results, their side of the marketing circle.

You have a great advantage if you meet face to face with your potential client (and anyone else who might be interested) to go over your proposal and pricing. Waiting for a response to a written proposal (that the client is reading by herself, comparing with others, and fainting if the numbers are too high) is risky. You can continue the financial discussion more easily if you're sitting in front of her.

- **Subtract Value If You Lower Your Price**
  Negotiating experts agree that if you're asked to lower your prices and you want to keep talking, you should definitely reduce what you give as well. Do not eliminate the main components of what will make your consulting successful, but consider cutting some training, research, or report writing that is not crucial, in return for the lower cost. Drawing from Alan Weiss, "The client has the choice as to how much value justifies what investment, but should never have the choice of benefiting through your sacrificing your margins. This is not collaboration. This is a transfer of wealth from you to the client." Giving up something for nothing also erodes your image. You don't want to be the cheapest consultant in town. It's fair to stand firm at some point. If necessary, part ways politely, and be glad that this person is not your full-time boss.

- **Save Time for Your Job Search**
  This is critical! When you come to the end of your consulting work or project, what are you going to do next? Hopefully, you're becoming indispensable while consulting because you're spotting problems that need to be solved on a full-time basis. If you immerse yourself solely in the present project, however, you will fall way behind in planning for your future. One consulting firm I worked with called this period "running off a cliff." Consultants had no income the months after a major project was completed if they didn't develop some new business when they were in their peak crunch period with their current clients. Remember Wile E. Coyote, the cartoon character, chasing the roadrunner off a cliff, with legs still going ninety miles a minute when he finds himself over the abyss? When you look down and see that your leads have dried up and your network has disappeared, you can anticipate a crash.

  Your need to protect time for your job search is a negotiating point. Just don't articulate it as such. Your scheduling needs are on your side of the marketing circle, so you bring them up only to imply that there is competition for you. "I appreciate the compliment of your wanting me to be here full-time during the project, Sheila, but that wouldn't be the most cost- or time-efficient way to structure its implementation. We should talk about an employment arrangement if that is the goal. You'll be able to reach me on my private cell phone if you have questions, but a lot of this can be done much more reasonably off-site. You'll be seeing me multiple times each week and this project will come in on time and on budget, just as we've planned." There is no guarantee that a consulting assignment will turn into a job, so don't take on a full-time assignment unless you really want to. A lesser commitment, say ten to fifteen hours a week with your favorite firm, is ideal. Approach it from the firm's point of view. "The practices we set up are more likely to become habit if I train an operations manager who then supervises the day-to-day integration. He'll establish his authority faster if I'm not there watching him constantly." Subtle, aren't you? What you said is correct; you just wriggled out of being on-site every day and made a proposal that was in the firm's best interest all at the same time.

- **Get the Agreement in Writing**
  If a proposal isn't already in place, take the initiative. You're the consultant, so you have a standard letter of agreement that you use (right?). You can get started sooner, and you can make sure the letter says exactly

what you want it to if you write it yourself. It should start with a description of the company's problem, the scope of your project, the methods you would use, and your anticipated outcomes, timing, and cost. Don't make it too long. Its primary purpose is to clarify the process for both of you.

Now you have a method for setting both your consulting rates and your compensation as an employee. You can provide an employer (or a client when it's for consulting) with a breadth of choices. There's more than one outcome to the negotiating process that could satisfy you both. If you look at the different ways that you could package yourself, and the different ways that an employer could hire you, you clearly have multiple ways to reach an agreement. How can he say "no"?

## Wrap-Up

Here's a riddle for you. What's the difference between negotiating with a car salesman or a real estate broker and negotiating with your new boss, at least for as long as you're working for her? Do you know the answer already? You can't walk away from your boss. With the way you've negotiated your compensation, however, you won't need to. You actually built your relationship when you demonstrated your ability to act professionally, calmly, with humor, and with awareness of both parties' needs. You prepare ahead of time, you know what's going on in the marketplace, you listen, and you solve problems. You're going to be a pleasure to work with.

# Conclusion:
# You Don't Have One

Does not having a conclusion to your career (until you're ready for it, of course) sound like the good news or the bad news? If you love your work, it should be the good news, and you now know how to create work you love. The goal is to enjoy your work and be thoroughly engaged with it for as long as you choose to be.

We've talked about dramatically increasing your choices, flexibility, and security as you build your professional skills and your reputation. You now have solid career management skills; building your professional skills will be an ongoing requirement. As you become increasingly well-recognized in your area of expertise, both inside and outside your company, your reputation will grow and so will your New Job Security. People will start coming to you or will be more receptive when you approach them because your excellent reputation will have preceded you. You're setting yourself up for both short- and long-term success when you start consciously managing your reputation.

## Making Your Reputation,
## Not Just Letting It Happen

"I didn't realize that I could consciously manage my reputation," a sales director told me after a seminar. It's not that hard, and it has a big payback. This is not about bragging or boasting. It's about letting others know how you can help them and about staying tuned into external business forces. You have a reputation whether you want one or not. You might as well make it work for you.

Let's assess your current reputation before working to enhance it.

### 👉 Growing Your Reputation

1. Write down how you would like to be known in three years. Would you like to be recognized for your technical expertise, your powerful position in your current company, your ability to balance being a great parent with your work (yes, you can include personal goals), your skill in developing people? Three years isn't far off, so be as specific as possible.
2. Next, write down your assessment of your current reputation.
3. Then find out what your current reputation really is. You have a couple of options. If you're currently employed, check to see whether your company offers 360 evaluations. These are evaluations that survey a handful of people whom you select from various levels on the organizational chart. The individuals are not identified with their feedback.

Another option is to hire someone to do a 360 for you if you're concerned about not getting straight answers from people. If you're currently employed and plan to use your own coach, be sure to alert your boss that you're working on your professional development and that you or your coach will be talking to some people as part of it. Don't surprise her; she may just be impressed and use you as a model. You can interview people yourself if you design the questions well and if you promise to say nothing and just take notes. You can use a coach if you want the interviewees to be more objective and candid. Your call. Regardless, survey people who have different perspectives on your work and stay away from people who might be potential employers. You want to save them for later.

Who would you like to solicit feedback from? People who have worked above you, below you, and lateral to you are good choices.

Three questions ought to elicit the information you want:

- What should I do more of?
- What should I do less of?
- What should I keep the same?

If you tell people before your appointment that you're doing some market research on yourself and give them these three questions ahead of time, you might get more thoughtful results. If they're doing you a favor, is there anything you could offer them in return?

Before going to work on building your reputation, consider the structure behind a reputation. There are many ways to become and remain a star that are consistent with your values and personality. A scientist will present his research at professional gatherings and publish in his industry's journals. Though this is seen as a professional responsibility, promoting the advancement of science for all, it also builds the scientist's reputation. Choose methods that work for you. If you base your choices on helping others, you create win-wins along the way.

*There are five main avenues for developing your reputation:*
- *Executing your job well*
- *Connecting with external groups such as professional and industry associations*
- *Writing and publishing*
- *Speaking and teaching*
- *Networking (internally and externally) by helping others*

You may find additional approaches that work well for you. Take a look at the graphic on developing your reputation, and see which activities interest you.

## DEVELOP YOUR REPUTATION: BECOME A STAR

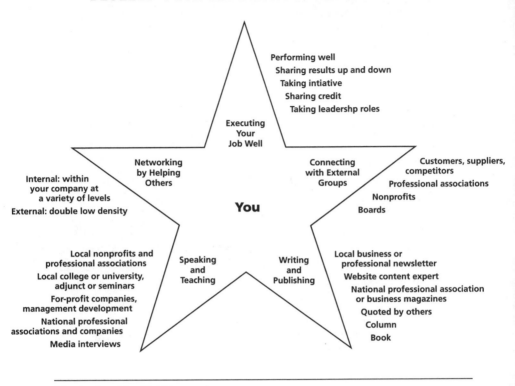

Performing well
Sharing results up and down
Taking intiative
Sharing credit
Taking leadershp roles

Executing
Your
Job Well

Networking
by Helping
Others

Connecting
with External
Groups

Customers, suppliers,
competitors
Professional associations
Nonprofits
Boards

Internal: within
your company at
a variety of levels
External: double low density

**You**

Local nonprofits and
professional associations
Local college or university,
adjunct or seminars
For-profit companies,
management development
National professional
associations and companies
Media interviews

Speaking
and
Teaching

Writing
and
Publishing

Local business or
professional newsletter
Website content expert
National professional association
or business magazines
Quoted by others
Column
Book

Reputations are built and changed by behaviors, not by wishes. As you accomplish the above goals, add more. They are habit forming because you're often helping and sharing with others in the process. Marketing for Mutual Benefit pays off.

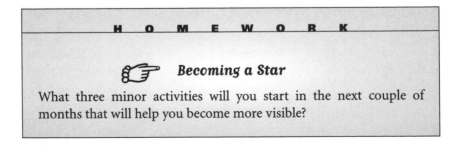

## H O M E W O R K

### ☞ *Becoming a Star*

What three minor activities will you start in the next couple of months that will help you become more visible?

# Leveraging Your Track Record
# from Now into Retirement

Consciously managing your reputation not only pays off when you're working full-time, it also pays off when you decide to slow down. Notice that I didn't say "stop" because my bet is that you won't want to stop working completely for a long time. Think of your career as a hike up and down a comfortably sized mountain rather than a dive off a springboard. A dive off a springboard requires a disciplined approach and focus, which is admirable, but after a rapid peak and some acrobatics, it's over in a flash.

People don't really want that for retirement.

Even if you suddenly have an enormous amount of money, which some people did in the early 2000s, early retirement isn't all it's cracked up to be. I frequently see people who are coming out of early retirement after a couple of years because they're bored. You have a good brain or you wouldn't be where you are today. There are only so many golf strokes the brain can analyze before it wants some new stimulation. If you live to be eighty years old, do you really want twenty to forty years of "retirement"? You and your spouse might kill each other first.

Demographics have changed. You're going to live longer, be more active, and have blood flowing through less-clogged arteries than your grandparents. In other words, you have a longer career to plan for than the traditional, hang-it-all-up-at-sixty-five norm. You have a variety of skills you can "unbundle" as you hike down the hill. During an active retirement you can concentrate on the work that you enjoy the most. The operative word I use with preretirement coaching is "taper." What skills do you enjoy using that you would like to "taper" out on? Use your career management skills to identify target markets that would consume these skills. Your well-established reputation will pay off in spades. The challenge, however, is this: *don't wait until you're ready to change your lifestyle to develop your reputation.* Waiting until you're sixty-four to develop a reputation as an expert in logistics management so you can start doing some consulting in that field when you're sixty-five is like closing the barn door after the cows are out: too little, too late. Start thinking about where your passions and pleasures are now, when you can do some reputation building around them and develop the relationships you'll need to carry you out on what will become your taper.

Tim combined his values with his work skills to find a meaningful segue into an active retirement.

Tim was still physically and mentally young at fifty-four when his company was acquired by a larger instrumentation company. His expertise was in sales and marketing. He had traveled the world not only managing the sales and distribution of products, but actually improving the quality of life in third-world countries on multiple occasions with his company's water filtration processes and systems. In addition to "doing good" in his professional life, Tim was active on the board of a well-known hospital and on the vestry of his church.

After the acquisition, it was time for Tim to move on. He could have gone after a similar job, and had a résumé toward that end if something irresistible should surface. With a strong values orientation, however, he wanted to explore mentally engaging, values-driven work that would also give him more flexibility in his schedule. Income wasn't as strong a concern as when his children were younger. Now, quality of life was increasingly important.

Tim focused on the types of nonprofits that were of the greatest interest to him: those whose mission involved the environment and conservation. Focus pays off, just as it does in full-time job searches. Most functions in the for-profit world are easily transferable to the nonprofit arena, as long as you take it upon yourself to find the right vocabulary. Tim's skills in sales and marketing transferred into fundraising and business development. He used these skills as an entry point.

His goal was to combine his skills (sales and marketing), his knowledge (developing people and operations and closing deals), and his values (giving to others, conserving and protecting the environment). Although his work experience was with for-profit firms, he had spent significant amounts of his personal time supporting nonprofit operations. He wove these threads into his résumé to show his transferability and to acquire the flexible lifestyle he wanted.

Tim repackaged his expertise, changed his vocabulary, and focused on the new market and its issues, which lowered the resistance of several targeted nonprofits. (Just because you're ready for them doesn't mean that they're ready for you.) Strategy and planning paid off, as always.

He is now on various boards of his choice, writing strategic plans for several organizations and building marketing programs for groups that truly need them. Not one of these were traditional job openings. He created them all by unearthing needs in conversations. He's making a difference. He has the type of job security and flexibility that he wants because he knows how to shape a new job rather than waiting for the right openings to develop. Tim's having fun.

Did you see how Tim took the initiative in his planning (Strategy #1: Take Control) and shaped his outcome as a result? In the process, he needed to help other people (gave away some of his marketing and fundraising expertise) to obtain his goal (a more value-driven position), which is Strategy #2: Market for Mutual Benefit. He stopped looking for job openings (Strategy #3: Stop Looking for Jobs) because what he liked doing—strategy and marketing—didn't exist as full-time jobs in cash-strapped nonprofits. His networking (Strategy #4: Network As the Norm) led to the meetings that led to the work that he wanted. Without clever negotiating (Strategy #5: Negotiate in Round Rooms), all his efforts would have been satisfying, but pro bono. Once he proved himself, compensation in different forms followed.

Take a stab at your long-term goal by doing the following homework. You will give yourself a great gift: a vision to test your career decisions against. Don't worry. If you change your mind after a while, you can substitute another goal that is a better fit. Over time, you'll have an increasingly clear idea about where you want to head.

Just as you want to build skills that allow you to stay competitive and reach your goal, you can deconstruct these skills when you start considering active retirement or a more flexible lifestyle. Ex–presidents of the United States open up law practices and build houses for nonprofit organizations. What would you like to do?

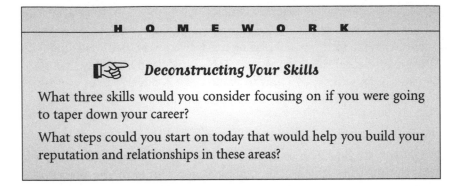

👉 *Deconstructing Your Skills*

What three skills would you consider focusing on if you were going to taper down your career?

What steps could you start on today that would help you build your reputation and relationships in these areas?

Try out your ideas. "I want to be considered an expert in lean manufacturing within my company and within the industry of semiconductor manufacturing." "I want to be known for setting up great human resource functions for small companies when they reach a critical mass and need to develop their own HR systems." If you test your ideas now, you'll have time to find the one that proves most interesting before leaving full-time employment. You have a lot to look forward to.

## You've Got the New Job Security

Congratulations! You know how to Take Control, determining your value, defining your skills clearly to others, and enjoying yourself in the process. You know how to Market for Mutual Benefit, identifying the hot buttons (BoSoC) of your target groups, then getting your needs met by meeting theirs. The strategy to Stop Looking for Jobs has hopefully raised a whole range of options for you. You can find problems and package yourself as the solution in ways that you choose. You already knew that to Network as the Norm should be a priority, though it's been easy to put off until now. Now that you have a structure that makes your time investment more manageable, you can sustain and grow both your network and yourself. Knowing how to Negotiate in Round Rooms isn't to be reserved solely for compensation discussions when entering a new company. You know how to do your negotiating homework, be creative, and present the outcomes that you want in terms that motivate the listener to agree, whether it's your employer or your teenager. You have the five new strategies under your belt. You're on a roll.

Keep the momentum going. As you continue to practice the five new strategies, you will build your reputation and manage your career successfully for as long as you choose. Instead of waiting for others, you now know how to make things happen for yourself. Your hands are on the steering wheel.

Practicing these five new strategies puts the New Job Security where it belongs, inside of you, by building minor daily practices in the five areas. Start now. Actually doing something rather than just thinking about it will uproot job security from the company's domain and move it into yours. What will you do today to begin the transfer? Would you like to check your local business newspaper to learn where contracts have been awarded recently? Would you like to set up a database for managing your contacts? How about joining a committee in a professional association or talking to someone who is working in an industry that might be of interest to you? The choices are endless and often are a lot of fun. The point is to plunge in. The next time someone asks you how your work or your job search is going, smile. You'll know where you're headed and you'll have the means to get there because you've taken control of your own career management. You have the New Job Security.

# Appendixes

# Appendix A

## WHAT HAPPENED? WHY ARE YOU LEAVING?

The questions "What happened?" and "Why are you leaving?" are perennial favorites. Turning these questions to your advantage and directing the conversation toward the future are your two objectives.

1. Answer the question, "Why are you leaving?" using the most positive interpretation, not "washing dirty linen." Take no more than ten to fifteen seconds to answer, covering just the high points and, ideally, the company's point of view as well.

2. Describe the opportunity. Explain why the parting will actually be an opportunity for you. Reflect a positive attitude. You're in control, showing strength.

   "This will actually be an opportunity for me because it will allow me to concentrate on . . ."

3. Envision the future. How will the companies that you're considering benefit from your transition and from your unique set of skills?

   "As a result, I am looking for a company that . . ."

4. Ask a question. It gets the other person talking and moves the conversation toward future possibilities. Relate your question to the positive characteristics you mentioned above in number three. Make your question broader than just asking about a job opening.

   "Am I correct in assuming that you . . . (have plans to introduce X products, want to convert to X type of system, and so on)?"

   "Are you aware of any companies that want to . . . (grow their international sales, turn around their operations, and so on)?"

**217**

# Appendix B

Strength that I'm demonstrating in this story:

Describe a **P**roblem.
("Sales were going downhill and we couldn't get our new products out of R&D . . .")

Describe specific **A**ctions you took to resolve the problem. Speak in bullet points, very simply and clearly. Use "I" rather than "we."
("The first thing I did was to call the team together . . .")

Describe the **R**esults of your actions. Quantify them whenever possible.
("As a result of the new systems and revised products that I introduced, within two quarters we were able to increase . . .")

What additional strengths, skills, and assets does this story demonstrate?

# Appendix C

## ELEVATOR STORY

Create your own Elevator Story.

- Introduction
  "I have over _____ years of experience in _____."

- Three Skills
  "What I particularly enjoy doing is _____."

- Two Results
  "As a result, I have been able to _____."

- Question
  "Are you aware of any _____?"

# Appendix D

Ben Rogers
ben@yahoo.com • 765-987-6543
International Marketing

Target List*

| Automatic Test Equipment | Measurement Equipment |
|---|---|
| Dynatup Impact Products, Canton, MA<br>  Loren Allison, GM | AEMC Instruments, Boston, MA<br>  Winthrop Teel, COB |
| GSI Lumonics, Laser Systems Div,<br>  Wilmington, MA<br>  Jim Leonard, CEO<br>  Michelle Lewis, CFO<br>  John Wren, VP Marketing | Analog Devices, Trans & Indus Products,<br>  Wilmington, MA<br>  Ray Bowyer, COB<br>  Jerald Christopher, President<br>  Jim Keith, CFO |
| Hewlett-Packard, Scope Communications,<br>  Marlborough, MA<br>  Peter Mayfield, GM<br>  Scott McCleskey, Marketing | Beede Electrical Instruments,<br>  Penacook, NH<br>  Walter Horne, CEO/Pres<br>  Peter Nicholas, VP Sales/Marketing |
| Inspex, Billerica, MA<br>  Tervo Goldston, COB/CEO<br>  Brian Hastings, CFO<br>  Robert Abbott, VP Marketing | Elmwood Sensors, Pawtucket, RI<br>  Henry Donato, President<br>  Barrie Gollinger, VP Finance |
| LTX Corp, Westwood, MA<br>  Samuel Dunlap, COB<br>  Roger Fiske, President/CEO<br>  Joan Filipone, SVP<br>  Ed Ohlmstead, VP, Mixed Signal Div | F.V. Fowler Co, Newton, MA<br>  Lydia Fowler, COB/CEO<br>  Uldis Jacob, EVP<br>  Steve Carter, Int'l Marketing |
| Micro Robotics Systems, Chelmsford, MA<br>  Neil Schmidt, President/CEO<br>  Dan McCarthy, VP Marketing | Hottinger Baldwin, Marlboro, MA<br>  Joseph Lombardo, CEO/Pres<br>  Marianne Ray, Sales and Marketing<br>  Jeff Taylor, CFO |

*Names have been changed to protect the innocent.

| | |
|---|---|
| Teradyne, Inc, Industrial/Consumer Div, Boston, MA<br>    Alex Kwok, COB<br>    David Joslin, Div Mgr<br>    Julie Eckstein, Marketing | MKS Instruments, Andover, MA<br>    John Silver, COB<br>    Peter Simmons, President<br>    Janet Aubrey, VP Worldwide Sales |
| ThermoSpectra Corp, Franklin, MA<br>    Thel Gollinger, COB<br>    Daniel Miller,President/CEO<br>    Jon Whitney, VP/CFO | Setra Systems, Boxboro, MA<br>    S.Y. Blythe, COB/CEO<br>    Jack Denis, President<br>    James Adrien, VP Sales |

# Appendix E

## THE MARKETING CIRCLE

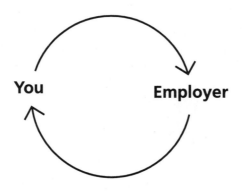

You          Employer

# Appendix F

## Creating a Job

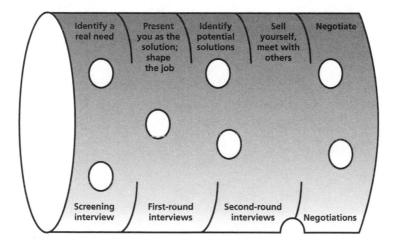

Identify a real need | Present you as the solution; shape the job | Identify potential solutions | Sell yourself, meet with others | Negotiate

Screening interview | First-round interviews | Second-round interviews | Negotiations

## Applying for an Existing Job

# Appendix G

## CATCH YOUR VALUE WAVE

**Industry:**

**Function:**

**Industry Trends**

**Company Needs**

**Your Strengths**

You, setting up a meeting:

_____

_____

_____

_____

_____

_____

_____

_____

_____

_____

_____

_____

# Appendix H

Colleagues in most recent job (including bosses and staff):

_____

_____

Colleagues in former jobs (including bosses and staff):

_____

_____

Vendors:

_____

_____

Customers:

_____

_____

Competitors:

_____

_____

Social friends and neighbors:

_____

_____

Relatives:

_____

_____

Clubs:

_____

_____

College alumni:

_____

_____

Bankers, consultants, lawyers, accountants, stockbrokers:

_____

_____

Professional associations:

_____

_____

Sports:

_____

_____

Church or clergy:

_____

_____

Volunteer, common interest, political, or civic groups:

_____

_____

Doctors:

_____

_____

Other:

_____

_____

# About the Author

Pam Lassiter is the Principal of Lassiter Consulting, a nationwide private practice firm that consults with companies and individuals on career management services and systems. A consultant in career management for over twenty years, Pam has designed programs, seminars, and training sessions for companies that are restructuring their workforce or implementing internal career development systems. Her work with individuals focuses on directing searches of senior-level executives towards timely, satisfying conclusions; and her corporate work focuses on improving employee productivity and retention. With an undergraduate degree from the University of Texas in English/Spanish, a master's degree from Boston University in psychological counseling, and graduate coursework in vocational development and business management, Pam lives in Boston, Massachusetts.

# Index